BLACK FILMS AND FILM-MAKERS

Also by Lindsay Patterson *(Editor)*

BLACK THEATER: *A 20th Century Collection of the Work of Its Best Playwrights*

A ROCK AGAINST THE WIND: *Black Love Poems*

BLACK FILMS
AND FILM-MAKERS

A COMPREHENSIVE ANTHOLOGY FROM
STEREOTYPE TO SUPERHERO

COMPILED WITH AN INTRODUCTION BY Lindsay Patterson

DODD, MEAD & COMPANY
NEW YORK

ISBN: 0–396–06843–X
Library of Congress Catalog Card Number: 73–11545

Printed in the United States of America
by The Cornwall Press, Inc., Cornwall, N.Y.

The following acknowledgments are made for permission to reproduce the
material indicated:

"Of Motion Pictures, Radio, The Press and Libraries" by Lawrence Reddick. Copyright © 1944 from *The Journal of Negro Education*. Reprinted by permission of the author. "Folk Values in a New Medium" by Alain Locke and Sterling A. Brown. Copyright © 1930 from *Folk-Say: A Regional Miscellany* edited by B. A. Botkin and published by University of Oklahoma Press. Reprinted by permission of University of Oklahoma Press. "Uncle Tom Will Never Die!" by Arthur Draper. Copyright © January 1936 by *New Theatre Magazine*. "Beige, Brown, or Black" by Albert Johnson. Copyright © 1959 by the Regents of the University of California. Reprinted from *Film Quarterly*, Volume 13, Number 1, pages 38–43, by permission of The Regents. "Pro-Negro Films in Atlanta" by Gerald Weales. Copyright © 1952 by the National Board of Review of Motion Pictures, Inc. Reprinted with permission of *Films in Review*. "The Death of Rastus: Negroes in American Films Since 1945" by Thomas R. Cripps. Copyright © 1967 by *Phylon* (Atlanta University). Reprinted by permission of *Phylon*. "Which Way the Black Film" by Richard Wesley. Copyright © 1973 by *Encore* magazine. Reprinted by permission of the author. "The Birth of *Birth of a Nation*" by Bosley Crowther. Copyright © 1965 by The New York Times Company. Reprinted by permission of *The New York Times*. "Hearts in Dixie (The First Real Talking Picture)" by Robert Benchley. Copyright © 1929 by *Opportunity Magazine*. Reprinted by permission of *Opportunity Magazine*. "Carmen Jones: The Dark Is Light Enough" by James Baldwin. Copyright © 1955 from *Notes of a Native Son* by James Baldwin. "It's Gonna Blow Whitey's Mind" by Lindsay Patterson. Copyright © 1968 by *The New York Times*. Reprinted by permission of the author. "In Harlem, a James Bond with Soul?" by Lindsay Patterson. Copyright © 1969 by *The New York Times*. Reprinted by permission of the author. "Sounder—A Hollywood Fantasy?" by Lindsay Patterson. Copyright © 1972 by *The New York Times*. Reprinted by permission of the author. "*Book of Numbers*" by Maurice Peterson. Copyright © 1973 by *Essence* magazine. Reprinted by permission of *Essence*. "The Negro Actor and the American Movies"

To
my nephews James H. Patterson III and Roger Lindsay Patterson
and to
Ruby Dee and Ossie Davis for the pleasure they have given
their friends and the universe.

Introduction

My Dear Son:

I have just seen some of those *new* black movies you have talked about so enthusiastically for sometime now, and I must say I was appalled. I found no virtue in them whatsoever. The plots were trite, the acting dreadful, and the technical direction awful. But what I objected to most was the inelegant use of language. If black people have anything going for them at all in America, it is their creative use of words and phrases.

I was appalled, too, at the violence in the films. You say that no one takes movie violence seriously. I disagree vigorously, for since the inception of television, moving pictures have steadily become less mysterious and awesome. When I was a kid we were intimidated by the images on screen, and Hollywood seemed larger than life. But that isn't true with your generation who is growing up in an era where the tragedies of the world are flashed daily before your eyes, with the result that nothing really shocks anymore. Man's inhumanity to man is all too often greeted with an automatic shrug.

Make no mistake about it, movies have a psychological and sociological impact on societies that is frightening. They set tones in morality and dress (one only has to walk through the urban centers of America to see how pervasive this influence is) for millions of people throughout the world. And I know for a fact that the existence of racial discrimination in some countries is a result of their populations having continuously viewed the black man as a foot-shuffling idiot in American films.

I remember quite well the first black movie I ever saw. It was in a topless tent on a vacant field under a dazzling Louisiana sky. White painted boards provided the projection screen, and backless wooden benches were our seats. Every fifteen minutes or so, there was a ten minute break while the projectionist-owner (a white man) changed reels on his single machine.

The movie was a western and awful. I don't remember the name of it (*Harlem on the Prairie,* perhaps?), but the star was a handsome, light-complexioned black man. When he wasn't riding his beautiful white stallion, he brawled, drawled and shuffled some. The audience howled—as only a black audience can—with derisive laughter. If anybody had told us that our black consciousness was being raised because we had finally glimpsed a black "hero" on screen, we would have told them they were mad.

A movie that did raise my consciousness was *Super Fly.* Of all the *new* black movies, it is the only one I continue to admire. It had an honesty and simplicity that haunts me even now. But because of what came before it and what has come after (cinematically speaking), few critics seemingly shared my admiration for it. All they could discern was another stereotype being acted out. But the movie presented an important message about the failure of American society to freely provide legitimate opportunities for its bright but impoverished young black men. Unfortunately, everybody focused on the sensational aspects of the movie, and this very valuable assessment about our society was lost in the hysteria about exploitation films.

That brings up the question of what black movies should be about. The hard reality is that most people don't want to be preached to or educated in a movie theater. They want to be entertained. I don't blame them, for after a gruelling day's work why should you have to sit through two and a half hours of political harangue about the unfairness and drabness of your existence. But a movie, whatever its intent, should, at least, strive for technical perfection, solid characterization and a coherent story line, rather than give the appearance of being thrown together with the speed and haste of a porno film.

But black movies—like porno films—have never been looked upon as a medium in which artistic perfection was sought, but as a device to make some producer rich. Most of the early black film companies were owned by persons who were interested only in turning a fast profit. Yet, there were a few film-makers who tried to make movies that were first rate and artistically true. Those producers, of course, had difficulty in being financed by banks, or attracting investors in their proposed products. The good movies that did manage to get made were financial flops, because there weren't enough black movie theaters throughout the country in which those movies could be shown. Nor did most black people attend all-black theaters, since they were usually dank, rat-infested fire contraptions. And white segregated theaters, of course, would not exhibit all black films.

Now that theaters are thoroughly desegregated and it has been conclusively proven that a huge black market for films exists, I have been wondering why some of the great black novels have not been made into movies. *Native Son* and *Invisible Man* would still make splendid films. So would the novels of current writers like Toni Morrison, Ishmael Reed, Alice Walker and Pauli Marshall. But you probably won't ever see a succession of good black movies based upon solid material until we build our own movie industry, which is doubtful in either my or your lifetime. Which is sad because even the movies in which blacks claim to have had a measure of control seemed locked in an ersatz formula that somehow renders the black experience artistically sterile. *Super Fly* seemed locked in no such formula. It was an original, which is why I liked it so much.

As a protest, some critics of black films have suggested that black actors refuse to act in artistically inferior properties. But that's like asking a politician to put a sack over his head in front of a television camera. Nevertheless, it's a problem the black actor has been struggling with for a long time. In the 1940's, when the NAACP set up an organization in Hollywood to examine screenplays that contained black characterizations, many black actors objected, and countered by establishing their own organization, which gave as its purpose the protection and safeguarding of the interest and employment possibilities of black film artists.

In the 1930's, Clarence Muse, one of the most talented early black actors, wrote a pamphlet in which he showed the black actor torn between two desires, "the giving of his best talent in a serious way to Negro audiences, or the winning of financial success as buffoon, clown, and dancer before white audiences." Today the dilemma is almost reversed: Should a black actor give the best of his talent before a predominately white audience, or seek financial success as a superstud or nigger before black audiences?

In 1972, four hundred black actors, directors, and writers met in Hollywood to form the Black Artists Alliance to "express common outrage at the gross and deliberate distortion of Black Life in motion pictures, television, radio and commercials." But the irony of it all was that many of those artists were appearing in or seeking employment in the very films they were condemning. For example, one of the organizers of the Alliance grudgingly admitted in interviews that he wrote a film script to "win with it commercially," but tried to defend it by stating that it contained some great message about black women (which, of course, it didn't). Whereas Fred Williamson honestly admitted in interviews that he was in black movies for the money, and if the white man was raking in the lion's share of the profits, so be it, as long as he was getting his.

But there are a few black actors and actresses like Cicely Tyson and Gloria Foster who won't accept anything that "degrades women or blacks," which means they are never going to work very much.

It may seem no big thing to you now that movie censors in the South routinely used to cut out Lena Horne singing the most innocent love songs in a film, or that Stepin Fetchit and Hattie McDaniel grew even more obnoxious and outrageous with each film appearance. But their roles had enormous impact on our lives. We were grateful to Lena Horne for never appearing before the public as less than a lady, but chagrined at Fetchit and Mc-Daniel because whites expected us to act like them for free.

We realized (and sympathized) that early black actors had a rough time breaking into movies. Most were maids who worked for white stars. Fetchit was a porter on a movie lot when he was *discovered*. But their financial success did not make it easier for us. Their screen images only drove the nails deeper into segregation. And Miss McDaniel only added salt to the wound by stating that it was better to "play a maid for $7,000 a week, than be one for seven."

Crazy as it may sound now, Hollywood at one time believed that only blacks would be successful in talking pictures (remember the first talking picture featured Al Jolson in blackface). Many of the great white silent film stars turned out to have horrible speaking voices, and so Hollywood turned to blacks. *Hearts in Dixie*, which brought Stepin Fetchit to the screen, was one of the results.

The year was 1929, and critic Robert Benchley said in a review: "Even granted that the sound could be made to come from somewhere near their mouths, the voice [of the actors] itself is impossible. They have either sounded like the announcer in a railroad station or some lisping dancing master, and the general effect has been to cause the public mind to revert to the good old days when subtitles were flashed on and the hero and heroine were not expected to give themselves away by talking. With the opening of *Hearts in Dixie*, however, the future of the talking movie has taken on a rosier hue. Voices can be found which will register perfectly. Personalities can be found which are ideal for this medium. It may be that the talking movies must be participated in exclusively by Negroes. But if so, then so be it. In the Negro the sound picture has found its ideal protagonist."

Also, during the twenties, black extras were abundantly employed, not only as slaves on plantations, but as Asians. A prime employment period was from 1924 to 1927, when over 17,000 extra and bit parts were filled by blacks. The peak period occurred in 1928, when about 10,000 black extra parts were cast. Charles Butler, who was himself black and responsible for recruiting black actors, stated that "the black extra received more money than any other extra in the industry except the Chinese."

But by 1946, the black extra was a thing of the past. Only 78 black men and 67 black women were registered with Central Casting. Hollywood was making war films, and though blacks were an integral part of the war effort this was not being reflected in movies. Black movies, on the other hand, never really got off the ground. Hollywood turned to Broadway and Europe for its "talking actors."

The fact is, black movies have never had a sustained period where actors, writers, directors, and technicians could perfect their craft. Even the rash of *new* films have now slowed to a trickle, and the much vaunted black movie boom of the early seventies has now become, it seems, a bust. Yet, I'm optimistic that one day we will see a plethora of films that are racially unselfconscious and excellent by any standards. That day will come. Meanwhile, contained in the following pages is a superb account of the road we've already traveled and are yet to travel, cinematically.

Your loving father.

Contents

Illustrations

SECTION I

NIGGER TO SUPERNIGGER

Lawrence Reddick

1   Of Motion Pictures

[1944]

Any visitor to neighborhood theaters will testify to their influence. Shouts, laughter, handclaps, yells, and tears are some of the more immediate effects of motion pictures on their audiences. That these experiences, which are often gripping, have an abiding influence is most noticeable in young people. The studies of the Payne Fund [1] document what we have all guessed from our own impression; namely, that ideas of love, clothes, manners, and heroism among adolescents (and others, of course) are directly traceable to movies. Many persons—especially young girls and old women—fall in love with screen heroes. Screen biography, newsreels, and travelogues are particularly effective in what they say about history, current events, and the peoples and places of the world. The implied associations that are indirectly suggested and repeated by the screen stories often leave residues that are more lasting than the evocative climaxes of the films.

In wartime, the portrayal of our enemies, our allies, and our own strength are definitely associated with sentiments and emotions. The national government realizes this and makes wide use of the movie as a medium for building and sustaining morale. Though there is no sure way of testing it, the movie play *Mrs. Miniver* probably did more to develop good will toward Britain

---

[1] One of the most useful volumes in this series is Herbert Blumer's, *Movies and Conduct.* New York: Macmillan Co., 1933; see also W. W. Charters, *Motion Pictures and Youth: A Summary.* New York: Macmillan Co., 1933.

among the masses of the American people than did all the speeches of all the diplomats combined.

It is, therefore, important to inquire into what such a powerful instrument for influencing the attitudes and behavior of so many persons has had to say about the Negro. Here we may expect to find one index as to what the American people have come to believe about the Negro, one key to popular stereotypes and the associations linked to them.

A check list [2] of important films shown in the United States that have included Negro themes or Negro characters of more than passing significance reveals that out of this total of one hundred, seventy-five of them must be classified as anti-Negro, thirteen as neutral—with equally favorable and unfavorable scenes—and only twelve as definitely pro-Negro. These measurements, of course, are rough and ready, yet they should be useful enough to indicate the main tendencies. Films are classified as anti-Negro when the Negro elements in them are limited to the stereotyped conceptions of the Negro in the American mind.[3] Films are classified as pro-Negro when the presentation advances beyond these stereotypes to roles of heroism, courage, and dignity. The overwhelming desire of the Negro people, as expressed through their critics, is to have Negro life admitted to the full range of human characterization, to eliminate the "race linking" of vice and villainies, and to have Negro actors on the screen treated "like everybody else."

As everyone knows, most of the films cannot meet this simple test. In them the Negro is exploited chiefly for comic relief. He is the clown, but seldom a magnificent clown; a buffoon; the butt of jokes, not the projector of them, except against himself. He may

2 This check list has been constructed from materials in The Film Library of the Museum of Modern Art. The Theatre Collection and the Schomburg Collection of Negro Literature of the New York Public Library.

3 The principal stereotypes of the Negro in the American mind are (1) the savage African, (2) the happy slave, (3) the devoted servant, (4) the corrupt politician, (5) the irresponsible citizen, (6) the petty thief, (7) the social delinquent, (8) the vicious criminal, (9) the sexual superman, (10) the superior athlete, (11) the unhappy non-white, (12) the natural-born cook, (13) the natural-born musician, (14) the perfect entertainer, (15) the superstitious churchgoer, (16) the chicken and watermelon eater, (17) the razor and knife "toter," (18) the uninhibited expressionist and (19) the mental inferior. These stereotypes supplement each other, though they are sometimes mutually contradictory. This whole subject will be developed elsewhere.

be an entertainer or a servant, who almost certainly will exhibit some of the following qualities: ignorance, superstition, fear, servility, laziness, clumsiness, petty thievery, untruthfulness, credulity, immorality, or irresponsibility, with a predilection for eating fried chicken and sliced watermelon. Within these limitations there are all sorts of variations. The Negro elements in films often arise out of situations involving human interest, real humor, and drama. There may be excellent acting. However, a rapid review reveals the ceiling above which the Negro on the screen is seldom, if ever, permitted to rise. It is significant that this ceiling on the screen is lower than the ceiling for the Negro in American life itself.

The Early Years

Motion pictures as popular entertainment are a twentieth-century development. Their history may be dated from 1902 when Thomas L. Tully opened the first theater exclusively for "moving pictures" in Los Angeles. Before 1915, despite constant improvements in technique and a rapidly expanding public interest in this cheap and thrilling amusement, the very best films of those days would be considered quite crude by modern standards. Uneven lighting and the quick, jerky movements and melodramatic gestures of the actors appear amusing now. Yet to contemporary audiences these films were marvelous. Even in these beginning years, when the movies were principally "peep shows," the Negro was presented in an unfavorable light. For example, in the prize fights, the Negro pugilist almost invariably was defeated by his white opponent.

In this pre-1915 era were such films of Negro life as the Rastus Series. The very titles of popular favorites like *How Rastus Got His Turkey* and *Rastus Dreams of Zululand* suggest the type of low comedy of these split-reelers. *Coon-town Suffragettes* was quite similar. *For Massa's Sake* tells the story of a devoted slave who wishes to be sold in order to pay the gambling debts of his master. Fortunately, his master discovers a gold mine and things end well before the final fadeout. *In Slavery Days* and *The Octoroon*, both released in 1913, show how tragic it must be for a white person to have a few drops of "Negro blood" in his veins. *The Debt* exploits the same theme with a somewhat original twist: a young man has a white wife and an octoroon mistress. They both have children who, when they have grown up, meet, fall in love, and almost marry before they discover their identity. *Uncle Tom's Cabin*, a perennial favorite, was first released as a three-reeler in 1910. The indictment of slavery in the original Harriet Beecher Stowe story was softened so as to make it acceptable to the South. The sight of Jack Johnson knocking out Jim Jeffries, ex-heavyweight champion of the world, was so disturbing to the "race pride" of white audiences, and conversely to Negroes as well, that this "prize-fight" film was banned.

"Birth of a Nation" [4]

The year 1915 is a great date in film history. This is the year of *Birth of a Nation*, which in terms of the advancement of the whole technique of presenting life on the screen made it the greatest film ever produced. It was the longest film ever made—twelve reels. It was the first film to be accompanied by a specially arranged orchestral score. It took a hundred thousand dollars and two years to produce. From the strictly artistic and technical point of view it was a masterpiece of conception and structure. Even today, it is important from this angle. At the same time, *Birth of a Nation* has remained, without question, the most vicious anti-Negro film that has ever appeared on the American screen. It was based upon the novels of Thomas Dixon, a Negro-phobe Southerner.

On March 3, 1915, the picture began its long career of arousing audiences throughout the country. It was a huge financial success. Nobody had ever seen anything like it before. It was the first film to be honored by a White House showing. This film spoke to the emotions through the eyes. It showed for all to see that the South was "right" about the Negro, that the North was "right" about preserving the Union, that Reconstruction, which elevated Negroes and some poor whites, was a shameful thing, that the virtue of Southern white womanhood had to be protected from "Negro

4 See also Section II, The Birth of *Birth of a Nation*.

brutes," and that when all seemed lost, the Ku Klux Klan heroically rushed in to save the day. An excellent summary of the social message of this film has been made by Jacobs:

The film was a passionate and persuasive avowal of the inferiority of the Negro. In viewpoint it was, surely, narrow and prejudiced. Griffith's Southern upbringing made him completely sympathetic toward Dixon's exaggerated ideas, and the fire of his convictions gave the film rude strength. At one point in the picture a title bluntly editorialized that the South must be made "safe" for the whites. The entire portrayal of the Reconstruction days showed the Negro, when freed from white domination, as arrogant, lustful, villainous. Negro congressmen were pictured drinking heavily, coarsely reclining in Congress with bare feet upon their desks, lustfully ogling the white women in the balcony. Gus, the Negro servant, is depicted as a renegade when he joins the emancipated Negroes. His advances on Flora, and Lynch's proposal to Elsie Stoneman, are overdrawn to make the Negro appear obnoxious and audacious. The Negro servants who remain with the Camerons, on the other hand, are treated with patronizing regard for their faithfulness. The necessity of the separation of Negro from white, with the white as the ruler, is passionately maintained throughout the film.[5]

In those days, liberals fighting in the cause of the Negro were not too many nor too strong. For example, the National Association for the Advancement of Colored People was but a few years old and in a sense had been founded because public opinion had shown itself to be so indifferent to the abuse of the Negro and the denial to him of elementary rights. Nevertheless, *Birth of a Nation* was recognized for what it was and was fought. Small riots broke out in Boston and a few other communities. The National Association for the Advancement of Colored People sought to have the film banned. Pamphlets and leaflets were issued against it. *The Nation* magazine called the film "improper, immoral and injurious . . . a deliberate attempt to humiliate ten million American citizens and to portray them as nothing but beasts." Dr. Albert Bushnell Hart, well-known historian at Harvard, pointed out the inaccurate and unfair picture given of the Union soldier "intended

[5] Lewis Jacobs, *The Rise of the American Film*. New York: Harcourt, 1939, p. 177.

to leave upon minds the conviction that in Reconstruction time the Negro soldiers freely plundered and abused whites of the South and were encouraged to do so by white officers." [6] D. W. Griffith, the film producer, rose to its defense with a pamphlet entitled *The Rise and Fall of Free Speech in America,* which included copious quotations from leading newspapers and magazines that had endorsed the film.

All this public commotion was a great boon to the box office. The film was banned in less than a dozen cities. The most objectionable scenes were "cut" in several other places. Since the movement was not at all strong enough to prohibit the showing of the film, it served as a great advertisement to thousands who otherwise might never have heard of it. This is not unusual in the history of social action programs. Nevertheless, for the first time the American people began to realize the power of the movie for social suggestion and for influencing life itself. *Birth of a Nation* was popular for a decade and doubtlessly did incalculable damage to race relations. Its glorification of the Ku Klux Klan was at least one factor that enabled the Klan to enter upon its period of greatest expansion, reaching a total membership of five million. Present-day attempts to revive the film usually have been beaten back by Negro, liberal, and radical groups. Revival showings today cut out the Reconstruction scenes, which are the most offensive.

The Talkie

The next great turning point in the development of the movie as a popular art form came in 1927 when the *Jazz Singer* made it clear that the "talking picture" would be the movie of the future. Al Jolson, in blackface, sang his songs well and captivated his audiences with the naturalness of his speaking voice. Definitely, a new dimension had been added to this form of mass entertainment. Between the *Birth of a Nation* and the *Jazz Singer* were about two dozen films with important Negro characters or scenes. About all these followed the usual pattern. None, save *Free and*

6 These quotations are from "Moving-Pictures" scrapbooks in the Schomburg Collection of the New York Public Library.

Equal, even attempted to approach *Birth of a Nation* in a direct appeal to race hatred. *Free and Equal* was a cheap imitation of the real thing. It failed miserably in its attempt to capitalize upon the popularity of the anti-Negro-equality theme. *The Nigger* was more objectionable in title than in content. It was an adaptation of Edward Sheldon's novel, *The Governor.* With one or two exceptions, films between 1915 and 1927, when they treated the Negro at all, adhered to the stereotypes.

The movie industry experienced a great expansion as a result of the introduction of the "talkie." Since Negroes are generally accredited with highly musical voices, it might be expected that this new medium of sound would open up new opportunities to them in Hollywood. In a sense this was true. In the period from 1927 to 1939 (when the next great anti-Negro picture was produced), the number of Negro parts in Hollywood films greatly increased. Let us see how often the stereotypes were departed from.

There were, to begin with, the *Our Gang* comedies of child life. This series was first started back in the days of the silent film. Comparatively speaking, their record for fair play was well above the average. Some of the films may be classified as pro-Negro in that the humor and pathos which come to children were presented without any "race angling." The children were not separated. They played together, easily and naturally, though in some of the films there was a tendency to place the Negro child in a somewhat more ridiculous or subservient position. The Negro child actors, with one exception, were brilliant and winsome. Even now film fans speak with enthusiasm of Sunshine Sammy, Farina, and Stymie. Buckwheat did not come off so well nor was he (or she) so well cast. Occasionally, Negro movie fans would protest about a line here or a situation there, but on the whole, *Our Gang* maintained itself as one of Hollywood's few contributions to better Negro-white relations.

Another attempt of Hollywood to do better by the Negro may be noted in one of the all-Negro features which appeared in 1929. King Vidor, with appropriate newspaper flourishes, produced *Hallelujah.* This was his first talking picture. It was also the first, Hollywood-produced, all-Negro feature. Technically, it registered

certain advances; sociologically, there may be some doubt. Nina
Mae McKinney and Daniel Haynes were the stars. The scenes were
laid in the cotton fields and city dives of the South. There was the
eternal struggle between good and evil as symbolized by a man of
God and a woman of the devil. Naturally, this gave many opportunities for preaching, shouting, baptizing, soul saving, spirtual
singing, dancing, gambling, love-making, and general good times.
A double premiere for the film was held in New York City at the
Astor Theater downtown and the Lafayette Theater in Harlem.
Most of the reviewers and the daily press liked *Hallelujah*. Some
of the Negro newspaper critics did, too. W. E. B. Du Bois, usually
hard to please, said that it was "beautifully staged under severe
limitations . . . a sense of real life without the exaggerated farce
and horseplay, . . . marks *Hallelujah* as epoch-making." [7] However, there were those who disagreed. Letters to the editor spoke
of King Vidor's "filthy hands reeking with prejudice." Another
commentator referred to *Hallelujah*'s "insulting niggerisms." Almost everyone seemed to like that "sweet little copperish brown-
skin," Nina Mae McKinney.[8]

Hallelujah was significant in that it gave Negro actors important
roles and did not exhibit the crude insults that disturbed Negro
patrons; however, it did not advance very far beyond the usual
stereotypes, and as everyone could see, being all-Negro was by that
token a jim-crow film. It was a box-office failure. Did it fail because
the producers were too timid or because they themselves were
prisoners of the popular stereotypes of the Negro? If they believed
the stereotypes were true, when they attempted to tell "the truth"
they still portrayed stereotypes. One historian of the American
movie had this to say:

In undertaking *Hallelujah*, Vidor also said he was primarily interested
in showing the Southern Negro as he is. The deed fell short of the
intent. The film turned out, however, to be a melodramatic piece
replete with all the conventionalities of the white man's conception of
the spiritual-singing, crap-shooting Negro.[9]

[7] *Crisis*, October 1929, p. 356.
[8] These quotations are from the Schomburg Collection scrapbooks.
[9] Jacobs, *op. cit.*, p. 458.

During this same year another all-Negro feature was presented to the public by Hollywood. This was *Hearts in Dixie*. Stepin Fetchit was the star. His great art was used to drive in deeper than ever the stereotype of the lazy Negro good-for-nothing.

The two most controversial "Negro films" of this period were *Emperor Jones* and *Imitation of Life*. Paul Robeson was the star in the screen version of Eugene O'Neill's play. With few exceptions, critics in the daily press praised this as one of the best films of the year. The Negro critics were divided. Some thought that it was well that a Negro emperor should be shown and that a white man, for the first time, could be presented on the screen as his lackey. Others, however, emphasized the pullman-porter, chain-gang, and voodoo scenes. Before the final act, Robeson, the emperor, is grovelling on his belly in the spirit-infested jungle. The *Chicago Defender* carried Robeson's picture under the caption "Attacked by Film Fans." One writer charged O'Neill and Hollywood with the purpose of presenting the Negro as "essentially craven." [10]

The controversy over *Imitation of Life* came to such a point that Fannie Hurst, the author of the novel by the same name, and Sterling Brown, who was then writing criticism for *Opportunity* magazine, were the principals in a clash of opinion. In criticism of the self-effacing Negro character, Brown wrote: "once a pancake, always a pancake." Fannie Hurst thought that Negroes should be a little more grateful for the "break" which she had given them in her novel and which carried over into the screen story. Editorials in the Negro press were rather unanimous in their praise of Louise Beavers and Fredi Washington as actresses, but they expressed annoyance and disgust at many scenes. In one of these Miss Beavers tells her former mistress that she does not wish to take her share of the profits from their joint pancake business and move into a home of her own; rather, true to the role of the devoted servant, she desires to remain "on the premises" to serve her white "ma'am" and "to rub your little feet every night when they are tired, just like I always used to do." Apparently, all the ex-Negro maid wanted for herself was a big funeral with white horses. "Peola,"

[10] *Ibid.*

the name of the maid's mulatto daughter who either wanted to be white or, at least, enjoy all the privileges that the daughter of the white woman enjoyed, became for a time a widely used term in Negro conversation. The comment of the *Literary Digest* was quoted with approval by many Negro newspapers:

The real story, the narrative which is merely hinted at, never really contemplated, is that of the beautiful and rebellious daughter of the loyal Negro friend. She is light-skinned, sensitive, tempestuous; she grows bitterly indignant when she sees that the white girl with whom she has been reared is getting all the fine things of life while she is subjected to humiliation and unhappiness.

Obviously, she is the most interesting person in the cast. Her drama is the most poignant, but the producers not only confine her to a minor and carefully handled subplot, but appear to regard her with a bit of distaste. They appear to be fond of her mother, because she is of the meek type of old-fashioned Negro that, as they say, "knows his place," but the daughter is too bitter and lacking in resignation for them.[11]

Space prohibits more than a bare mention of many other films. The favorable Negro films make a short list. Among them were *Arrowsmith*, which included Clarence Brooks as a dignified Negro doctor in the West Indies (a reviewer for the Associated Negro Press termed this "the best legitimate part ever allotted to a colored actor in the history of the movies"); *Flying Down to Rio*, in which Etta Moten sang and a chorus danced the "Carioca"; *The Spirit of Youth*, which told the story of the life of Joe Louis and *The Singing Kid*, in which Cab Calloway and Al Jolson pal about on equal terms before Calloway and his band render their musical numbers.

Huckleberry Finn, with Rex Ingram in the "Nigger Jim" role, did show the passionate wish for freedom on the part of the runaway slave and the human response to this sentiment on the part of the unspoiled youngster. *Dark Rapture* was one of the few authentic films of Africa to reach the commercial theater houses. *Dark Sands* and *Sanders of the River* were British-produced films of Africa. Paul Robeson was the star in both. Opposite him were Nina Mae McKinney and Princess Kouka, beautiful enough lead-

[11] December 8, 1934.

ing ladies who were, this time, given sufficient scope to display their artistic talents. In this regard these pictures were above the average, yet they were, after all, justifications and apologies for colonial imperialism. *Sanders of the River*, for example, was advertised as the story in which three white men held at bay a war-crazed empire of three million natives. Robeson, though majestic enough in his own kingdom, is made to appear subservient before white men. At one point in the story an African chief asks Robeson, "Whose dog are you?" This was, a critic said, one of the frank and delicious moments of the film.[12]

The films unfavorable to the Negro make a long list. There were, for example, the *March of Time* newsreels on Harlem voodoo and Father Divine; various Stepin Fetchit pictures like *Judge Priest* and *Carolina* (with Hattie McDaniel); various Bill Robinson pictures like *The Little Colonel, The Little Rebel* and *Steamboat 'Round the Bend*; various Clarence Muse pictures like *So Red the Rose*, in which one little white Southern girl from the big house routs a plantation insurrection by slapping the face of one of the Negro insurrectionists. Louis Armstrong appears in Bing Crosby's haunted house café in *Pennies From Heaven. King Kong* and *Baboona* were typical African films with the usual emphasis upon the naked, "primitive," black savages who consider every blonde a goddess and every trader or missionary a god. These African films sometimes went so far as to show an animal absconding with a native woman or actually eating a native man as in *When Africa Speaks. Trader Horn*, though ambitious and expensive, was pointed out to be false and misleading. In *The Green Pastures*, another all-Negro feature, Hollywood turned the rather majestic and dignified play into a light, and for the most part, ridiculous travesty. In *Show Boat* Paul Robeson got a chance to do some magnificent singing. However, he was merely a roustabout with the maid-cook Hattie McDaniel as his wife. "Moran and Mack" continued the stereotyped blackface minstrel tradition with *Hypnotized.*

12 Schomburg Scrapbooks.

The Era of "Gone With the Wind"

With *Gone With the Wind,* the creation of a motion picture became a national event. Already the country had "gone wild" over the novel. By 1939, the year the film was made, more than 2 million copies of the book had been sold. When to this were added reprints, cheap editions, and serialized versions, it meant that half the book-reading public in the United States had read Margaret Mitchell's super "best seller." It was advertised in the *American Historical Review* as the greatest historical novel ever written by an American.[13]

This wide interest was kept at fever heat by skillful publicity. Hollywood's search for a suitable Scarlett O'Hara lasted for a year, brought forth thousands of candidates, and finally ended up with the selection of an English actress, Vivian Leigh. When the filming actually began there was some sensational or intriguing story about it each week, to keep the public interest from lagging. Before the production was completed, some two years and $3.7 million had been spent. The great day came on Thursday, December 14, 1939. All eyes turned to Atlanta, Georgia—sometimes called the capital of the South—for the long-awaited world premiere. Below the Mason and Dixon line it was a day of glory. For Atlanta it was more than a holiday. Confederate flags and the festival spirit pervaded the town. Several governors of neighboring states were on hand. Newspapers editorialized at length and published corrected versions of the "Rebel Yell."

The South was right. *Gone With the Wind* said in the most effective manner possible that the antebellum South, that wondrous land of beauty and happy slaves, had been destroyed by Union soldiers and carpetbaggers. The Negroes in the film, as in the novel, did not want to be free. They were shown as liars, would-be rapists, mammies, and devoted field hands. All of this was so interwoven with the story, presented so beautifully in technicolor, with all the arts of sight and sound coordinated, that the effect on the unsuspecting patron was irresistible.

The parallels with *Birth of a Nation* are instructive. Both were

13 October 1936, p. vii.

about the South, the Civil War, and the Negro. Both were remarkable films from the artistic and technical point of view, though *Gone With the Wind* was a bit too long (3 hours; 45 minutes) and the last half was less competent than the first half. Both were huge financial successes—as early as 1940 it was estimated that *Gone With the Wind* would gross $60 million.[14] Both were great as anti-Negro propaganda, but differed in their approaches. While *Birth of a Nation* was direct, *Gone With the Wind* was subtle. The social consciousness of the nation had developed to such a point that the inflammatory appeals of 1915 were not permissible in 1939. Perhaps there was little need for the former obviousness. The art of suggestion had matured.

Some critics felt that where *Birth of a Nation* ended, *Gone With the Wind* began. The latter completed the job of wiping out of the public mind the "Northern" view of slavery, Civil War, and Reconstruction, replacing it with the traditional "Southern" view. Ideologically the South had won the Civil War. The defeat which it suffered on the field of battle was more than repaired by its victory over the minds of the American people through history books, novels, and now the motion pictures. Some critics felt that the final touch to this victory came with the award to Hattie McDaniel of an "Oscar" from the Academy of Motion Picture Arts and Sciences for her role as "Mammy."

Despite the triumph of the film, a vigorous fight was waged against it. During the production period the National Association for the Advancement of Colored People and other groups were successful in getting some of the most offensive scenes eliminated or, as in some instances, softened. The film as finally released was not as bad as the novel. Perhaps these concessions were the reasons that the NAACP did not lead or even join in the fight against the showing of the finished product. This fight was led by groups like the National Negro Congress, certain Negro newspapers, and "left" political groups. The *Socialist Appeal* denounced the film as a glorification of the old South. Virtually all of the other radical groups did likewise. But it was the Communist Party which carried

[14] In June 1944 the producers estimated that 63.5 million persons in the United States and Canada had seen *Gone With the Wind*.

on the most consistent struggle against it. To begin with, the motion picture reviewer who refused to expose the anti-Negro bias of the film was fired from the staff of the *Daily Worker*. Editorials, articles, cartoons in this newspaper and in the *New Masses* blasted *Gone With the Wind* as "vicious," "reactionary," "inciting to race hatred," "slander of the Negro people," and "justifying Ku Klux Klan." The New York State Committee of the Communist Party resolved that:

Gone With the Wind revives every foul slander against the Negro people, every stock-in-trade lie of the Southern lynchers. While dressed in a slick package of sentimentality for the old "noble" traditions of the South, this movie is a rabid incitement against the Negro people. The historical struggle for democracy in this country which we have come to cherish so dearly is vilified and condemned. The great liberator, Abraham Lincoln, is pictured as a tyrant and a coward. Not only is this vicious picture calculated to provoke race riots, but also to cause sectional strife between the North and the South just when the growth of the labor and progressive movement has made possible the increasing unity of Negro and white, in behalf of the common interests of both.[15]

Negro leaders in Harlem, Brooklyn, other Northern cities, and in a few Southern communities condemned the film. The National Negro Congress issued news releases and handbills and joined with other Negro and "left" groups to picket theaters where the film was shown. Some trade unions and units of the American Labor Party in New York supported these moves. This large effort to have the film banned, withdrawn, or boycotted was altogether unsuccessful, even in Negro neighborhoods. But it did serve to further "educate" the public to something of an awareness of anti-Negro elements in motion pictures and the power of the movie for developing social attitudes.

The net effect of such a film on the public mind can only be guessed. Walter White himself said that whatever sentiment there was in the South for a federal antilynch law evaporated during the *Gone With the Wind* vogue. At least one Southern child, who had seen the film, is reported to have told his Negro nursemaid that

[15] *Daily Worker*, January 15, 1940.

this servant would still be a slave and "Daddy would not have to pay you" but for the Yankees.

Since "Gone With the Wind"

Since 1939 the story of the Negro in motion pictures must be summarized and telescoped. Generally speaking, from the Negro angle, the films have improved. Some of the most objectionable ones were like *The Texan* and *Santa Fe Trail.* In the former a lone, drunken Negro in the uniform of the Union army staggers down the street of a Southern city during the Reconstruction period and blurts out "Gangway for the United States Army." In the latter the abolitionist hero, John Brown, is transformed into an inhuman fanatic. In the *Prisoner of Shark Island,* one unarmed white man audaciously approaches Negro troops with guns pointed toward him and commands, "Put that gun down, Nigrah!" And the Negroes, true to Hollywood, say to themselves, "He means it. He's no Yankee. He's a Southern white man." Obediently, they put their guns down.

Mr. Washington Goes to Town was advertised as the first all-Negro feature comedy. Its general tone may be indicated by the confession of one character in the film that "pork-chops is the fondest thing I is of." *Tennessee Johnson* was fought by the National Negro Congress, "left" groups, and trade unions as being anti-Negro and antidemocracy in the sense that it glorified President Andrew Johnson and his cooperation with the "Southern Bourbon aristocracy." This film, too, was modified at the suggestion of the NAACP prior to its release and again the NAACP declined to join in the public fight against it. However, more other-than-Negro support for the fight against this film was mobilized than ever before. Perhaps this was largely responsible for the box-office failure of this production.

On the other hand, most of the films within the past five years have been above this level and some have been far above it. *Keep Punching*, though a second-rate production, told a straightforward story of the life of the pugilist Henry Armstrong. Joe Louis returned to the screen in *This Is the Army*. Here the parts given to

Negroes were not particularly distasteful in themselves, but they were small parts, confined to the usual singing and dancing with a zoot-suit background. Withal, the Negro soldiers never got mixed up with the white soldiers, even in the fun making. *Tales of Manhattan* was remarkable not in that it repeated the familiar stereotype of the superstitious Negro, but that a "great and progressive" artist like Paul Robeson should accept such a role. Robeson, as before, responded to public criticism by saying that he did not realize what he was doing until he got too far into his lines and contract to turn back. He volunteered to join a picket line if one should be thrown around any theater showing the film. In one episode Robeson and Ethel Waters, as two farmworkers, find a wad of money that has fallen from an airplane. They are made to appear so credulous as to believe that the United States currency came from Heaven. It should be added, in all fairness, that before the sequence is concluded Robeson does get a chance to speak brave words of security for all. Some critics admitted that his role "might have been worse."

Fury and *The Ox Bow Incident* are two of the few American-made films that show the lynch mob. These represent high points for Hollywood courage. This courage, however, is not unlimited. For example, in *Fury* there is no Negro. In *The Ox Bow Incident* there is a Negro but he is not the lynch victim, nor does the lynching take place in the South. Nevertheless, the lynch spirit is shown. It is not glorified. As a matter of fact, the symbolism is so skillful in *The Ox Bow Incident* that the leader of the mob is a Southerner, and the lone Negro in the story—Leigh Whipper—is shown to be on the side of "justice, humanity and civilization." Incidentally, Whipper had a role of similar importance, calling forth sympathy and understanding, in *Of Mice and Men*. *Proud Valley* (also known as *The Tunnel*) is unusual in that a Negro appears as the star of a film in which all the other actors are white. However, the locale is not the United States nor are there any love scenes which involve him. Instead, the Welsh miners do a great deal of singing and digging in the mines. Robeson, the star, comes off well. Altogether this is a great step forward for the film industry.

Young Pushkin, produced in Russia, was the straight story of the early life of Alexander Pushkin, the Russian poet of part Negro ancestry. This story was told without the slightest "race" consciousness. No American film has ever reached this height. The three American-made films that perhaps came nearest to it were: *In This Our Life, Bataan,* and *Sahara. Arrowsmith,* produced back in 1931, is about the only other Hollywood film that goes into their class. All of these depart from the stereotypes.

In *In This Our Life* (Warner Brothers), an earnest, truthful, energetic Negro lad, speaking perfect English, refuses "to take the rap" for the wreckless, neurotic, Southern belle, who, in a fit of temper (her sister's husband did not keep the rendezvous with her), runs down a child with her automobile. The Negro boy, despite threats and bribes, refuses to "Uncle Tom." Instead, he "talks back" and airs the Negro problem with courage and dignity. Incidentally, this Negro boy is presented as a clerk and law student—not, as usual, a cotton picker or a tapdancer. This picture won a place on the Honor Roll of Race Relations for 1942. *Bataan* told the story of the last ditch stand there of American soldiers against the Japanese enemy. There is a Negro soldier—Kenneth Spencer —who is drawn as naturally and sympathetically as are any of his half-dozen companions. They all behave like men. The NAACP presented an award to Warner Brothers for this creditable production. In *Sahara* (Columbia), the French Negro soldier—Rex Ingram—is handsome. He is perhaps the first Negro on the sceen who has been permitted to have a white man as his personal servant—a captured Italian soldier. The Negro soldier is allowed to be brave and intelligent. He uses his hands as a cup for the dripping water that quenches the thirst of the whole group. As a climax this Negro, in the face of gunfire, overtakes a fleeing Nazi, physically overcomes him, and pushes his blonde head down into the desert sand. This may be the first time ever that any Negro— even a foreign Negro—has been permitted by Hollywood to assume a heroic role while killing a white man, even an enemy.

Four all-Negro films illustrate another positive, though limited, development. *Dr. George Washington Carver* was a feature built around the life and work of the scientist. Not a first-rate production, yet it was important historically. It has been reported that at least one Hollywood studio is interested in a full-length story of Carver's life. *Cabin in the Sky* exhibited the stereotypes, yet these were softened considerably. For example, the line "eating fried chicken all the time" was deleted from the theme song of the film. The Negro couples who dance and sing do so with grace and restraint. They are attractive couples. When the inevitable brawl occurs in the cabaret, the participants fight with guns and not with the traditional razors. Lena Horne, here as elsewhere, is permitted to be a beautiful girl. Ethel Waters is given a chance to do some real acting and the jokes are not necessarily derogatory to the Negro. *Stormy Weather* was one of those great star-studded musicals. It contained no particular indignities, though, again, the Negro is an entertainer. Within this limitation, all sorts of talents are displayed. Especially noteworthy are the dances of the Nicholas Brothers and Katherine Dunham. However, this film, like all other Negro films, is jim crow. In that sense it is false and objectionable.

The Negro Soldier, produced under the auspices of the War Department itself, is significant because of this sponsorship and because, for the first time, the story of the Negro in the wars of the United States has been told through motion pictures. The terrific struggle "to educate" the War Department and the film producers to this point is a great tale yet untold. An additional effort has been necessary in order to assure a wide distribution and presentation of the film to other-than-Negro audiences. The three chief objections to *The Negro Soldier* have been (1) it is too long for a "short" and too short for a full-length feature, (2) it slides over the Civil War period (in which some two hundred thousand Negroes fought on the Union side) in order to avoid hurt to Southern sensibilities, (3) it does not present the real problems of the Negro in the army. Despite these objections, plus the fact that it is, too, a jim-crow picture, this film is considered an important step forward.

Pattern of Change

Thus, from these brief notes the social function of the movie in the realm of race relations should be clear. The following generalizations seem to be justified:

1. That the Negro is usually presented as a savage or criminal or servant or entertainer.
2. That the usual roles given to Negro actors call for types like Louise Beavers, Hattie McDaniel, "Rochester," Bill Robinson, Clarence Muse, and various jazz musicians.
3. That other groups such as Orientals, Mexicans, and South Europeans are sometimes presented unfavorably, but no religious or racial minority is so consistently "slandered" as the Negro.
4. That films have improved somewhat during the present war.
5. That when an attempt is made to improve the treatment of the Negro on the screen, the improvement usually takes place within the limitations of an all-Negro film.
6. That these limitations on the Negro are also important as limitations on the development of the movie as an art form and as an organ of democratic culture.

The testimony is virtually unanimous from those who are aware of the treatment of the Negro by the movie that such portrayal is inaccurate and unfair. Directly and indirectly it establishes associations and drives deeper into the public mind the stereotyped conception of the Negro. By building up this unfavorable conception, the movies operate to thwart the advancement of the Negro, to humiliate him, to weaken his drive for equality, and to spread indifference, contempt, and hatred for him and his cause. This great agency for the communication of ideas and information, therefore, functions as a powerful instrument for maintaining the racial subordination of the Negro people.[16]

If all this is true, it goes without saying that any real program of correcting the mistreatment of the Negro by the movie industry must include basic changes in the social order of which the movies are a part. But more immediately and directly such a program would surely need to consider:

1. The use of noncommercial movies that treat the Negro favorably. There are any number of worthwhile films that have been produced

[16] Lester Granger, executive secretary of the National Urban League, among others, has said: "One of the greatest handicaps that the Negro has to face in his fight for complete integration into the American social scene is the persistent American stereotype which portrays him as a criminal, potential or actual, or as a stupid, doltish clown." Quoted in the *New York Post*, April 17, 1937.

or distributed by government agencies, labor unions, film libraries, or other educational institutions. The entertainment quality of this type of film is being constantly improved. Churches, schools, libraries, clubs, YMCAs, and other organized groups could make wide use of these inexpensive shows.

2. Production of more and better films by Negroes themselves. Frankly, most of the movies made by Negro producers have been of third-rate quality. Yet the success of Oscar Micheaux with his melodramas suggests what could be done if those who know better would help.

However, the main effort must be concentrated on the commercial film—Hollywood. The question has been asked many times: why does Hollywood treat the Negro so. As the *New York Age* put it, "When will Hollywood producers have the guts and moral courage to give a true-to-life version of Negro characters when they are intimately associated with white characters?" [17] The first answer may be that most of the Hollywood producers believe that they are presenting the Negro "as he is." But beyond this superficial naïveté, it is to be remembered that the movie industry is a money-making business. It has been said that Hollywood will produce anything that it can get away with *that will sell.* This may be an extreme generalization, but one important executive of the movie industry himself has said:

We are in the game to make money, not to make friends or enemies. We produce whatever it pays to produce, regardless of color or creed of the subjects. In order to realize adequate profits on a production, distribution must be nation-wide. It does not suffice that the East, West, and North accept Negro pictures, and the South refuses to accept pictures wherein Negroes are starred.[18]

And the South does insist upon the color line upon the screen. There have been Southern associations against "social equality" on the screen. Some of these, like the Southern Film Association, go so far as to object to all-Negro films like *Hallelujah* since Negroes are the stars in them.

[17] February 23, 1935.
[18] The *Afro-American*, May 17, 1930. For a more recent statement see interview with Samuel Goldwyn as quoted in the *Los Angeles Tribune* February 28, 1944.

The strategy of those working for better treatment of the Negro, accordingly, must be worked out in terms of the profit motive of the industry. Hollywood will respond to the proper pressures just like everything else does. The following steps may be suggestive:

1. There should be local committees for cultural democracy as part of the race relations betterment organizations. These should be affiliated to a national committee of this sort.
2. Such committees should undertake sufficient research to document, chapter and verse, the generalization that the Negro is inaccurately and unfairly presented on the screen.
3. The widest dissemination ought to be given to this information so that the movie-going public, movie critics, actors, screen writers, and producers will be aware of these facts.
4. Direct contact should be established and maintained with all the elements that enter into the production and distribution of films. This means that such conferences as those of Walter White and Wendell Willkie with Hollywood executives should be repeated and that the organizations of the screen writers, actors, distributors, film reviewers, and so forth should be worked with and induced to impose upon themselves a code such as has been worked out by the Emergency Committee of the Entertainment Industry. Negro actors in particular must be supported when they refuse to accept "Uncle Tom" and "Aunt Jemima" roles.[19]
5. All the devices of leaflet, news story, picket line, and so forth should be used to "educate" theatre-goers to the end of organizing boycotts of anti-Negro films. A good start may be made with the 500-odd theaters in Negro neighborhoods. But the fight must extend far beyond these limits. A special effort should be made to gain the support of progressive, liberal, religious, and labor-union-conscious groups.
6. Present censorship councils and boards of review should be worked with to include treatment of the Negro in films as part of their codes. These bodies include not only the movie industry's self-imposed Will Hays office but The National Legion of Decency, National Board of Review, and various religious, civic, and state councils.

[19] Lena Horne once said: "All we ask is that the Negro be portrayed as a normal person. Let's see the Negro as a worker at union meetings, as a voter at the polls, as a civil service worker or elected official." *PM*, July 8, 1943.

7. Though the Office of War Information has declined to advise Hollywood on the question of the treatment of the Negro, it and other
governmental agencies may be persuaded to throw their great influence in the right direction as is now done with reference to roles or
scenes that may be offensive to Latin America, China, and other
parts of the world. As a beginning the government might ban the
use of such terms as "nigger," "darky," "pickaninny," "smoke,"
"sambo," "coon," and "WACoon."

Alain Locke and Sterling A. Brown

2   Folk Values in a New Medium

[1930]

I

From the traditional sentimentalities of the moving-picture version of *Uncle Tom's Cabin* to anything approaching true folk values is a far way—not to be reached without at least one turning. That they should have been so notably attained in the next Hollywood venture in the portrayal of Negro life, *Hearts in Dixie*, is, after all, something of a modern miracle. It was a result of sincere experiment and a determination to overdo rather than miss the truly genuine, no doubt inspired by the sobering risk of large financial outlay but nevertheless as much the result of good luck as of the rewarded virtues of good management. *Uncle Tom*, with the exception of fairly genuine type portrayal on the part of James B. Lowe in the title role, had yielded on the Negro side little beyond the conventional values of blackface comedy and traditional sentiment. Everything was type reduced to formula, vacillating between the oversentimental and the overrealistic. Still, two things were definitely accomplished—the box-office possibilities of Negro themes were thoroughly demonstrated, and the values of Negro folk life advanced several steps beyond Octavus Roy Cohen farce and comedy. Hollywood jumped at the new lesson, and the first all-Negro talkie was the result.

Hearts in Dixie[1] caught Negro life at a level angle without much

[1] See also Section II, *Hearts in Dixie*.

distortion, and in spite of some sporadic tinting from the plantation tradition and occasional intrusion of slapstick comedy, projected a really moving folk idyl on the peasant level. The usual
types are there—the Daddy, Uncle, the Mammy, and the inevitable
pickaninnies, but in this group they are real flesh and blood Negroes evoking a spontaneous and genuine human interest. In fact,
they have real individuality. Lazy Gummy is new because he is
crafty as well as lazy; the grandfather, too, because he is ambitious
and discerning as well as pious, loyal, and humble, and little
Chinquapin because, though the most lovable of pickaninnies, as
we see him leave on the river steamboat to go "up Nawth to
school," we feel that he might just as reasonably turn out a Booker
T. Washington as a roustabout or a longshoreman. The story is
sketchy; too often a slender skeleton for heavy coatings of "human
interest" and "local color"; but, nevertheless, *Hearts in Dixie* is the
truest pictorialization of Negro life to date. It is to the credit of
both the story and the production that, while they do not fully
exhaust the full depths of Negro life and character, they do not
perpetuate the old libels and the hackneyed caricatures.

To all this rather negative virtue, the acting adds something
really positive—another dimension that makes the chief roles
spiritual revelations of some fundamentals of Negro folk character.
Clarence Muse, Eugene Jackson, and Stepin Fetchit bring to a
focus qualities lacking in all previous movie productions of Negro
life, and rare even on the legitimate stage except in dramas like
Porgy—spontaneity, naturalness, unself-conscious charm. With
Muse the grandaddy has lost his "Uncle Tom" posturing, except
in a few obviously directed sob-moments; the children are spontaneous and unaffected. There is real depth to both the humor and
the pathos, and the absence of the clownish leer and the minstrel's
self-pity are real steps toward the genuineness of Negro emotion.
Of course, most genuine and spontaneous of all is Stepin Fetchit,
who contributes the still more typical quality of infectious rhythm
and mercurial change of mood. Indeed never before has this primitive capacity for becoming an incarnate emotion been more
graphically portrayed. Stepin Fetchit in this picture is as true as
instinct itself, a vital projection of the folk manner, a real child

of the folk spirit. In fact, it is the emotional vibrancy of the race, reflected in the acting and singing, that is the propelling force vitalizing the spectacular machinery and photography of this picture, and it is as evident in the trained artistry of Muse as in the wholly untrained and naïve being of the incomparable Fetchit.

Throughout, perhaps the greatest artistic triumph is that of the Negro voice in song and in speech. A fortunate shift from the obvious realism of the movies stakes the whole effect of the church scene and sermon on the sound of the preacher's voice booming through the closed doors of the pine-boarded chapel. Fine vocal effects are gotten in the more stereotyped but attractive cotton-field and levee scenes, but here, cut away from all dependence on stock pantomime, the Negro voice achieves an artistic triumph and becomes a more purely Negro thing, for once—a true peasant gem in a genuine setting. At points like this, with the glitter of "paste jewels" in mind, one wonders if happy accident or deliberate insight cleared the way for such thrilling glimpses of the folk spirit. Of course, if so, then with respect to this whole range of American life, the most conventional of the American arts has overleapt the claptrap conventions of generations.

II

Unfortunately *Hallelujah* relies heavily on the usual claptrap. It is obviously ambitious, attempting to fuse elements as diversified as Cohen's humor and *Porgy's* rhythmic design, as Berlin's mammy songs and the spirituals. It results in a potpourri, made no more palatable by its great dependence on rather stale ingredients. For instance, at the time set for the moving beauty of the baptism scene, we must have the commonplace anticlimax of a fat woman's falling in the water, with all the ridiculous corollaries. There is the threadbare belated wedding service with the eldest son serving as best man.

As this comes from Hollywood, we should probably be resigned to the trick plotting; to the coincidences such as the accidental death of the brother, the clouds breaking at the right moment in Zeke's conversion; to the silliness of waiting for a husband to come home before eloping noisily out a back window, although the husband has been away at work all day; to the unintelligible stupidity of Zeke as preacher, inconsistent with his projected character; to the Elmer Gantryism crudely overlaid with a poorly popularized Freud. We resign ourselves to a great deal, hoping that the milieu will be permitted to show, without too drastic an alteration, something of its own verve, and beauty, and dignity. The hope is not entirely vain.

There is first of all the singing. It is so good that it makes one reflect rather bitterly on the forfeited possibilities of the whole picture. Here are mellow, full voices, spontaneous and enthusiastic; making something rich and strange out of even the theme song—"The End of the Road." Such a transformation wasn't easy, because this song has really no connections with any point farther south than the lower East Side. Daniel L. Haynes, from his "Cotton, Cotton" to his simply moving "Going Home," is satisfying, and close to sources. Nina Mae McKinney seems to get something of Market Street into her "St. Louis Blues," something of the newer recklessness which may be one rendering of the folk classic. The old mother's lullaby while putting the children to bed is genuinely folk, and one of the highest points of the many high points in the singing. But most authentic of all, one feels, is the hypnotic effect of Victoria Spivey's wail, "He's gone,"—a chant that recalls the weird moans that have made this young artist's name a byword among the folk.

The more obvious type acting of Miss McKinney as Chick and of William Fountaine as Hotshot, siren and villain respectively of the piece, furnishes no such folk values as the nuances of some of the other characters. One would be bold to say that the triangle isn't a folk situation, but certainly this one smacks too much of Hollywood. The acting of Spunk, the kid brother who idolizes the strapping Zeke, is fine; Missy Rose is good; and the mother is priceless. They identify themselves with folk material; with the others, even at their best there is overacting and condescension. Chick is too consciously arch, Zeke seems too determined to speak dialect as the years have mistaught us that it should be spoken. But the mother makes up for much of this.

The dialogue is not memorable. Few lines seem to have the homeliness, the pungency, the imagery of folk speech at its best. Missy Rose's "Ah kin heah its heaht beatin'!"—with the new watch to her ear—and Mammy's splendidly scornful "You'd ought to be thankful he laid his holy hands on you," are shining examples of the few bits of dialogue that stick to the memory.

The plot, as may be gleaned, is hardly folk but Hollywood; the hero, lured by the vamp, who deserts him for the roué, expiates and returns chastened to the waiting girl, "at the end of the road." Sentimentality such as this is not in the best Negro folk tradition. Even so, however, *Hallelujah* is important. Its pioneering, its very failures, promise a great deal.

III

In these two pictures Hollywood has taken Negro life out of the conventional rut and advanced it almost to a point of vital realism. If acting and pantomime could have been brought up to the level of singing and dancing and speech, one might call even the present situation artistically satisfactory. For all their exploitation of local color, the settings such as the cotton bottoms, the levee, and the rock quarry are far too brief and patchy to give a seriously sustained background for values that have the highest artistic potentialities. What is most interesting is to see how trite plot, farce, and melodrama can be redeemed by folk versions of the primary emotions, and artificial, overcoached acting by instinctive racial tricks and mannerisms. These glimpses of a rich background promise great things if developed by the sensitive and courageous hand of one familiar with the Negro folk genius, and if received by an audience willing to forget something of what tradition has led it to expect.

Arthur Draper

3 Uncle Tom Will Never Die!

[1936]

What Hollywood thinks of the American Negro is best expressed by the roles given him in the motion picture. He may be the lazy, good-for-nothing comedian, exemplified by Stepin Fetchit and Sleep'n Eat; the simpleminded child of *Green Pastures*; the servile, "good nigger," Uncle Tom; the popeyed distortion of a hotcha performer in a Harlem nightclub interpreted so many times by Bill Robinson, "Fats" Waller, and Jennie LeGong; or the viciously antagonistic threat to white supremacy, cause of "race riots" and "lynching parties." It is this latter distortion with which the films are just beginning to deal, appropriately enough at a moment when, throughout the Deep South, Negro and white workers are beginning to get together jointly to fight for better living conditions in such organizations as the Sharecroppers' Union and that of the mineworkers and steelworkers in Birmingham.

Paramount's *So Red the Rose*, the film version of Stark Young's best-selling novel, with Margaret Sullavan, Walter Connolly, Janet Beecher, and Randolph Scott in leading roles, deliberately portrays the Negro masses of the South as stupid, sullen rioters. At the same time, it presents Daniel Haynes, the Adam of the stage version of *Green Pastures*, as the loyal Uncle Tom who is supposed to win the audience for the producer's conception of the Negro's place in American life.

The story is a libelous presentation of Southern Negroes of the

30

Civil War period. It pictures their revolt from their owners as based only upon laziness, greed, and hysteria. In the picture, its leaders are opportunists, misleading a simpleminded people.

The hope that this picture of the Negro will be popular throughout the jim-crow South led Paramount to send its director of advertising and publicity, Robert M. Gilham, on a tour of the Southern states for the purpose of enlisting the aid of such organizations as the Daughters of the Confederacy to assist in the exploitation and publicizing of the picture. This cooperation was not difficult to secure, and as a result, the picture had a simultaneous "preview" opening at each of the eleven capitals of the original states of the Confederacy. The "patriotic" organizations sent letters to all their members, no less than sixty thousand such promotional letters being sent out by the Daughters of the Confederacy alone.

Paramount knew what it was about when it started making this picture. One of its publicity stories pointed the problem succinctly: "Sociological experiments are by no means the purpose of film making and the few daring souls who have invaded this most controversial of all fields have met with disastrous failures." Paramount was already beginning to worry about this "sociological experiment."

"Yet there is a tendency in 1935," the release continued (and it has been published in scores of newspapers throughout the country), "to depart somewhat from the standardized forms of screen literature and to liberalize this media to conform to modern tolerance and thoughts." Thus, Hollywood must believe, and is passing on this belief to the American public, that *any* portrayal of a Negro in an American film is "a modern tolerance" and that the cinema's vicious conception of Negro characters is "a modern thought."

In the same publicity release, Hollywood takes pride that "there has been a marked decrease in that form of intolerance which specializes in the drawing of color lines and your colored performer of merit now shares marquee distinction with the whites." Yet, in Hollywood, his salary is lower; he is discriminated against on a jim crow basis, and you have never yet seen the photograph of a Negro actor, other than an artist's drawing or a cartoonist's caricature, displayed in a newspaper ad created in the offices of either the studios or the film distribution companies. Think back on the advertising campaign that sold *Emperor Jones* and *Sanders of the River*. No photograph of Paul Robeson was ever used in the advertising of either of these pictures.

So Red the Rose was directed by King Vidor, maker of *The Big Parade, Hallelujah, Our Daily Bread* and *The Wedding Night*. It was his expert handling of large groups in these pictures that have made them outstanding American films. But, how did King Vidor get the two hundred Negro members of the cast of *So Red the Rose* to depict the portrait of their race that he wished American audiences to see—a portrait, by the way, that is completely at variance with the historical documents of Du Bois and Beard. Another of Paramount's own publicity stories tells the tale:

It is in the slave quarters that most of Vidor's large group shots are taken. Hundreds of dishevelled negroes were photographed there. Negroes in jubilee spirit, chanting and singing the spirituals and folk songs which today are classics in musical history.

But this scene of jubilee and happiness filmed early in the morning took on a grimmer aspect in the afternoon's work. The slave quarters were the scene of rebellion; the chants changed to ominous growls as the negroes, goaded on by a leader, left this peaceful plantation scene to answer Marse Lincoln's call to liberty.

Vidor is familiar with the colored mind, and sympathetic as well. This perhaps accounts for his unusual interest in the black man and for his understanding of his likes and dislikes. And so, before he turned his cameras, he spoke to this mob for at least fifteen minutes, giving them a simple word picture of negro life during the period of slavery, stressing too the significance of the event which gave them their freedom.

The director holds the opinion that the colored race is the most difficult of all people to handle as a group in the making of motion pictures. Fundamentally living only for the joy they get out of life, they are inclined to laugh at serious things and this native comedy sometimes is difficult to overcome when sheer drama is necessary.

King Vidor took this day's work most seriously. He outlined his story to his colored group and made some of them cry through a somewhat maudlin presentation of the evils which their ancestors were supposed to have suffered. This had the effect of putting them in the proper mood and the rapid change from happiness to a sullen anger was accomplished without delay. (Author's emphasis—Editor.)

To placate the jim-crow confederacy, the publicity stories go on to point out that ". . . the director has constructed a large camp at Sherwood Forest for the blacks. They have their separate mess tents, their hospital and sleeping quarters and a huge entertainment tent where they congregate at night to put on a remarkable impromptu show."

To this tent at night, "most of the stars of the company go for relaxation. Margaret Sullavan, Randolph Scott, Walter Connolly, Daniel Haynes, and the supporting cast sit at a front row bench and watch long-legged Darby Jones dance until he falls into a state of exhaustion—a performance of primitive fervor that would panic a sophisticated Broadway audience."

It is entirely possible that King Vidor may have had little to say about the writing of the screen play for this picture. The film was given into the hands of producer Douglas MacLean, now off the Paramount lot, himself Southern born, raised by his "mammy," and many lines in the picture were drawn out of his own "experience."

The picture tells the story of an old, feudal, Southern family during the Civil War. Its treatment of its slaves is humane, understanding from the "white God" point of view. At no place in the story is hinted the encroachment of the industrialists who turned feudal plantation life into the "outdoor factory." Such a picture might have shown the speedup, beatings, starvation of the slaves, might have given American audiences an honest clue into the "revolt of the slaves" that took place during the Civil War. Thus, when the slaves on the Bedford plantation revolt, there is no sympathetic basis upon which they may turn against their white masters. One sees only crazed Negroes turning against the gentle hand that has cared for them so many years.

They revolt simply because Clarence Muse, in the role of Cato, a slave, holds before them the possibility of a life of laziness and greed; because he fans a hatred for the white folks that has no foundation in the motivation of the picture.

Thus, the first Northern cannon ball that falls on the plantation is the signal for the hysterical scream from a "kitchen Negro": "A message from Abe Lincoln, dat's what dat is! Abe Lincoln done sent a cannon ball to tell us he ain't far away! Abe Lincoln done sent the word!"

And when William, the "Uncle Tom" butler, played by Daniel Haynes, tells the coachman to walk the horses before stabling them, this is the reply: "I've unhitched horses for the last time. Let the white folks unhitch their own horses . . . I'se gonna be free—that's what I am." And hysterically shouting, he runs toward the slave quarters in an ecstatic frenzy, shouting "Free! Free! Free for true!"

In the slave quarters a scene of rebellion is pictured. Cato, the ringleader, is on a stump. The answers to his questions come like a choral response.

"You been slaves long enough, ain't ya?"

"Yes! That's right!"

"You want what belongs to you, don't ya?"

"Yes! Ain't it true? Thass right!"

"Are you going to take what belongs to you?"

"Yes! Yes! We sho' is!"

"Or wait until somebody else eats it up?"

"No! No! No we ain't!"

"All this is yours! Go and get it!"

Then is pictured a scene in the barns, sties, and pens, with the Negroes greedily lunging for pigs, nabbing squawking chickens, driving off horses, shouting, "I got mine! I got mine!"

And Cato declares, "Before long we'll all be sitting in the golden chairs in the big house . . ." He gets into the carriage. "Now we're goin' to the warehouse and gets ourselves things. It all belongs to us now! We're the kings!"

And there he builds up the frenzy that possesses them. "We are free! No more work! Marse Lincoln has given us de land! Has given us de houses! Not another day's work! Yankee army in blue coats coming down de road to give us everything to eat! No more plowing . . . no more breaking new ground . . . no more planting . . . no more chopping cotton! Just sittin' in the sun!"

It is the daughter of the house of Bedford (Margaret Sullavan) with her little brother (Dickie Moore) who breaks the revolt. She is worried lest sound of the shouting be carried to the manor house where her father is dying. And the methods she uses are so simple that they deny the seriousness of the slaves' rebellion. It is the old, sentimental, "Uncle Tom" attitude that ends the riot; after shaming one of the ringleaders with a single slap in the face, she reminds the rioters that they are all her friends, the friends who raised her from childhood, that she is their "little white bird," that they must continue to be "good." Chanting a hymn they follow her to the manor. When Malcolm Bedford dies, the slaves quietly disperse and leave the plantation.

It would be manifestly unfair to King Vidor to ignore some of the splendid directorial touches upon which his reputation is based. One of the most amusing scenes in the picture is the satire on Southern pride marching off to war, personified by Walter Connolly, as head of the Bedfords, who doesn't believe in the South's cause until he is wakened one night by the flat of a Union sabre on his broad posterior. Then, suddenly, the cause becomes alive and he turns the house out to find the beautiful uniform he once wore to a Governor's reception. For Marse Bedford is going off to war, attired as a Southern gentleman.

On the other hand it would constitute a negligence not to point out to Mr. Vidor that if *So Red the Rose* succeeds at the box office in the South it will be at the cost once again of provoking even sharper racial lines than exist in these states at the present time, of provoking an even greater hatred by the whites for the Negroes, of breaking the solidarity between workers of all races that is today beginning to change the Old South of infamous reputation into a New South built on workers' pride.

Albert Johnson

4   Beige, Brown, or Black

[1959]

The late 1940s, a brief period of sociological experimentation in American film making, contained several works dealing specifically with problems involving Negro characters. Such films as *Home of the Brave, Pinky, Lost Boundaries,* and *No Way Out* were particularly memorable because they attempted to portray the Negro in a predominantly white environment; and as a figure of dramatic importance, the Negro has long been overlooked or carefully avoided on the screen, chiefly because of the refusal of Southern theater exhibitors to book such films. The United States Motion Picture Code's rule regarding the depiction of Negro characters, notoriously outdated, has only managed to keep in effect a rigidly stereotyped view of a race whose economic and intellectual status has risen to such a degree since 1919 that one tends to look upon most Negro screen actors as creatures speaking the language of closet drama.

American drama has suffered from a lack of Negro playwrights (not to mention Negro screen writers) who are able to present their characters in authentic and dramatically informative situations, for certainly few racial groups in this country flourish so actively on a level of melodrama, except perhaps the Puerto Ricans in New York, and yet, the two most successful stage works about contemporary Negro life are based upon the same rather bland premise: the sudden acquisition of a large sum of money by a middle-class family (*Anna Lucasta* and *A Raisin in the Sun*). These plays succeed because they honestly develop character in an all-Negro milieu on a nonstereotyped basis—they reveal the Negro to audiences with the same sympathy and insight with which Sean O'Casey exhibited the Irish in *Juno and the Paycock*. So far, so good, but what has happened in the American cinema since the forties regarding the plight of the Negro?

First of all, the Supreme Court decisions regarding integration of Southern schools, in 1954, once more brought the entire question of Negro-white relationships to the attention of the world. The incidents ensuing from this historic decree have yet to be conveyed in either stage or screen terms, and apparently, no one is courageous enough to do anything about it, but, at any rate, the Arkansas affair stirred interest in the Negro race once more as a focus for drama. Secondly, it was apparently decided by various Hollywood producers that a *gradual* succession of films about Negro-white relationships would have a beneficial effect upon box-office returns and audiences as well. The first of these films, *Edge of the City* (1956), is the most satisfactory because it is the least pretentious. The performance by Sidney Poitier (the Negro actor whose career has most benefited by the renaissance of the color theme) was completely authentic, but true to the film code, any hint of successful integration must be concluded by death, usually in some particularly gory fashion, and so, Poitier gets it in the back with a docker's bale hook. The most constructive contribution of *Edge of the City* to film history is one sequence in which Poitier talks philosophically to his white friend, using language that rings so truthfully and refreshingly in the ears that one suddenly realizes the tremendous damage that has been nurtured through the years because of Hollywood's perpetration of the dialect myth. The film was praised for its honesty, but its conclusion was disturbing; audiences wanted to know *why* the Negro had to be killed in order for the hero to achieve self-respect.

Strangely enough, this promising beginning of a revival of American cinematic interest in interracial relationships took a drastic turn with Darryl F. Zanuck's lavish production of *Island in the Sun* (1957). The focus changed from concern for an ordinary friendship between men of different racial backgrounds to the theme of miscegenation, considered to be, in Hollywoodian terms, a much bolder and more courageous source of titillation.

This film, made solely for sensationalistic reasons, was supposed to depict racial problems on the fictional West Indian island of Santa Marta, but it became simply a visually fascinating document without a real sense of purpose. Against a background of tropical beauty, a series of romantic attachments and longings are falsely attached to a group of famous personalities, each of whom is given as little to do as possible.

Harry Belafonte, a Negro singer who has risen to the astonishing and unprecedented stature of a matinee idol, was presented as David Boyeur, a labor leader for the island's native population, and his obvious attraction for a socially distinguished white beauty, Mavis (Joan Fontaine) created a furor among the Southern theater exhibitors, who either banned the film or deleted the Belafonte-Fontaine sequences. Actually, there were no love scenes between the two, only glances of admiration and dialogue of almost Firbankian simplicity. In fact, Boyeur's decision not to make love to Mavis is evasive and full of choplogic, and every indication is given that poor Mavis will literally pine away thereafter among the mango trees. On the other hand, a Negro girl, Margot (Dorothy Dandridge) is allowed to embrace and eventually marry a white English civil servant (John Justin) and although their life on Santa Marta is segregated, they finally sail happily off to England together at the end of the film. And so, the crux of the matter of miscegenation is again at the mercy of the film production code. Although "color" is the most important problem on the island, it seems that a white man may marry a Negro girl and not only *live*, and live happily, but that a Negro man and a white woman dare not think of touching. There is an odd moment in *Island in the Sun* when (after watching Mavis yearn for Boyeur in sequence after sequence) the Negro reaches up and lifts her slowly from a barouche, holding her waist. The shock effect of this gesture upon the audience was the most subtle piece of eroticism in the film, and only the lack of honesty in the work as a whole made this hint of a prelude-to-embrace seem realistic.

Island in the Sun also stirred other concepts about color, for the problem of concealed racial ancestry is introduced, bringing out all sorts of moody behavior on the part of a young girl, Jocelyn (Joan Collins) and her brother, Maxwell (James Mason). Jocelyn attempts to break off her engagement to an English nobleman, but he ignores her racial anxieties and is willing to chance the improbabilities of an eventual albino in the family. Maxwell, however, is driven into gloom, drink, and eventual murder, one feels, because the Negro skeleton in the family closet has thoroughly rattled him. The entire film is certainly important as a study of the tropical myth in racial terms, and even Dandridge's character, though she comes out of the whole business fairly happily, is not entirely free from the stereotype of the Negro as sensualistic, for, at one point, she performs a rather unusual Los Angeles–primitive dance among the Santa Marta natives, an act that is quite out of character, if one knows anything at all about the problem of class consciousness among the Negroes themselves in the West Indies.

Miss Dandridge has been continually cast as the typically sexy, unprincipled lady of color, in all-Negro films like *Carmen Jones* (1956) and *Porgy and Bess* (1959), as well as in a singularly appalling film called *The Decks Ran Red* (1958), in which she is the only woman aboard a freighter in distress and, naturally, is pursued by a lusty mutineer, with much contrived suspense and old-hat melodrama. It is ironic, under the circumstances, to recall that this actress's dramatic debut in films coincided with that of Belafonte in *Bright Road* (1955), a minor work about a gentle schoolteacher and a shy principal in a Southern school.

The commercial success of *Island in the Sun* led to the decisive movement in Hollywood to make films dealing specifically with the theme of miscegenation. The color question appeared in the most unusual situations, particularly *Kings Go Forth* (1958), an epic cliché of wartime in France, where two soldiers (Frank Sinatra and Tony Curtis) find it nicer to be in Nice than at the front. Sam (Sinatra) falls in love with Monique Blair (Natalie Wood), whose parents are American, although she has been reared in France. Monique lives with her widowed mother and reveals to Sam that her father was a Negro. Exactly *why* this is introduced is never really clear unless it was intended to bring some sort of adult shock to a basically *What Price Glory* situation, for even Mademoiselle from Armentières is fashionably under the color line in contemporary war films. There is also a triangle complication, for while Sam is away, Monique becomes infatuated with Britt (Curtis) after hearing him play a jazz solo on a trumpet. This implies that even Monique's French upbringing cannot assuage the jazz tremors of her American Negro heritage. Of course, nothing is solved in the film. Although Sam and Britt go through a baptism of fire and limb loss, their characters are molded out of a screen clay pit as tough-talking, hard-drinking, callous hedonists, and the fact that both love *and* racial awareness are merged in their personalities is supposed to be basis for poignancy; besides, marriage with Monique is only weakly suggested at the conclusion of the film. Perhaps the most unfortunate part of *Kings Go Forth* was its adherence to the lamentable Hollywood practice of casting a white actress in the part of a mulatto heroine, thereby weakening even further an already unsuccessful attempt to jump on the bandwagon of popular film concepts regarding hardhearted American officers falling madly in love with foreign girls of another race. *Kings Go Forth* convinced one that racial films were once more in vogue, and the so-called taboo theme was simply a "gimmick."

Although it attempts boldness, *Night of the Quarter Moon* (1959) only belabors the question of intermarriage. Ginny (Julie London) marries a wealthy San Franciscan, Chuck Nelson (John Drew Barrymore) while on a vacation in Mexico. When she reveals that their marriage might cause them trouble because of her racial background (she is one-quarter Portuguese-Angolan, which is, one supposes, cause for some sort of genetic alarm), Chuck tells her that such statistics only bore him. However, the film erupts into a succession of violent and racially antagonistic episodes on the part of Chuck's society-minded mother (Agnes Moorehead), the San Francisco police force, and the neighbors. The fact that Chuck is a Korean war veteran, susceptible to mental blackouts and fatigue, creates an odd impression about American film myths of this nature. It would seem that war veterans are more susceptible to miscegenation, and that certain environments, like the Caribbean or Mexico, actually put one into that frame of mind that considers

racial backgrounds to be of major insignificance, eventually leading to intermarriage. All of this chaos leads to one of the most
incredible courtroom sequences in film history, during which
Ginny's Negro lawyer (James Edwards) strips the blouse from her
back in front of the judge so that her skin color can be revealed
as white. *Night of the Quarter Moon* did contain one notable
feature, however. It showed an adjusted, sophisticated, and extremely articulate interracial couple, Cy and Maria Robbin (Nat
Cole and Anna Kashfi), and Maria's summation of a white man's
general attitude toward a quadroon is a very forthright and adult
statement that takes one by surprise.

It is, indeed, the social position of an individual who is able to
pass for white that seems to bear most interest for film makers,
and it was only a matter of time (twenty-eight years) before a remake of *Imitation of Life* (1959) would appear. Fannie Hurst's
novel, a tear-jerker, could possibly have been a fine film, considering the different film techniques and audience attitudes of 1931
and 1959. However, the earlier version of the film is the more
honest of the two, if only for the fact that the mulatto girl, the true
figure of pathos, was played by Fredi Washington, a Negro actress.
But the basic premise that any Negro girl with a white skin is
doomed to despair on a social level is maintained in a most unreal
and almost farcical manner. The clichés are kept intact and aimed
at the tear ducts, and once more, one cannot help feeling that a
Negro screen writer might have been able to bring subtlety into
the characterizations. *Imitation of Life* is a hymn to mother love,
a popular fable of ironic contrasts between the light and the dark
realms of racial discrimination. A famous actress, Lora Meredith
(Lana Turner), and her daughter, Susie (Sandra Dee), are devoted
to the Negro maid, Annie Johnson (Juanita Moore), and her
mulatto child, Sarah Jane (Susan Kohner). But it is the behavior
of Sarah Jane as a beautiful young woman that is handled falsely.
Living in a nonsegregated environment in a Northern metropolis,
surrounded by the glamour of Lora's world of the theater, it is
inconceivable that Sarah Jane would be made to feel inferior by
people around her, especially since she is not, by any stretch of the
imagination, obviously a Negro. It is equally incomprehensible

that Sarah Jane's taste in clothes would not be affected by the chic apparel of both Lora and Susie, both of whom symbolize a world to which she very much wants to belong. The final stroke of absurdity lies in the sequence in which Sarah Jane is savagely beaten by her white boy friend (Troy Donahue) when he learns that she is a Negro, implying that anyone who attempts to step out of an established class structure, racially or otherwise, must be subjected to physical violence. This attitude (equally out of place in a film like *Room at the Top*) comes as a shock and reflects a dangerous kind of moralizing. As if inner anguish is not enough for an individual who is unable to successfully "pass" for white, or move from one social strata to another, one must behold such a character actually beaten up and thrown into the gutter.

In *Imitation of Life*, Annie's funeral is epic sentiment in the charlotte-russe tradition, complete with a spiritual by Mahalia Jackson—an episode that is completely fictional and as incredible to Negro spectators as it is to white; and Sarah Jane's psychological maladjustment never leads one to imagine that she would so blatantly embrace her Negro heritage by hysterically throwing herself upon her mother's coffin; also one is never told what the girl eventually does or becomes. What is not understood by the makers of *Imitation of Life* is that a Negro's sympathies are with Sarah Jane, *not* Annie, and that contemporary audiences are able to discern the finely hypocritical dictums of the fake solution, the outdated stereotypes of the code, and, in a sense, the anti-integrationist's point of view.

The Negro character in the 1950s is very much the hero or heroine in isolation, and the cinema never quite illustrates this quality of "invisibility" and frustration as often as it should. Perhaps the most effective presentation of this particular aspect of racial adjustment is *The World, the Flesh and the Devil* (1959), in which Ralph Burton (Harry Belafonte) finds that he is the only person alive in New York City after some great destructive force has swept away all human existence. The horror of loneliness in New York, a potential Angkor Vat surrounded by steel foliage, is brilliantly evoked, at once underlining one's contemporary fears of sudden, radioactive destruction, and emphasizing the symbolic figures of the Negro hero alone in society.

The appearance of two white people throws the film back into the world of color consciousness. Sarah Crandall (Inger Stevens) meets Ralph, and for a time they exist together, but he insists upon maintaining separate living quarters. The racial issue remains symbolically in his mind, though, in reality, it is gone with the civilization around them. When Benson Thacker (Mel Ferrer) arrives, however, a triangle is created, a wall of simple-minded cliché obscures the true situation, and after a gun battle and fight, the men declare peace, join hands with Sarah, and walk into the oblivion of Wall Street together.

This parable exemplifies today's approach to the theme of inter-racialism; vague, inconclusive, and undiscussed. Like a fascinating toy, American film makers survey the problem from a distance, without insight, and guided by a series of outmoded, unrealistic concepts regarding minorities. The major irony is this: that in a country where life is actually lived quite freely with races so intermingled, it is still difficult to capture this sense of freedom, of humanity, this robust diversity of backgrounds of American life upon the screen. As far as motion pictures are concerned, the Negro character remains mysterious because he is the most diversified by background, by color, and by regional dialect, and considering the number of films involving Negroes, the race as a whole is inadequately represented on the screen. Represented solely by limited night-club entertainers and recording artists, and only a few outstanding young actors (Poitier, Belafonte, and Henry Scott, who has appeared in only one small role so far), it is no wonder that audiences cannot get a sense of truth between the black, brown, or beige images that vary so greatly from celluloid to reality, from mythology and stereotype to history and drama.

Gerald Weales

5　Pro-Negro Films in Atlanta

[1952]

When the editor of *Films in Review* asked me to do an objective survey of the reactions in Atlanta to such pictures as *Pinky, Home of the Brave,* and *Intruder in the Dust,* I agreed to try, even though I have never seen a survey that was objective.

I should not have agreed to try. As I began the interviews that would supply the material for this article, I fancied that I wore my objectivity with a certain dignity. But I was rather uncomfortable. When I began to write, I found my prejudices affecting my adjectives and parenthetic expressions and destroying my objectivity. I have, therefore, abandoned the pretense. I shall try to present the various reactions to these movies as honestly as my prejudices permit.

I should, first of all, make my prejudices known. I am white, in my twenties, and although I grew up in a part of southern Indiana where racial discrimination and racial hatred are in too wide evidence, I attended nonsegregated schools. In the small town from which I come the intermingling of Negroes and whites ends after graduation from high school. Often the feeling of distrust or distaste or ridicule which many whites have toward Negroes arises, or is strengthened, in the postschool years.

I seem to have escaped this. I attended college in New York City, where I may have been strengthened in the opinions that I hold because once again I worked and studied in an atmosphere that seemed more interested in an individual's abilities than in his color. My prejudices were formed. I am angered and disgusted by any act or statement that passes judgment on an individual solely on the basis of his race. I am not, however, a crusader. I now teach in the South. I do not expect to change the face of the racial situation, although a face-lifting is, in fact, in process. I do not think myself noble for holding these beliefs. They are, fortunately, shared by a great many people, both Northern and Southern. I do not state them in order to be commended or condemned, but only so the reader may know the orientation of the author of what follows.

My first problem in gathering material was to ascertain which of the racial films had been shown in Atlanta, and I was thereby obliged to consider the work of the Atlanta censor, Miss Christine Smith. A municipal appointee, she naturally shares the shortcomings common to all censors: a certain amount of human error and caprice. She must decide which movies are likely to inflame Atlanta's moral and social danger spots. Her decisions are subject to review, on appeal, by a board that is also Atlanta's Library Board. Usually this board upholds Miss Smith, but there have been instances of the board ruling against the censor's decisions both to permit and to prohibit the showing of films. But most often Miss Smith's decisions are not appealed.

Miss Smith resents the continual interest in her treatment of racial pictures, for she feels that a large part of her work, that involving morality, is ignored. Miss Smith speaks freely about the rules which determine her decisions. In general, she refuses permits, or demands cuts, on two grounds—either because films invite the breaking of Georgia laws, or because they might tend to incite the audience to violence. These two rules of thumb are sufficiently broad to give the censor a certain amount of personal elbow room in making her decisions. She has banned only three films with distinctly racial themes: *Lost Boundaries, Imitation of Life,* and *Birth of a Nation.* The last two have played in Atlanta in the past, but have not received a city permit during the period in which Miss Smith has served as censor.

The subject of both *Lost Boundaries* and *Imitation of Life* is passing (i.e., Negroes passing themselves off as whites), which certainly violates the segregation laws of Georgia. Since, in Miss Smith's opinion, these two films present passing favorably, they have been banned. *Pinky* also treats of passing, but because the heroine decides to remain a Negro, the picture stays within Georgia law and may be shown. However, the scenes involving the kiss between Pinky and her white suitor were cut, since an interracial kiss is obviously nonsegregated and might be interpreted as an invitation to break the segregation laws. *Show Boat* was permitted even though Julie was apparently still passing at the end of the picture, for she was in the lounge of the riverboat with the rest of the passengers. Perhaps it was comeuppance enough that she had to watch her beloved showboat sail down the river away from her with her beloved Magnolia aboard. Similarly, a scene was cut from *Home of the Brave* showing whites and Negroes together at a school dance, even though the school was Northern and nonsegregated.

Birth of a Nation was banned because the violence of some of its scenes might incite audience emulation. Miss Smith uses the banning of this picture to defend herself against the charge that her censorship is one-sided, though she insists she needn't deny such a charge since she carries out only her legally prescribed duties. Also for fear of possible violence, part of that scene in *Pinky* in which the two toughs attempt to pick up the heroine, and the scene showing police brutality, were cut, as were some of the riot scenes in *The Well*.

Atlanta, then, has had a chance to see *Intruder in the Dust*, *Pinky*, and *Home of the Brave*, with only the first uncut. Films such as *Red Ball Express* and *Bright Victory*, in which the problem of race hatred figures as a minor theme, have also played. *The Quiet One*, which depicted the onset of psychosis in a Negro child in Harlem, played noncommercially under the sponsorship of both white and Negro groups. *The Well* began a commercial run too late in August of this year to have been seen by most of the people interviewed in the course of this study.

The censor and one of the Atlanta reviewers imply that the distributor did not try to book *No Way Out* into Atlanta because its violence made it a likely prospect for banning. The distributor, however, explained that no theater or other booking outlet in Georgia has been willing to take the picture. The picture has not been ruled on by the censor.

Of Atlanta's first-run houses, only two, the Roxy and the Fox, have facilities for Negroes. *Pinky* is the only one of the racial films that played at either of these houses. A large number of Negroes will not attend segregated movie theaters, just as they will not attend other segregated events, such as the concert series in the City Auditorium. Many of these Negroes will not attend Negro houses either. For many years one booker handled all the Negro houses and the film fare was extremely poor. The majority of pictures in Negro theaters are still the cheap and sensational ones, though at least one Negro house has been attempting to bring in the better films. The physical condition of some of these houses, the dirt and the noise, have kept people away. Many Negroes go to see films, if they see them at all, only when they visit some city in which they are free to enter any theater and sit in any section of it.

Of the pictures involving race relations that played Atlanta, only *Pinky* was a box-office success—so much so that one booker called it a "classic," a term with which the trade describes a long-term box-office draw. On its first run at the Roxy, not only the gallery, but the balcony (ordinarily white) was reserved for Negroes. It played three weeks and drew large crowds in both white and Negro second-run houses. The other racial movies have done only average business.

The reason for the success of *Pinky*, at least with the white population of the South, probably lies in its final conventionality. The possibility of passing, and of interracial marriage, titillates a certain kind of mind. *Pinky* offered this sensation, plus a good solid ending in which the heroine decided to remain a Negro, which could easily be read as a testimonial to the rightness of the Southern view of the Negro. To cap this all-round bargain, the aristocrat-servant roles played by Ethel Barrymore and Ethel Waters hid racial indignity beneath a fine example of personal dignity.

A second difficulty in collecting material inhered in the touchy subject of the films in which I was interested. Southerners speak warily on racial matters. This is particularly true in a city like Atlanta, which has a large, active, and intelligent Negro population and a great amount of white-Negro cooperative activity. Politicians, particularly, step carefully around the racial question.

For instance, the mayor of Atlanta, who on occasion has shown a certain enlightenment in these matters, particularly when the National Association for the Advancement of Colored People held its convention in Atlanta last year, refused me an interview. The refusal came not from the mayor, but from his secretary, and the reason given was that the mayor knew nothing about these films. This could easily be true, but a little suspicion is not unreasonable under the circumstances. Again, the state adjutant of the American Legion, when reached by phone, refused to discuss the subject. In all cases I sought not the individual, but the opinion, and offered to make anonymous any views which might not be politically wise. But who would believe a man writing an article for a Northern publication?

I have been able, however, to get a wide range of opinion from those I have interviewed. I made no attempt to take a scientific sampling, to list the reactions to the movies on a percentage basis. Most of my interviews were with the articulate, the intellectual segment of the population—educators, journalists, professional men.

The range of opinions about these movies in Atlanta's white population runs from those who are afraid the films may have some effect on the racial status quo, to those who pray that it will. Perhaps the best example of the extreme conservative is the following quotation from a review of *Red Ball Express* by Fred D. Moon, movie reviewer for the Atlanta *Journal*: ". . . producer Aaron Rosenberg and director Budd Boetticher have become so involved in proving that white and Negro troops just love to work and play together, that they've missed the drama of their theme. The thing boils down to a mediocre war melodrama, heavily larded with love-thy-brother angles . . . It should go to town when it hits the colored circuits."

Another Atlanta newspaperman, a Southerner whose protestations that he is without prejudice suggest the "some-of-my-best-friends-are-Negroes" brand of liberalism, had a strangely paradoxical attitude. He thought that racial films had absolutely no value educationally, yet he deplored the use of propaganda in them. His insistence that films be kept clear of ideational slants, coupled with his belief that the slant isn't slanting, suggest both an uneasiness and a wishful thinking concerning racial matters that are never explicit in his statement of his beliefs.

His view of the ultimate scource and intention of the propaganda (always in the pejorative sense) in these films was common. Not a few Atlantians dismissed these films as coming from the North, as an attack on the South.

A variation on the theme that interracial movies are ineffectual was succinctly stated by a theaterman who had been born in the North but had lived in the South for fifteen years. He declared that the pictures impressed only those who had already accepted the interracial thesis.

One white man long active in work against discrimination (not just on racial grounds) suggested that these films may be a part of a changing community pattern, like the experiences of Southern whites with Negroes in the army—the proverbial drops of water disintegrating the rock of prejudice.

For these films to have this limited effect, it is necessary that the audience identify with the Negro protagonist. One traditional Southerner, a literate and articulate teacher, was able to explain his identification with Lucas Beauchamp in *Intruder in the Dust* by insisting that the picture is not about Lucas being a Negro at all, but about the necessity for the recognition of the dignity of each individual man. This is true, of course, but before such an explanation becomes valid the primary acceptance of the Negro Lucas as a human being must be made.

The reaction of many young people, particularly young men, to *Home of the Brave* was much the same, if less articulate. Perhaps because the hero of *Home of the Brave* as a soldier had participated in experiences they had had or expected to have, many young male students at Georgia Tech found they identified with the hero, often against their desires. In an essay attempting to discuss this picture, one boy, an Atlantian, after struggling with and finally accepting the friendship between the Negro and the white man in that picture, ended with this about-face: "As a final statement, I would like to say that I don't believe the Negro will ever take the place of or replace any white man's position in life. They will never mix congenially!"

There was further evidence of this kind of response to this film in a report given to me by a woman, a native Georgian, whose experience in public relations and in interracial work has sharpened her powers of observation in this particular field. She sat through *Home of the Brave* several times just to observe audience reaction. She reported that a heavy tension settled over the audience as it realized what kind of picture was being shown, but that after several minutes relaxation set in. The relaxation in turn gave way to the tension that any audience feels when it becomes involved in the suffering of the hero. By the time the doctor is forced to abuse the paralyzed soldier with racial epithets, the audience was plainly, audibly with the hero. This woman did not regard this audience sympathy as conversion to the idea of racial equality. Nor were the reactions recorded in the essays of the young boys, described above, evidence of any such conversion.

Negro intellectuals think even less of the educational value of these films. Most of them felt that the presentation of the Negro, even in the supposedly sympathetic pictures, was false, stereotyped, or too special to be of general application or interest.

A Negro businesswoman, who had shelved early ambitions for a theatrical career because she would have been restricted to a career of portraying servants, greatly resented the Hollywood presentation of the Negro in so-called serious films. Like so many other Negroes, she cited the stereotype of *Pinky* as an example. Pinky's grandmother, the washerwoman replete with bandana and shack, she regarded as a variation on the loyal mammy.

Only one of the Negroes interviewed, a librarian possessed of wry humor, made an effort to explain the stereotype. She admitted that there are Negroes of the mammy type that Waters played in *Pinky* and that small Negro boys gobble watermelon, but she resented the continued depiction of such Negroes because many people would think the whole Negro race is composed of nothing else. She despised the stereotype, not because it has no basis in truth, but because it is a partial truth that misrepresents a whole people. She also considered the eye popping of the Negro boy in the graveyard scene in *Intruder in the Dust* another example of the stereotype spilling over into a serious movie.

Several Negroes suggested that the incidents around which these films are built are too specialized, often too melodramatic, to have any widespread influence. Some have violence—murder, a race riot —as a plot device. A well-known Negro professional woman pointed out that the Negro's problem is not so much one of potential violence as of the continual abrasive effect of small incidents, the piling up of insults, the quotidian gnawing at human dignity in an atmosphere of distrust and prejudice.

Perhaps the solution is the junking of the whole concept of the racial picture, for the continued treatment of the Negro as a "problem" forces him into a new kind of stereotype. The films praised most highly by the Negroes I interviewed were those in which the Negro takes part in action as a man, not only as a Negro. The two instances most cited were Canada Lee's role in *Lifeboat*, where although appearing as the ship steward, again a servant, he was allowed dignity and intelligence, and Leigh Whipper's role of a Negro preacher in *The Ox Bow Incident*, in which his was one of the few voices raised against the lynching of the two white men.

A leader of the Negro community in Atlanta, who formerly held a position of importance in an educational institution in New York City, where he studied the Negro as he appeared in entertainment and educational fields, believes that the salvation of the Negro as a human being lies with the Negro himself. By organized insistence on equalitarianism, through such organizations as the NAACP, he believes, Negroes will finally achieve equality of status. This belief determines his opinion of the films in question. He chose to praise *The Well* and *No Way Out* because in those two films the Negroes fought their own battle on equal grounds, club for club, tirejack for tirejack, and won. He attacked *Intruder in the Dust* because in it the Negro community did not rally to the defense of Lucas, who had to be saved by the white boy and the old white lady with the help of only one Negro, the boy who was continually frightened. He admitted, however, that although the Negroes in the city in *No Way Out* and the town in *The Well* might be ready to fight their own battle, it was highly unlikely that in the small Mississippi town depicted in *Intruder in the Dust* the Negro community would make the display of power he wished it would. His distaste for William Faulkner's racial opinions distorted his reaction to that picture. But his dislike for *Intruder in the Dust* is more understandable than his enthusiasm for *No Way Out*. Though the Negro fights for himself in that picture, the interracial violence which it exploits hardly offers an acceptable solution to racial problems.

Even as incomplete a survey of Atlanta's reactions to racial movies as this one indicates that these movies were unsatisfactory to most whites and Negroes.

Paring the individual reactions down to some kind of pattern, we find three major attitudes: 1) disapproval by a large section of the white community that does not favor any change in the relations between the races; 2) disapproval by Negro intellectuals who think these pictures sidestep the issue; and 3) the admission by those whites and Negroes who would like these films to be educationally effective that they are so only in a very limited way.

Thomas R. Cripps

6 The Death of Rastus:
Negroes in American Films Since 1945

[1967]

Students of the film have been divided over the issue of just what movies communicate. Those closer to the era of the behaviorists such as Lenin and Jane Addams believed that movies molded opinion. They held that films have a proven effect upon behavior because the experience of movie-going, unlike theater, is "extrasocial" and thus a clear identification takes place between filmed image and the mind of the viewer.[1]

More recent observers argue that the film is a kind of reflector of values. Siegfried Kracauer postulates a cinema as a social communicator of deep layers of Jungian collective meanings and psychological dispositions.[2] Given this assumption, each viewer's back-

[1] Paul G. Cressey, "The Motion Picture Experience as Modified by Social Background and Personality," *American Sociological Review*, III, 4 (August 1938), 516–25. For brief comments by earlier observers, see Thomas R. Cripps, "The Negro Reaction to the Motion Picture 'Birth of a Nation,'" *Historian*, XXV, 3 (May 1963), 344–62.

[2] For various shades of opinion on the effects of motion picture viewing, see Hortense Powdermaker, "An Anthropologist Looks at the Movies," 80–87; Norman Woelfel, "The American Mind and the Motion Picture," 88–94; Allan A. Hunter, "A Clergyman Looks at the Movies," 95–97; Leo C. Rosten, "Movies and Propaganda," 116–24, all in *Annals of the American Academy of Political and Social Science*, CCLIV (November 1947). For estimates of value transmission to various audiences, see Mildred J. Wiese and Stewart G. Cole, "A Study of Children's Attitudes and the Influence of a Commercial Motion Picture," *Journal of Psychology*, XXI (January 1946), 151–71 (in which the authors found that a movie gave support to "their uncritical conception of an idealized America," 170); Siegfried Kracauer, "Those Movies with a Message," *Harper's*, CXCVI, 1777 (June 1948), 567–72, who warns that message movies may show the fragility of that which they wish to promote. See also Frederick Elkin, "Value Implications or Popular Films," *Sociology and*

54   BLACK FILMS AND FILM-MAKERS

ground determines what he gets from a film; that is, he captures what is usable to himself. "He utilizes the picture situation," as Franklin Fearing puts it, "in the process of coming to terms with the larger environment." [3] Thus movies form attitudes in a chance way, depending on biases already held by the audience members individually. They have residues of imagery from older movies through which they view new images. Thus they may evade, misinterpret, or miss the point of a film's persuasion. In some cases a boomerang effect is achieved: that is, the viewer comes away believing more strongly in the attitude opposite to the one presented by a film. German audiences, for example, missed the point of the problem movie, *Blackboard Jungle*, taking it to be a documentary with Glenn Ford the only professional actor.[4]

At least one critic, after seeing Stanley Kramer's movie about the hysterical paralysis of a Negro soldier, concluded that *"Home*

Social Research, VIII, 5 (May-June 1954), 320–22, who more recently and scientifically argues that even an Abbott and Costello comedy may have an unconscious "social function" of suggesting values, though less obviously with a problem or message film.

[3] Franklin Fearing, "Influence of the Movies on Attitudes and Behavior," *Annals of the American Academy of Political and Social Science*, CCLIV (November 1947), 70–79.

[4] Russell Middleton, "Ethnic Prejudice and Susceptibility to Persuasion," *American Sociological Review*, XXV, 5 (October 1960), 679–86. For arguments for the persuasiveness of propaganda films, see, among others, Albert L. Goldberg, "the Effects of Two Types of Sound Motion Pictures on the Attitudes of Adults Toward Minorities," *Journal of Educational Psychology*, XXXIX (May 1956), 386–91; L. E. Raths and F. N. Trager, "Public Opinion and 'Crossfire,'" *Journal of Educational Sociology*, XXI (February 1948), 345–68; Irwin C. Rosen, "The Effects of the Motion Picture 'Gentleman's Agreement' on Attitudes toward Jews," *Journal of Psychology*, XXVI (October 1948), 525–36; and C. I. Hovland *et al*, *Experiments on Mass Communication* (Princeton, 1961). For statements critical of the efficacy of film propaganda, see, among others, Eunice Cooper and Helen Dinerman, "Analysis of the Film 'Don't Be a Sucker': A Study in Communication," *Public Opinion Quarterly*, XV (Summer, 1951), 243–64; Eunice Cooper and Marie Jahoda, "The Evasion of Propaganda: How Prejudiced People Respond to Anti-Prejudice Propaganda," *Journal of Psychology*, XXIII (January 1947), 15–25; S. H. Flowerman, "Mass Propaganda in the War against Bigotry," *Journal of Abnormal and Social Psychology*, XLII (October 1947), 429–39; Herbert Hyman and Paul B. Sheatsley, "Some Reasons Why Information Campaigns Fail," *Public Opinion Quarterly*, XI (Fall, 1947), 413–23; J. E. Hulet, Jr., "Estimating the Net Effect of a Commercial Motion Picture upon the Trend of Local Public Opinion," *American Sociological Review*, XIV (April 1949), 263–75; Hans Zeisel, "A Note on the Effect of a Motion Picture on Public Opinion," *American Sociological Review*, XIV (August 1949), 550–51 (cited in Middleton). For the reaction to "Blackboard Jungle," see Joseph Axelrod, "German and Austrian Reaction to the 'Blackboard Jungle,'" *School and Society*, LXXXV, 2105 (February 16, 1957), 57–59.

of the Brave will convert no one; in some observers (because of the unintentionally implied cowardice of the Negro), it could have the effect of confirming prejudice." A social scientist who studied the attitude creation of the move biography of Sister Kenny found it a weak propaganda agent simply because the audience respondents did not attribute accuracy and seriousness of purpose to motion pictures. Other critics have pointed to ethnic and national attitudes and minority relationships as other factors in the successful transmission of images by the film. As Kracauer has put it:

Hollywood and any national film industry for that matter is both a leader and a follower of public opinion. In portraying foreign characters it reflects what it believes to be the popular attitudes of the time, but it also turns these often vague attitudes into concrete images.[5]

Thus in American motion pictures in-group self-images will become the norm of behavior, and all the jangling diversity of ethnic groups will round off into a broadly based white, Anglo-Saxon, Protestant type. Some minority groups have contributed to this kind of negative stereotyping by their protests against reprehensible typing. Witness protests by Italians against *The Untouchables* and protests by Negroes against *Birth of a Nation*. The result is not an elimination of the stereotypes but instead the continuation of the least objectionable of them. As Terry Ramsaye stated: "the multitude can chuckle at Step'n Fetchit and laugh with Rochester, but they will woo and win with the Gables, the Taylors and the Coopers." Thus villainous Negroes stay off the screen at the price of making "the negro [sic] so amusing and agreeable that an audience is always pleased at the appearance of a black face." [6]

[5] Robert Hatch, "Movies: Good Intention," *New Republic* (May 16, 1949), 22–23; *Hulet, op. cit.*, 263–75; Siegfried Kracauer, "National Types as Hollywood Presents Them," *Public Opinion Quarterly*, XIII, 1 (Spring, 1949), 53–72.

[6] Margaret Farrant Thorp, *America at the Movies* (New Haven, 1939), 130; for other popular criticisms of unintentioned stereotyping in message movies, see Kracauer, *op. cit.*, 567; Dore Schary, "Our Movie Mythology," *Reporter*, XXII, 5 (March 3, 1960), 39–42; Hollis Alpert, "D for Effort," *Saturday Review*, XLII (October 3, 1959), 29.

The combination of these two factors produces a kind of selective censorship. The history of film censorship in America is a long, tedious tale of the suppression of the sins of the Puritans. As Sterling Brown has pointed out, seven stereotypes of Negroes can be isolated: the contented slave, the wretched freeman, the comic Negro, the brute Negro, the tragic mulatto, the local color Negro, and the exotic primitive. The elements of these types include laziness, filth, sensuality, and crime, so that it is as though white America is torn between two conclusions: Negroes are America's antidemocratic nightmare and Puritan conscience and must be suppressed, or they must be depicted publicly as the stereotype because it sustains the myth of Anglo-Saxon purity.[7]

In practice a compromise has been struck. The private censorship code of the motion picture producers of America proscribes all the vicious elements of the stereotype and tolerates the ridiculous elements. Thus, through the 1930s and 1940s, only racial comics such as Rochester, Willie Best, and Mantan Moreland (as Charlie Chan's valet) crept into American films.[8] The effect in recent films has been that Negroes must still remain segregated even as the imperatives of segregation diminish in reality. A normal sexual role, for example, continues to be denied to Negroes. Sidney Poitier, in the widely acclaimed *Lilies of the Field*, is as effectively denied a full characterization by the presence of the nuns as costars as, say, Lena Horne was in the musicals in which she was consigned to a vaudeville act that bore no relation to the plot line.

In a sense the producers' code makes movies a technological equivalent to folk art. Their dependence on the box office makes

7 Sterling A. Brown, "Negro Characters as Seen by White Authors," *Journal of Negro Education*, II, 2 (April 1933), 179–203. For the most recent of studies of censorship and its effects, see Murray Schumach, *The Face on the Cutting Room Floor* (New York, 1964), pp. 279 ff, Appendix III.

8 See Cripps, *op. cit.*, for an earlier example of the striking of the bargain. For a copy of the Hollywood motion picture producers' code, see Schumach, *op. cit.*, Appendices. For a recognition of the compromise in advice given to young screenplay writers, see Walter B. Pitkin and William M. Marston, *The Art of Sound Motion Pictures* (New York, 1930), pp. 25, 62, one of several "how-to" books in which the authors advise young writers to "study closely the vogue in pictures" in order to determine what sells. A handy chart delineating the various racial taboos is appended.

them, at the same time, a reflection, a distortion, and an exaggeration of American life. If "Hollywood is the mass unconscious," the theater is the place where wishes are gratified, where (according to Marlon Brando) "people . . . correlate what happens on the screen with their own experience." One of Walker Percy's characters expresses this mythical quality:

Our neighborhood theater in Gentilly has permanent lettering on the front of the marquee reading: Where Happiness Costs So Little. The fact is I am quite happy in a movie, even a bad movie. Other people, so I have read, treasure memorable moments in their lives. . . . What I remember is the time John Wayne killed three men with a carbine as he was falling to the dusty street in *Stagecoach*, and the time the kitten found Orson Welles in the doorway in *The Third Man*.[9]

It can be seen that although movies are a "symbolic expression of life," they can shape "value patterns" to a degree only and then not in the efficient way assumed by the earlier observers.[10]

Socially conscious Hollywood producers have accepted this view to some extent. Many are self-conscious and guilty about the charge that Hollywood's achievements in race relations over the long run have been anti-Negro from *Birth of a Nation* to *Gone With the Wind*. But it would be difficult to imagine a different condition in view of the social scientists' vision of movie makers as essentially followers of, rather than creators of, mores. They would have had to crusade, "which Hollywood seldom does except for the most certain and established causes." [11] What is basi-

[9] For development of the concept of the mass unconscious, see Siegfried Kracauer, *From Caligari to Hitler* (Princeton, 1947); the cinema criticism of Parker Tyler, especially *Hollywood Hallucination* (New York, 1944), pp. 231–238, 244; for the Brando comment, see Richard Dyer McCann, *Hollywood in Transition* (Boston, 1962), p. 187; for less technical comments, see Jean Benoit-Levy, *The Art of the Motion Picture* (New York, 1946), pp. 196–201, 217–18; Robert Hughes, *Film: Book I* (New York, 1959), pp. 3–24, 35–60; Gilbert Seldes, *The Public Arts* (New York, 1956), pp. 191, 210, 298; Henry James Forman, *Our Movie Mad Children* (New York, 1935), *passim*; Walker Percy, *The Moviegoer* (New York, 1962), pp. 12–13.

[10] For fairly recent statements of the efficacy of film propaganda, see J. P. Mayer, *Sociology of the Film* (London, 1946), pp. 167–68, 49, 17–18, 25; Martha Wolfenstein and Nathan Leites, *Movies: A Psychological Study* (Glencoe, Illinois, 1950), p. 307.

[11] Dore Schary, "Censorship and Stereotypes," *Saturday Review of Literature*, XXXII, 18 (April 30, 1949), 9–10; Louis Kronenberger and John T. McManus, "Mo-

cally a scientific argument has its layman's equivalent: that is, the liberal position that movies should "both symbolize and effectuate a revolution in the imagination and behavior," as opposed to the conservative notion that because movies are one of the "principal influences of the modern world in the determination of the character of our people and our society" producers have a moral responsibility to seek what is right—a consensus. Thus to the conservative "controversial pleading and the pursuit of theoretical and experimental causes should have no place in the theatrical film." [12]

Censorship has been one of the most persistent influences on the maintenance of stereotypes. Southern censorship has taken the most exaggerated stances. In Atlanta, *Lost Boundaries* and *Imitation of Life* were banned *in toto* as inciting to violence or lawbreaking. Of all the movies in the 1940s about Negroes, only Faulkner's *Intruder in the Dust* was uncut. In 1945 *Brewster's Millions* was banned in Memphis because Eddie Anderson stood too close to, and seemed too friendly with, Helen Walker. Even an innocuous film such as *Island in the Sun* was either protested or banned in Memphis, New Orleans, Jacksonville, and Montgomery, because white citizens' councils and the Ku Klux Klan saw it as "immoral and indecent" because of the implied equality of the characters of Harry Belafonte and Joan Fontaine.[13] Where there is no censorship on racial grounds, producers, sensitive to protest from both Negroes and whites, have reduced Negro roles to ambivalent ciphers. Otto Preminger's *Carmen Jones*, as James Baldwin has pointed out, is not believable precisely because the role of Joe (played by Belafonte) is reduced to a nullity for fear of stereotyping Negro sexuality. Typically, any breaking of the color line, perhaps expressing the unconscious reservations of liberal

tion Pictures, the Theater, and Race Relations," *Annals of the American Academy of Political and Social Science*, CCXLIV (March 1946), 152–58.

12 Martin S. Dworkin, "The New Negro on the Screen," *Progressive*, XXIV, 11–12 (November-December 1960), 33–36; Martin Quigley, "Importance of the Entertainment Film," *Annals of the American Academy of Political and Social Science*, CCLIV (November 1947), 65–69.

13 Gerald Weales, "Pro-Negro Films in Atlanta," *Phylon*, XIII, 4 (Winter, 1952), 298–304 (reprinted from *Films in Review*, November 1952); Philip T. Hartung, "Trillions for Brewster," *Commonweal*, XLII, 4 (May 11, 1945), 94–95; *New York Times* (July 4, 18; August 17, 1957; November 25, 1949).

movie makers, is met by violence. In Robert Wise's *Odds Against Tomorrow,* Belafonte is burned to death unrecognizably, along with a racist played by Robert Ryan whom he fought, the obvious implication being that to resist segregation is to die. In *Broken Lance,* Spencer Tracy dies pointlessly after his interracial marriage to Katy Jurado.[14]

Tragedy can be barely averted only when non-Negroes are involved, as in *Broken Arrow* (American Indians), *Bhowani Junction* (East Indians), and *Love Is a Many-Splendoured Thing* (Chinese); or when Negroes are saved by the sacrifice of a white friend, a kind of symbolic atonement for lynching, as in *Home of the Brave* and *Intruder in the Dust*; or when white actresses play Negro roles, as in, most recently, *Kings Go Forth.*[15]

The story of Negroes in American films since 1945, therefore, is not only the story of the death of Rastus, or Sambo, or Uncle Tom, but the rebirth of a complete man as yet unnamed. The story, so far, has three parts: up to 1954, Negroes as a social problem; through the 1950s, Negroes as emerging characters yet bearing the vestiges of Rastus; and finally, from the varied themes of the 1960s, the beginnings of the fully articulated character. The first intimations of the end of the Negro stereotype were seen in the anti-Fascist war movies: Dooley Wilson's wise piano player in Warner Brothers' *Casablanca*; Rex Ingram's Senegal soldier in *Sahara*; and Canada Lee in Alfred Hitchcock's *Lifeboat.*[16]

Shortly after the vogue of war movies ended, the cycle of racial message movies began. Stanley Kramer's *Home of the Brave,* adapted from Arthur Laurents's polemic against anti-Semitism, was the first in 1948, followed by Louis de Rochemont's *Lost Boundaries* and Elia Kazan's *Pinky.* By 1952, with Clarence Brown's *Intruder in the Dust,* the cycle had spent itself, not so

14 James Baldwin, "Life Straight in de Eye," *Commentary,* XIX, 1 (January 1955), 74–79; Martin S. Dworkin, "The New Negro on the Screen," *Progressive,* XXV, 1 (January 1961), 38.

15 Henry Popkin, "Hollywood Tackles the Race Issue," *Commentary,* XXIV, 10 (October 1957), 354–57; Martha Wolfenstein and Nathan Leites, "Two Social Scientists View 'No Way Out,'" *Commentary,* X, 4 (October 1950), 388–91; Albert Johnson, "Beige, Brown, or Black," *Film Quarterly,* XIII, 1 (Fall, 1959), 38–43.

16 Dorothy B. Jones, "Tomorrow the Movies: IV. Is Hollywood Growing Up?" *New Republic,* CLX, 5 (February 3, 1945), 123–25; Dworkin, *Progressive,* XXIV, 10, 39–41.

much departing from the old stereotypes but creating a new one: that of Negroes who cannot be fulfilled without the sacrifice of, or the support of, white men. As a case in point, James Edwards, the Negro in *Home of the Brave*, goes on a mission to a Japanese-held island where his best friend, a white man, is killed. Edwards feels a dual guilt at his friend's death, first, because he is glad that he personally survived, and second, because he had wished his friend dead after an argument in which he had been called a racial epithet. Falling victim to hysterical paralysis, he is taken to the base psychiatrist who induces Edwards to walk again by hurling the same epithets at him, symbolically implying that Negroes can be fulfilled only on white men's terms. At the end of the film the audience sees a fraternal scene in which Edwards and a one-armed white man depart, suggesting Negro-white equality only as long as the whites are not complete. In *Pinky, Lost Boundaries*, and *Intruder in the Dust* the problems of Negroes are resolved in each case at the pleasure of upper-class white society. So little came from the cycle of problem movies that Negroes nearly disappeared from the screen completely in the early 1950s.[17]

By the mid-1950s the cycle had achieved only a few side effects. The all-Negro exploitation films such as Robert Gordon's *Joe Louis Story* and James Wong Howe's *Go Man Go*, a cheap program movie about the Harlem Globetrotters, declined in numbers. The South's romantic "lost cause" mystique became tarnished and its decadence in the manner of Tennessee Williams was emphasized in a rash of movies. Indians began to get sympathetic treatment in several Westerns.

After 1954, cinema Negroes became, not a problem for whites to comprehend, but symbolic figures of the struggle against oppression. In the strident *Blackboard Jungle*, only Sidney Poitier is allowed to struggle successfully against the tide of urban poverty.

17 See Dworkin, *ibid*. Except for this series of articles there is no treatment of Negroes in films after 1948. For an inadequate survey of the years before 1948, see Noble, *The Negro in Films* (London: Skelton Robinson [1948?]); for rather doctrinaire-Marxist comment on history and propaganda, see V. J. Jerome, *The Negro in Hollywood Films* (New York, 3rd printing, 1952); John Howard Lawson, *Film in the Battle of Ideas* (New York, 1953); and Gordon Kahn, *Hollywood on Trial: The Story of the 10 Who Were Indicted* (New York, 1948).

In Darryl Zanuck's movie of Alec Waugh's *Island in the Sun*, it is Harry Belafonte, until then a popular nightclub singer, who plays the dynamic labor leader; and in Robert Wise's tightly directed crime thriller, *Odds Against Tomorrow*, it is again Belafonte who is the criminal at war with both society and his Southern racist accomplice.[18] Only occasionally did the old Negro intrude upon the new Negro tragic hero-as-victim, as in Otto Preminger's gaudy production of *Porgy and Bess* in 1959.

By the 1960s, institutional racial equality had become socially acceptable behavior in many areas of America. One heard occasional liberal voices even from a closed society such as Mississippi.[19] Churches began to break their long silence on the issue of race.[20] Professional associations opened their doors to Negroes. No longer news was the marriage of the famous Negro actor, Sammy Davis, Jr.; nor Lyndon Johnson, late of Texas, dancing at his inauguration with the wives of the various darker-skinned men in attendance. Such rapid change was accepted in varying degrees. The intellectuals and the well-to-do had nothing to fear from it. The middle-class houseowner nervously accepted it in every neighborhood but his own. Older people and working-class people tended not to accept it at all. These varying degrees of acceptance of change were reflected in a tripartite cinema of the 1960s. A comparable case can be seen in the film treatment of juvenile behavior in the highly literate *David and Lisa* by Frank and Eleanor Perry; the middle-brow, guilt-evoking *Rebel Without a Cause*; and the sensational exploitation movie, *Untamed Youth*; each one dealing with the same subject, but in three distinct styles. Similarly, as Negroes intrude upon the collective consciousness of America they evoke a similar set of divergent images.[21]

18 Dworkin, *Progressive*, 36–38.

19 For a recent example of liberal Southern comment, see James W. Silver, *Mississippi: the Closed Society* (New York, 1964).

20 For a criticism of the silence of the churches on social issues, see Peter Berger, *The Noise of Solemn Assemblies* (Garden City, 1961).

21 In dealing with the films of the 1960s, I have not supplied complete information about producers, releasing companies, and directors because they would be of little bibliographic value. Typically, in periodical indexes, films are listed by title, then journal in which a review or article appeared. Those few libraries that keep active files of film reviews also catalogue by title, as do the various Library of Congress film copyright volumes.

At the lowest level of exploitation of racial themes is Stephen Borden's *My Baby Is Black*, which depicts a love affair between a Negro medical student in Paris and his white girl friend. The audience is titillated by shots of the two in embrace, alternated with scenes of vicious rejection of the Negro by the girl's parents. Another cheap exploitation film of the 1960s was Larry Buchanan's *Free, White, and 21*, in which a Negro, Frederick O'Neal, is accused of rape and acquitted. The film's gimmick is that near the end, the audience is asked to "vote" as jurors to determine O'Neal's guilt or innocence, after watching a plot that clearly shows him innocent. After he is acquitted, a lie detector test showing the jury is wrong is introduced into the film. The prosecutor, playing every string of the lurid rape theme, asks rhetorically whether we do not "love the Negro too much." Both films express clearly the undercurrent of white proletarian reservations toward the assimilation of Negroes into American life.

In the middle-brow movies of the 1960s, many New Negro social roles are depicted, usually no more than one in each film. In Hubert Cornfield's *Pressure Point*, Sidney Poitier plays a prison psychiatrist whose patient is a racial psychotic played by Bobby Darin, who is an anti-Roosevelt, anti-Semitic fascist. Thus the audience is led to accept a Negro as a doctor, if for no other reason than that the psychotic cannot. Another break from the stereotype is even more literally stated in Millard Kaufman's *Convicts Four*. The standard blues-humming Negro convict gives way to a prepossessing, aggressive convict played by Sammy Davis who, upon being assigned a new cellmate, a murderer, announces that he is not to be called "shine," that he is never to be asked to sing or dance, and finally that it is he to whom tribute is owed if the new man wishes to be protected from the hazing by the other inmates. The result is a unilateral white paper announcing that hereafter Rastus is dead.

In many movies small chips have been made in the stereotype. In Robert Aldrich's psychological murder mystery, *Whatever Happened to Baby Jane?*, all the whites are afraid, psychotic, or cheap crooks. Only the Negro maid is a balanced human being. She is like an enduring Faulkner Negro moved to a Northern city. In John Frankenheimer's *Manchurian Candidate,* dignified middle-class Negroes appear as window dressing. Warner Brothers announced that forty Negro extras appear in their comedy, *Kisses for My President.* In Gordon Douglas's *Rio Conchos,* Jim Brown plays a courageous Negro soldier immediately after the Civil War. The only racial stereotype is a lazy, serio-comic Mexican played by Tony Franciosa. All the Southerners in the film are outlaws whose commander is insane and lives in a mock-up facade of a Southern mansion, which symbolically burns to the ground in the last scene in the picture.

Occasionally the old stereotypes recur. In John Ford's *Man Who Shot Liberty Valence,* Woody Strode plays an Uncle Tom who shuffled off camera after being hit with a bucket of whitewash. In three Frank Sinatra comedies, Sammy Davis has played comic Negro Sambo types, especially in John Sturges's *Sergeants Three,* in which he plays Kipling's Gunga Din, renamed Jonah and moved to the American frontier.

It is in the so-called art movie, independently produced on a low budget for limited distribution in small urban theaters, where one finds the most sensitive view of Negroes in American life. Artistically, this kind of film attempts to deal with reality seriously, with little concession being made to market conditions, profits, or mass taste. The first limited success of this genre was John Cassavetes's *Shadows* (1960). Using unknown actors, Ben Maddow's script attempted to show the world of Negroes as closed and esoteric by juxtaposing it with the world of whites through the medium of the anxieties of a young girl who has been passing. On the surface, it would seem that Lela Goldoni's role is simply a repeat of many other white actresses who have played Negroes, including Jeanne Crain's *Pinky,* Flora Robson in *Saratoga Trunk,* and Yvonne de Carlo in *Band of Angels.* There is not the cheap, sexually charged situation of the earlier films, but only the contrast of two worlds and the need, in American society, to choose one or the other. Similar to *Shadows* was Shirley Clarke's *Cool World,* which also used unknown or amateur actors and which was shot on location in Harlem from various concealed angles. The result is a fast-paced film about the habitués of the cool world of small-time gangsters, junkies, and prostitutes. The movie is not a racial message or a plea to white America to send aid, but a story that uses a real part of Negro America without apology. There are sensual scenes, shots of narcotics addiction, drinking, wrecked and poor families, but the film does not piously say, "Look at the way these Negroes behave." It is a film about poor people who live in a city. The failure of the film, if it has one, is that few people saw it, even though in the Negro neighborhoods it was retitled *Cool World in Harlem* and luridly advertised.

The best evidence of the death of Rastus is Michael Roehmer's 1965 production, *Nothing But a Man*, the story of a marriage of a Negro railroadworker played by Ivan Dixon and a Negro school-teacher played by Abbey Lincoln. They live in a small Southern town that is seen as a physical, unnamed presence pressing upon them in dozens of small ways. The pressures seem about to destroy the marriage, as they destroyed the life of the railroadworker's father. The theme is not, What are Negroes like? which would be a return to the stereotype, but rather, How do people behave under strain? How do they survive? How do they live as persons when the society sees them as types?

Social change has thus compelled a comparable change in some artfully made movies about Negroes; while a few other movies still deal in the old sensationalism of the contradictory stereotypes of comedy, sexuality, brutality, and laziness. Neither is the norm for American movie-going behavior. In most middle-brow films of the 1960s, Negro characters had changed into perfectly abstinent, courageous paragons of virtue as stifling and destructive of mature characterization as the old Rastus stereotype. This new unreality is evident in the absence of adult sexual behavior in the films of Sidney Poitier. In *Blackboard Jungle* women characters were carefully segregated from Poitier; in *The Defiant Ones* he is chained to a male character and confronts no women; in *Raisin in the Sun*, he is married, but residing in his mother's crowded apartment; in *Lilies of the Field* his costars are a gaggle of nuns; in *The Long Ships*, he is an African prince who, despite his large harem, has taken an oath of chastity. One can still wonder when a commercial film will put all the parts of *the* Negro together into a whole man.

Richard Wesley

7   Which Way the Black Film

[1973]

To put it bluntly, black movie making, in its current stage, is hopelessly shallow. It is controlled primarily by persons who have nothing on their minds except the desire to make money. Questions of art, relevancy, *truth* have little to do with what they are all about in any real sense. To be sure, there are notable exceptions, but they are so few and far between that they are very nearly buried in the garbage that came before and after them. The black film, as a genre of cinematic art, is degenerate, debased, and an insult to the integrity of audiences of black people, who, starved for the sight of *anything* black on the silver screen, flock to see these manifestations of celluloid prostitution.

These "blaxploitation" films are characterized by an overwhelming lack of creativity, not to mention morality. Technically, the long shot and the close-up seem to be about the only camera shots directors can come up with. In addition, most of the current crop of these films are merely glossed-over versions of earlier, more successful white films. *Shaft* is a modern-day Sam Spade (from the *Maltese Falcon*), *Cool Breeze* is a black version of *The Asphalt Jungle*, and *Blacula* is a black Count Dracula. Needless to say, Hollywood and the Negroes involved in this ridiculously inept practice of legalized plagiarism seem not at all concerned about the low quality of what they are doing.

As with most of the pablum that rolls out of Hollywood, these "black" films are escapist in nature, in addition to being violent, sadomasochistic in some instances, sexploitative in most cases, and overall devoid of believability or humanity. These films, for the most part, portray blacks outwitting the white man at every turn, or else beating him to death. Quite naturally, an oppressed people will relate in a positive manner to such pictures. But these films have created a "legal" white whipping boy—the gangster. The white gangster or the hopelessly crooked white cops are the only white villains blacks are allowed to deal with. Mere low men on the totem pole. Never mind the corrupt federal officials who fail to safeguard black people attempting to vote in the South. Never mind the "jive" meat and produce inspectors who continuously allow substandard foods to find their way into the supermarkets and grocery stores of black communities. Don't deal with the Strom Thurmonds, James McClellans, *et al.*, who are daily engaged in activities designed to stifle the lives of the black, Chicano, Puerto Rican, native American, and poor. No. Let these "niggers" see their heroes deal with the most obvious villains only.

Although the bulk of "blaxploitation" films have come from the decrepit bowels of a withering Hollywood, there are a few that have come from the efforts of independent black film makers. Generally, these are poorly made, as witness *The Bus Is Coming*, *The Final Comedown*, or *Georgia, Georgia*. All were hobbled with bad photography, amateurish acting, pretentiousness, sloppy editing, poor directing, and moronic promotion. It is these black film makers who are most disappointing, for they have acquired the means of putting together motion pictures. And they have invariably managed in one way or another to make movies that are best forgotten. Even the best of these black-controlled films have too much going against them. They are always lacking *something*: artistry, insight, or something else. One always leaves the theater feeling less than satisfied.

Black film makers, whether producers or directors, also seem fearful of striking out on their own and setting up their own distribution houses, film studios, and movie houses. With more than one hundred black theater playhouses now functioning on an ongoing basis, it is possible to begin the establishment of a black movie circuit for independent black film makers, and move to control as much of the economics of the making of these movies as possible.

I'm not just talking through my hat. Fifty years ago, the late Oscar Micheaux, the first black film maker, used to shoot films— feature films, not documentaries—in New York and rural New Jersey, then tour black communities throughout the North and South exhibiting his finished product. In order to do this, he established contacts with various black civic leaders, churches, social clubs, and businesses and asked them to assist in setting up places where he might show his films. Eventually, he encouraged these same people to help finance the films. Micheaux was able to produce and exhibit films in this manner for more than thirty years, right up into the 1950s, utilizing only the relatively limited economic base black people had in those days. However, this lesson is lost on most of the young black film makers of today. In one instance, a group of blacks got together, raised the money for a film from a group of black businessmen, and then got a white executive producer, and turned their film over to a major white movie studio for distribution. They have done well, for it is a successful movie, but the white movie company is doing even better. Is it little wonder, then, that we are still slaves one hundred years after the emancipation?

Other black cine-men (and cine-women) hire themselves out to major white studios as story consultants, researchers, script doctors, etc., and color a particular screenplay (pun intended) to make it "relevant." Check the credits of *The Legend of Nigger Charley* and you will see the name of a very prominent black historian-scholar. Observe the credits of the unlamented *Slaves*, and you will find that one of our better black novelists *wrote the screenplay*.

Yet, there have been black men who have tried to rise above these restrictive circumstances. Melvin Van Peebles and Christopher St. John have both managed to produce films in which they retain a bulk of the profits as well as present thought-provoking and controversial themes. Their films are technically sound, valid pieces of work and artistry. Both are examples of black men controlling their own work in a field that until a few years ago denied they even existed.

Van Peebles, with *Sweet Sweetback's Baadasssss Song*, showed that it was possible for blacks to maintain rigid control over every aspect of their work, as well as the profits. He even proved that it was possible to produce a good film without the aid of racist film unions. Christopher St. John followed suit with his film, *Top of the Heap*. Both men now find themselves in a position to move on and make other films utilizing a method they proved can work. Their movies are highly creative, cinematically employing a wide variety of camera shots and special effects; employing surrealism, mythology, folklore, bawdiness, and *imagination* to tell their stories uniquely. Their films therefore stand out from the rest in the sense that they are truly *black* films; that is to say, films dealing with blacks that employ techniques and cinematic ideas not generally common to the white film.

However, questions of the artistic worth of these two films are being raised by numerous black critics, and such queries must be dealt with. I confess to having mixed emotions about both films, despite my overall admiration of the work put into them. I question whether or not Van Peebles should have used his talents to make a political statement within the framework of a pornographic film (read his book, *Sweet Sweetback's Baadasssss Song*) and whether or not Christopher St. John should have assumed so many roles—author, producer, director, and star—in his own picture. This same criticism can be directed at Van Peebles. It seems to me that the scope of both films is limited as a result of their overkill in personal involvement.

Sadly, the above are momentary smooth spots on a roughhewn surface. Until black men like Berry Gordy, Jr. James Brown, Al Bell, Eugene Dickerson, and other black millionaires can find some way to pool resources and form their own film companies, it will be the Melvin Van Peebleses and Christopher St. Johns who will do the work that must be done.

In another reality, it should be pointed out that there is no reason for me to believe that the current "blaxploitation" film craze should continue to expect support from the black community. That they do is in large part due to the fact that Hollywood has conditioned the American public to accept mediocrity. Look at the fact that American voters continuously vote politicians into office and seldom statesmen—the black community is part of that public.

The black community, at some point, will rebel against these films and cease to support them in large numbers, no matter what kind of billing they receive. This is already happening with such films as *Soul Soldier, Hammer, Slaughter,* and *Melinda,* none of which is doing well in New York City. To have truly *made* it, you've got to have made it in Gotham.

The bulk of protest against these films has thus far come from the black intelligentsia (media, artists, critics, scholars). But now the protests are coming from the "bloods on the block" who, in reality, are the ultimate determinants in whether or not the films will be financially successful. These are the people who are growing tired of being pandered to, weary of being portrayed as modern-day Stepin Fetchits in jump suits, as whores, pimps, violence-prone thugs, and so on. When the "black people people" (as Ed Bullins once called them) revolt, the age of the black films as a product of crass exploitation will end.

But the flame must burn brightly just once before it goes out, hence we have *Shaft, Cotton Comes to Harlem,* and *Super Fly* thrust upon us. But these films are enjoying tremendous success for another reason: The blacks who worked on them were successful in employing something called "the black style." And the films have successfully combined the elements of action, color, tempo, mood, and music. These are the criteria that are dear to the heart of most black audiences because they are also part of the daily lives of black people as they eke out an existence on these bleak shores. When these criteria are successfully employed, the result is a movie as visually exciting as a James Brown show at its peak, as aesthetically satisfying as Muhammad Ali boxing, as electrifying as Walt Frazier's dribbling, and as slick as Maury Wills stealing second. The black style is in the way we walk, the way we have turned the English language into another language, and the way we dress.

Less successful are films such as *Come Back Charleston Blue*, *Shaft's Big Score*, or *Honky* (a real stinker) in which one or more style elements are missing. With the exception of *Honky*, these movies are sequels to highly successful originals. That they are not doing as well at the box office is indicative of the rumblings within the community. (According to one story reaching the east coast, Gordon Parks, Sr., the director of *Shaft* and *Shaft's Big Score*, was booed off the stage at last summer's San Francisco Black Arts Expo.)

But *Super Fly* is the end of it all. The image of the superhip, invulnerable black stud has now been exhausted. We have had our: black loner (*Slaughter*), black athlete-crime buster (*Hammer*), black private-eye (*Shaft*), black cop (*Cotton Comes to Harlem*), black cowboy (*Legend of Nigger Charley*), and black supercrook-with-a-heart-of-gold (*Cool Breeze*). All these images have now been incorporated into the form of a parasitic insect known as *Super Fly*. *Super Fly* outslicks them all—crooked cops, doublecrossing niggers, gangsters, and anyone who gets in his path—and gets away with the money *and* the girl. He also dresses better than *Shaft, Slaughter, Hammer,* or *Cool Breeze.* Unlike *Shaft*, who merely reacts, *Super Fly* shows that he can think as well as rough somebody off. He is *successful,* and contrary to popular belief, a lot of people don't relate to the drugs as much as they relate to his success. A mother of three told me she has sworn off black films like *Super Fly* since discovering that her child had learned the song, "Pusherman," from the movie word for word. Another woman spoke of seeing kids coming out of the movie imitating Super Fly snorting coke.

Any attempt to top *Super Fly* with an action-thriller film will only succeed in making it clear that the later film is trying to mimic the original. The black superhero films will no doubt continue to be made and some will make money, but I do not feel that the box-office receipts will be as overwhelming as in the past.

What this means is that more serious black films will come to the fore. Having exhausted the action-film genre, Hollywood and its Negro cronies will be forced to look into other areas. The more serious and *truthful* black films will then be made. They will come not only from Hollywood and integrated independent film companies (reluctantly), but from independent black film makers, as well. Such groups as Chamba Productions, Incorporated, in New York City, or the New Lafayette Film Company, now aborning in South Carolina. Young men like Cliff Frazier, St. Clair Bourne, Stan Lathan, Jim Allen, and others will make their presence felt.

The work of art known as *Sounder* is an example of the better black films. It emphasizes a strong story line, identifiable people, strength, action, pathos, the will to survive and grow, and love. *Sounder* is the finest film about black people since *Nothing But a Man* in 1965. The irony is that both were produced and directed by whites.

In conclusion, if black films are truly to take their place as a valid cinematic art form alongside the films of other cultures, then blacks *must* control them and they must work to raise their quality. The fact that black men have not really investigated some of the ideas of economic and artistic control pioneered by Oscar Micheaux; the fact that there are Negro actors available to do any jive role offered them; the fact that many blacks in positions to effect change are generally lacking in discipline, creativity, or insight, looks askance on the quality of the bulk of blacks involved in film making today. Are these people serious about their work, about creating a new and valid cinematic art form? Or are they simply reel/real-life Blaculas sucking black people dry while riding into the Promised Land of financial success?

Which way the black film?

SECTION II

MOVIE MILESTONES

Bosley Crowther

1. The Birth of *Birth of a Nation*

[1965]

On February 8, 1915, there occurred in Los Angeles an event that may well be regarded as the most outstanding in the history of American films—the premiere performance of a "photo-drama" that was to demonstrate to the world the vast potential of motion pictures, and at the same time, inflame the people of this country with emotions that recollection can rekindle even now. The film was David Wark Griffith's *The Birth of a Nation*, one of the greatest ever made, and beyond any question, the most explosive ever released in the United States.

Today, the story of the making and showing of this extraordinary film is more legend than history. There are varying accounts of how much money it cost to make it and how much money it has earned. One guess, as good as any other, sets the latter figure at $50 million, which, if true, would make it the biggest earner of all time, even bigger than its remarkable kinsman, *Gone With the Wind*.[1]

Certainly it was the largest and the longest film made up to its time. It ran for twelve reels, or almost three hours, which was three times as long as the standard length of a film in 1915. And it was the first American film to be exhibited on a two-a-day basis, in theaters and auditoriums, at an unheard-of two-dollar top admission price.

[1] As of January 1973, the gross (U.S. & Canada) for *Gone With the Wind* was listed by *Variety* as $77,030,000, but *The Godfather*, released in 1972, was listed as having grossed $81,500,000, making it the all-time box-office favorite.

More amazing was the revelation it gave of the tremendous potency of the then rather primitive motion picture when used with imagination, audacity, and skill. And most amazing, perhaps, were the disruptive and disturbing effects it had upon race relations in this country over a period of many years.

The Birth of a Nation was a highly pro-South drama of the American Civil War and the period of Reconstruction, and it glorified the role of the Ku Klux Klan. The effect of this was to generate a divisive, anti-Negro sentiment that outraged liberals and the pro-Negro organizations that were then gaining strength —notably the National Association for the Advancement of Colored People, which was six years old. Violent demonstrations generally marked showings of the film.

Indeed, its effects upon public sentiment might be compared to those of *Uncle Tom's Cabin* when it was published in 1852. In the North, it excited indignation; in the South, it "waved the bloody shirt." It undoubtedly gave much stimulation to the rise and growth of the modern Ku Klux Klan.

The irony of this famous picture is that it should have been such a superior achievement in the medium and yet such a disturbing social document. But it was probably the very fact of its effectiveness as a device for arousing sentiment in a nation still sensitive to the memory of the antagonisms and agonies of civil strife that attracted great attention to it and made for its great commercial success. And it was certainly the immensity of its impact that opened eyes to the social importance of films.

No one had any real notion until *The Birth of a Nation* that the infant movies could do anything more than amuse. Dustin Farnum playing "The Squaw Man" was just about the speed of that day—he and a splayfooted clown called Charlie Chaplin who was just coming into popularity in the Mack Sennett slapstick comedies. Art had been only vaguely hinted at with the appearance of Sarah Bernhardt in a forty-minute film called *Queen Elizabeth*, though a faint intimation of what was coming was contained in an Italian spectacle, *Quo Vadis?*, which ran for the unconscionable length of two hours and was offered on Broadway for one dollar.

Schooled in this environment was Griffith, a former playwright who had been acting in, and directing, "flickers" for the pioneer Biograph company in New York since 1908. In turning out dozens of one- and two-reelers, he had discovered and developed many of the now familiar and commonplace ways of making moving pictures more flexible and articulate.

With his cameraman, G. W. (Billy) Bitzer, he had learned to move the camera around and shoot a scene from more than one angle. He had worked out the use of the close-up. Most important, he had developed unusual ways of assembling shots and scenes to build up a narrative continuity with cumulative force. In 1913, his *Judith of Bethulia*, a Biblical drama which was the first American film to run four reels, clearly foretold his epic bent.

As the Kentucky-born son of a Confederate colonel, Griffith passionately felt that the South had been wronged severely after the Civil War. He believed that the white population had been abused and exploited by Northern carpetbaggers and Southern scalawags who had incited the emancipated Negroes, and he wanted to make a film on this theme.

In 1914, when he went to California to make movies for the Mutual company, he resolved to fulfill this ambition with a full-scale masterwork. He took for his story a novel entitled *The Clansman*, by the Reverend Thomas Dixon Jr., a former Baptist minister from North Carolina, upon which a highly fustian and unsuccessful stage melodrama had been based in 1906, and set to work writing a scenario.

The film was supposed to cost $40,000—a shockingly high figure in those days—but expenses mounted and passed this figure during filming in the late summer and fall of 1914. Griffith sought more funds. Meantime, scuttlebutt spread in the young community of Hollywood that the film was to be of unexampled magnitude. In its large cast were several actors who had previously worked for Griffith—Henry B. Walthall, George Siegmann, Mae Marsh, Robert Harron, Sam de Grasse, and Lillian Gish. The elaborateness of the project made its financing difficult. A special company, significantly called Epoch, was formed by Griffith, novelist Dixon, and Mutual president Harry Aitken when directors of the Mutual company would not take on the great cost.

In his book *The Birth of a Nation Story*, Roy Aitken, a brother of Harry and onetime secretary of Epoch, pins down the disputed cost of the film at $110,000—$59,000 raised by the Aitkens and the remainder by Griffith himself (through assorted sales of stock in a separate company of his own). The complexity and confusion of this financing is interesting today simply because it demonstrates the total lack of experience with, and skill for, anything of this sort in the comparatively modest movie industry of the time.

Even before the opening in Los Angeles, word got around that Griffith had an unprecedented film. The shooting of battle scenes with hundreds of extras and the knowledge that the drama dealt with the postwar rise of the Ku Klux Klan had alerted expectations. The film was rumored by some to be a sensation, by others it was described as "a dirty nigger picture." At that point, it was still known as *The Clansman*.

On the night it opened, Clune's Auditorium, a 2,600-seat showplace in Los Angeles (later the home of the Los Angeles Philharmonic), was packed. There was a heavy police detachment outside and inside to guard against a threatened demonstration. It was by far the most elaborate and exciting opening a motion picture had ever had—another "first" for this precedent-shattering picture and, indeed, the launching of the later, familiar "Hollywood premiere."

The audience's reaction was terrific. People were held spellbound and came away shocked and excited, exhilarated and dazed. It was notable that the drama not only encompassed an extraordinary sweep of time and events, but was made in a style that gave an unusual sense of immediacy and momentum to the inflammatory material it contained.

Beginning with the outbreak of the Civil War, it told, in highly melodramatic fashion, of the defeat, and then the recovery, of the South in terms of the relations of two families, the Camerons of South Carolina and the Stonemans of Pennsylvania. The first half (taken from another Dixon noved called *The Leopard's Spots*) described the outbreak of the war; the departure of the Cameron and Stoneman boys (who are friends) to join, respectively, the armies of the Confederacy and the Union; the bloody battles that followed; difficulties on the Southern home front; the slow defeat; the surrender at Appomattox; and the assassination of Lincoln.

The second half concerned the Reconstruction. The eldest Cameron son—the Little Colonel, a hero in the war—was in love with Elsie Stoneman, whose father was a senator and an impassioned champion of Negro equality. (The character was clearly modeled after Thaddeus Stevens.) Here the course of the drama ran from a lurid presentation of the arrogance of the freed slaves, urged on by carpetbaggers and scalawags, and the humiliation and violation of the whites, to the founding of the Ku Klux Klan by the Little Colonel and the triumph of that organization in saving members of both families from Negro terrorists and bringing order to the South.

High points were an attempted rape of the Cameron daughter by a renegade Negro and scenes of the rising and riding of the Klan.

Audiences were bowled over by the film's pictorial sweep, by its arrangements of personal involvements, by what was much later designated its "documentary quality." Even today, on seeing it, one is struck by the vividness with which Griffith made the viewer sense the eruption of a Civil War battle, the reek of carnage on a smoking battlefield, the dismal aspects of postwar desolation, the bold appearance of the charging Ku Klux Klan.

A decade after it was made, the great Soviet film director, Sergei Eisenstein, studied this film as an incomparable model of cinema technique while preparing for his classic *Potemkin*. He found in Griffith's style the origins of the basic method of cinema cutting or editing to which he gave the name "montage." And he later wrote that, for him and for others of the young Soviet directors of the 1920s, Griffith's film was "a revelation."

After the Los Angeles opening, the picture was brought east. Dixon took it to the White House to show to his old college companion, President Woodrow Wilson. Wilson, who was Southern born, was profoundly stirred. "It is like writing history with light-ning," he is reported to have said—perhaps the strongest endorse-ment any film has ever had. It was also shown to members of the Supreme Court and Congress.

At a preview showing in New York, Dixon is alleged to have been so stimulated that he leaped to his feet and shouted to Grif-fith at the climax, *"The Clansman* is too tame! Let's call it *The Birth of a Nation!"* That is the legend about how it got its name.

When the film opened at the Liberty Theater in New York on March 3, its reputation had preceded it. The NAACP, sup-ported by such vocal citizens as Rabbi Stephen S. Wise, Lillian D. Wald, and Oswald Garrison Villard, protested to Mayor John Purroy Mitchel that the film was an insult to the Negro race and that it would do untold damage. They besought the mayor either to ban the picture or to order cuts. The mayor did not stop the showing, but he had some scenes trimmed.

Openings at the Illinois Theater in Chicago and the Tremont in Boston followed within a few days after the New York opening. In each of these cities there were protests by the NAACP and by distinguished citizens. In Boston, there were angry demonstra-tions on the lawn of the State House and a violent disturbance in the lobby of the theater on opening night.

There was little journalistic criticism of motion pictures at that time. (The notice of the opening of the film in *The Times* was little more than a four-paragraph news report.) But a scathing denunciation of the movie was carried in the March 20 issue of *The New Republic.* It was written by Francis Hackett, the drama critic of that publication, and it crystallized the attitude of liberals throughout the country.

Bitterly attacking Dixon as a "yellow clergyman" because he "recklessly distorts Negro crimes to influence the ignorant and the credulous," Hackett quoted subtitles from the movie to illustrate his points:

Dixon shows the revolting process by which "the white South is crushed under the heel of the black South." "Sowing the wind," he calls it. On the one hand, we have "the poor bruised heart" of the

white South, on the other "the new citizens inflamed by the growing
sense of power."

We see Negroes shoving white men off the sidewalks, Negroes quit-
ting work to dance, Negroes beating a crippled old white patriarch, Negroes slinging up "faithful colored servants" and flogging them till they
drop. . . . And we see continually in the background the white Southerner "in agony of soul over the degradation and ruin of his people."
To hoochy-koochy music [there was a special musical score composed
by Joseph Carl Breil], we see the long pursuit of the innocent white
girl by the lust-maddened Negro and we see her fling herself to death
from the precipice, carrying her honor through "the opal gates of
death."

Having painted this insanely apprehensive picture of an unbridled,
bestial, horrible race, relieved only by a few touches of low comedy,
"the grim reaping begins." We see the operations of the Ku Klux
Klan, "the organization that saved the South from the anarchy of black
rule." We see Federals and Confederates uniting in a holy war "in
defense of their Aryan birthright." . . . The drama ends with a suggestion of "Lincoln's solution"—back to Liberia—and then, if you
please, with a representation of Jesus Christ in "the halls of brotherly
love"!

As a consequence of Hackett's criticism and the intensive oppo-
sition of the NAACP, which issued a special edition of its
publication, *The Crisis,* containing denunciations from many dis-
tinguished humanitarians, including Jane Addams and Dr. Charles
W. Eliot, the film was banned in many cities—Newark, Atlantic
City, and St. Louis, among others. Governor James M. Cox of
Ohio ordered that it not be shown in that state during the First
World War. It was also banned, at various times, in Kansas and
West Virginia.

Throughout the South it was shown and viewed with enthu-
thiasm. The sort of public response it met there was described by
John Hammond Moore, in a document published recently in the
Proceedings of the South Carolina Historical Association:

Beginning in October, 1915, when Spartanburg was the first community
in this state to see the motion picture . . . thousands of South Carolin-
ians thrilled to [its] stirring scenes. Men who once wore gray uniforms,

white sheets and red shirts wept, yelled, whooped, cheered and on one occasion even shot up the screen in a valiant effort to save Flora Cameron from her black pursuer. A carnival atmosphere reigned whenever this movie came to town.

A favorite and effective stunt to whip up excitement was to have a troop of horsemen dressed in the white sheets of the Ku Klux Klan ride through towns on their hooded horses in advance of showings of the film.

There can't be much doubt that the excitement generated by this film had a great deal to do with the inauguration of the modern Klan. The original Klan, which had come into being in 1866, was officially ordered disbanded by its Grand Wizard, General Nathan Bedford Forrest, the Confederate cavalry leader, in 1869, and was filed away as an incident in postwar history after a series of searching congressional investigations in 1870–1872.

But in 1915 a man named William J. Simmons, an ex-minister and former staff employe of the fraternal society, the Woodmen of the World, eager to have an organization of his own, took his cue from the enthusiasm in the South, for *The Birth of a Nation*. He assembled a group of followers and on Thanksgiving night in 1915, presided at the first meeting of the new organization on top of Stone Mountain outside Atlanta. A fiery cross was burned. Simmons had wanted to call his organization the Clansmen, but he found there was another organization registered under that name. So he picked up the original name, embroidered on it, and called his organization the Invisible Empire, Knights of the Ku Klux Klan.

In his book on the KKK, John Moffatt Mecklin says:

It will doubtless always be a matter of debate whether the influence of *The Birth of a Nation* was predominantly good or bad. It did undoubtedly make many aware for the first time of the wickedness and injustice of the Reconstruction period. The weakness of this picture does not lie so much in its exaggeration of the evils of Negro domination in the South . . . as in the fact that it shows the Klan only in its best aspects and before it had been made use of by evil men for the perpetuation of outrages even worse than those it was designed to eliminate.

The movie continued as a huge success all through the First World War, not only in this country but around the world. It earned Griffith a fortune—though he lost much of it on his next film, an even larger and more expensive project entitled *Intolerance*. This was his answer to those who had challenged *The Birth of a Nation* as an example of precisely that quality which the new film condemned. Griffith always felt that *The Birth of a Nation* told the truth about the South.

In recent years, prints of the film have been distributed—mainly for college and film society showings—but the NAACP still maintains an official objection to it.

While Griffith made many other pictures, and was the undisputed dean of American film directors in the 1920s, after that decade his fortunes waned. When he died in 1948, he was an impoverished and all but forgotten man. So, too, was Thomas Dixon, when he died in 1946. And Harry Aitken, who also made a fortune from the picture, lost it in later deals, faded from the scene as a film industrialist, and died poor nine years ago.

Robert Benchley

2 Hearts in Dixie
(The First Real Talking Picture)

[1929]

Ever since the inception of the talking movie, there has been a perfectably justifiable suspicion that it wouldn't work. There could be no doubt that sound could be made to come from some part of a screen on which figures were shown, sound that could be construed by eager and imaginative members of the audience to be coming from the mouths of the characters. But as for any illusion of speakers, that was more or less of a gamble.

One of the chief obstacles in the advance of the "talkies" has been the voices of the actors. Even granted that the sound could be made to come from somewhere near their mouths, the voice itself was impossible. They have either sounded like the announcer in a railway station or some lisping dancing master, and the general effect has been to cause the public mind to revert to the good old movie days when subtitles were flashed on and the hero and heroine were not expected to give themselves away by talking.

With the opening of Hearts in Dixie, however, the future of the talking movie has taken on a rosier hue. Voices can be found that will register perfectly. Personalities can be found that are ideal for this medium. It may be that the talking movies must be participated in exclusively by Negroes, but, if so, then so be it. In the Negro the sound picture has found its ideal protagonist.

With the exception of one character (easily the worst actor in the picture) the entire cast of Hearts in Dixie is colored. And people who have never been able to see anything at all in the "talkies" are convinced after seeing this one. There is a quality in the Negro voice, an ease in its delivery, and a sense of timing in reading the lines that make it the ideal medium for the talking picture. What white actors are going to do to compete with it is their business. So long as there are enough Negroes to make pictures, and enough good stories for them to act in, the future of the talking picture is assured.

The story of *Hearts in Dixie* is practically negligible. It is almost embarrassingly meager. There are scenes on a cotton plantation, with an occasional close-up of an old man, his daughter, and his grandchild in a casual family relationship. The mother dies; the child is left to the grandfather, and as the picture ends, we see the little boy leaving on the *Nellie Blye* to go up the river to school, with the grandfather waving "goodbye" as the boat toots its way up the river. There are times in the story when you are not sure that this *is* the story, when you wonder if there is a story after all. But there are never times when you care much, for you can hear the rich resonance of the voices and watch the unparalleled ease and grace of acting of the characters, and nothing else much matters.

Of course, entirely outside the main story (what there is of it) is the amazing personality of Stepin Fetchit. I see no reason for even hesitating in saying that he is the best actor that the talking movies have produced. His voice, his manner, his timing, everything that he does, is as near to perfection as one could hope to get in an essentially phony medium such as this. You forget that you are listening to a synchronized sound-tract that winds its way along the side of a photographic film. You forget that back of all this are weeks and weeks of dull, repetitive rehearsals and stupid bickerings in the office of the producing company. When Stepin Fetchit speaks, you are there beside him, one of the great comedians of the screen.

I happen to have have been in Hollywood when *Hearts in Dixie* was being made. I know that it could have been twice as good a picture as it is. I happen to know that Sloan, the director, is now in a sanitarium recovering from a nervous breakdown because his picture was tinkered with and cut to pieces to make a Jewish holiday. *Hearts in Dixie,* as originally made, was a great epic of the Southern Negro. To see the little snatches of it that have been left, snatches that only suggest the wild, elemental abandon of the original, is to realize why the movies can never be an artistic force in the community so long as they are in the hands of the present group of financiers. But, even as it stands, *Hearts in Dixie* is something worth seeing, because of the actors and the direction of the actors and the inevitable feeling that the moving picture can be made to talk with some degree of illusion.

In only one respect (aside from the direction of Mr. Sloan) has the interference of the white man been beneficial. This is in the comedy dialogue. For some reasons best known to Negroes themselves, when they are left alone to write their own comedy lines, they desert their native wit and mess around with what they seem to feel white folks *want* them to say. With the exception of *Blackbirds* there has not been a Negro show in which the comedy lines have not been execrable. They usually consist of the mispronunciation of big words, and such mispronunciation as even the most ignorant of Negroes could not possibly make. To this is added the inevitable fright that a Negro is supposed to fall into when confronted by ghosts, loud noises, and razors. This usually makes up the list of Negro comedy in the revues that they themselves have fashioned, and it is the most unfair of all the libels that the Negro creates against his race. For the real Negro comedy is as easy and unforced as that of Will Rogers (when his *is* unforced), and if it could be written into a revue, would easily be the most spontaneous of all American comic dialogue.

It is this heavy-handed childishness that the dialogue writers in *Hearts in Dixie* have avoided. The lines are funny and they sound genuine, but they are not based on mispronunciation. One of the funniest comedy scenes on any screen comes in *Hearts in Dixie* when Mr. Fetchit, after as arduous a courtship as his lack of energy would allow him to make, ends by asking the lady of his choice if she loves him. And when she admits that she has been won over by his charm and does love him, he says: "Then get me some more of those spare-ribs." It is all as effortless as Mr. Fetchit's comedy itself, and the white dialogue writers on Mr. Fox's lot have given the Negroes a better break than they have given themselves in the past.

The fact remains, however, that many people will remember *Hearts in Dixie* as the first talking picture in which the characters seemed really to talk, and will remember its Negro cast as the first real actors they ever saw in talking pictures.

James Baldwin

3. *Carmen Jones:* The Dark Is Light Enough

[1955]

Hollywood's peculiar ability to milk, so to speak, the cow and the goat at the same time—and then to peddle the results as ginger ale—has seldom produced anything more arresting than the 1955 production of *Carmen Jones.* In Hollywood, for example, immorality and evil (which are synonyms in that lexicon) are always vividly punished, though it is the way of the transgressor—hard perhaps but far from unattractive—which keeps us on the edge of our seats, and the transgressor himself (or herself) who engages all our sympathy. Similarly, in *Carmen Jones,* the implicit parallel between an amoral Gypsy and an amoral Negro woman is the entire root idea of the show; but at the same time, bearing in mind the distances covered since *The Birth of a Nation,* it is important that the movie always be able to repudiate any suggestion that Negroes are amoral—which it can only do, considering the role of the Negro in the national psyche, by repudiating any suggestion that Negroes are not white. With a story like *Carmen* interpreted by a Negro cast, this may seem a difficult assignment, but Twentieth Century-Fox has brought it off. At the same time they have also triumphantly *not* brought it off, that is to say that the story *does* deal with amoral people, Carmen *is* a baggage, and it *is* a Negro cast.

This is made possible in the first place, of course, by the fact that *Carmen* is a "classic" or a "work of art" or something, therefore sacrosanct and, luckily, quite old: it is as ludicrously unenlightened to accuse Mérimée and Bizet of having dirty minds as it is impossible to accuse them of being anti-Negro. (Though it *is* possible perhaps to accuse them of not knowing much and caring less about Gypsies.) In the second place the music helps, for it has assuredly never sounded so bald, or been sung so badly, or had less relevance to life, anybody's life, than in this production. The lyrics, too, in their way, help, being tasteless and vulgar in a way, if not to a degree, which cannot be called characteristic of Negroes. The movie's lifeless unreality is only occasionally threatened by Pearl Bailey, who has, however, been forestalled by Mr. Preminger's direction and is reduced—in a series of awful costumes, designed, it would appear, to camouflage her personality—to doing what is certainly the best that can be done with an abomination called "Beat Out That Rhythm on a Drum" and delivering her lines for the rest of the picture with such a murderously amused disdain that one cannot quite avoid the suspicion that she is commenting on the film. For a second or so at a time she escapes the film's deadly inertia and in Miss Bailey one catches glimpses of the imagination which might have exploded this movie into something worth seeing.

But this movie, more than any movie I can remember having seen, cannot afford, dare not risk, imagination. The "sexiness," for example, of Dorothy Dandridge, who plays Carmen, becomes quite clearly manufactured and even rather silly the moment Pearl Bailey stands anywhere near her.[1] And the moment one wishes that Pearl Bailey were playing Carmen one understands that *Carmen Jones* is controlled by another movie which Hollywood was studiously *not* making. For, while it is amusing to parallel Bizet's amoral Gypsy with a present-day, lower-class Negro woman, it is a good deal less amusing to parallel the Bizet violence with the violence of the Negro ghetto.

[1] I have singled out Miss Bailey because the quality of her personality, forthright and wry, and with the authoritative ring of authenticity, highlights for me the lack of any of these qualities, or any positive qualities at all, in the movie itself. She is also the only performer with whose work I am more or less familiar. Since even she is so thoroughly handicapped by the peculiar necessities of *Carmen Jones*, I should like to make it clear that, in discussing the rest of the cast, I am not trying to judge their professional competence, which, on the basis of this movie—they do not even sing in their own voices—it would be quite unfair to do.

To avoid this—to exploit, that is, Carmen as a brown-skinned baggage but to avoid even suggesting any of the motivations such a present-day Carmen might have—it was helpful, first of all, that the script failed to require the services of any white people. This seals the action off, as it were, in a vacuum in which the spectacle of color is divested of its danger. The color itself then becomes a kind of vacuum which each spectator will fill with his own fantasies. But *Carmen Jones* does not inhabit the never-never land of such bogus but rather entertaining works as *Stormy Weather* or *Cabin in the Sky*—in which at least one could listen to the music; *Carmen Jones* has moved into a stratosphere rather more interesting and more pernicious, in which even Negro speech is parodied out of its charm and liberalized, if one may so put it, out of its force and precision. The result is not that the characters sound like everybody else, which would be bad enough; the result is that they sound ludicrously false and affected, like antebellum Negroes imitating their masters. This is also the way they look, and also rather the way they are dressed, and the word that springs immediately to mind to describe the appallingly technicolored sets —an army camp, a room, and a street on Chicago's South Side, presumably, which Bigger Thomas would certainly fail to recognize—is "spotless." They could easily have been dreamed up by someone determined to prove that Negroes are as "clean" and as "modern" as white people and, I suppose, in one way or another, that is exactly how they *were* dreamed up.

And one is not allowed to forget for an instant that one is watching an opera (a word apparently synonymous in Mr. Preminger's mind with tragedy *and* fantasy), and the tone of *Carmen Jones* is stifling: a wedding of the blank, lofty solemnity with which Hollywood so often approaches "works of art" and the really quite helpless condescension with which Hollywood has always handled Negroes. The fact that one is watching a Negro cast interpreting *Carmen* is used to justify their remarkable vacuity, their complete improbability, their total divorce from anything suggestive of the realities of Negro life. On the other hand, the movie cannot possibly avoid depending very heavily on a certain quaintness, a certain lack of inhibition taken to be typical of Negroes, and further, the exigencies of the story—to say nothing of the images, which we will discuss in a moment—make it necessary to watch this movie holding in the mind three disparate ideas: (1) that this is an opera having nothing to do with the present day, hence, nothing, *really*, to do with Negroes; but (2) the greater passion, that winning warmth (of which the movie exhibits not a trace), so typical of Negroes makes *Carmen* an ideal vehicle for their graduation into Art; and (3) these are *exceptional* Negroes, as American, that is, as you and me, interpreting lower-class Negroes of whom they, also, are very fond, an affection which is proven perhaps by the fact that everyone appears to undergo a tiny, strangling death before resolutely substituting "de" for "the."

A movie is, literally, a series of images, and what one *sees* in a movie can really be taken, beyond its stammering or misleading dialogue, as the key to what the movie is actually involved in saying. *Carmen Jones* is one of the first and most explicit—and far and away the most self-conscious—weddings of sex and color that Hollywood has yet turned out. (It will most certainly not be the last.) From this point of view the color wheel in *Carmen Jones* is very important. Dorothy Dandridge—Carmen—is a sort of taffy-colored girl, very obviously and vividly dressed, but really in herself rather more sweet than vivid. One feels—perhaps one is meant to feel—that here is a *very* nice girl making her way in movies by means of a bad-girl part; and the glow thus caused, especially since she is a colored girl, really must make up for the glow which is missing from the performance she is clearly working very hard at. Harry Belafonte is just a little darker and just as blankly handsome and fares very badly opposite her in a really offensive version of an already unendurable role. Olga James is Micaela, here called Cindy Lou, a much paler girl than Miss Dandridge but also much plainer, who is compelled to go through the entire movie in a kind of tearful stoop. Joe Adams is Husky Miller (Escamillo) and he is also rather taffy-colored, but since he is the second lead and by way of being the villain, he is not required to be as blank as Mr. Belafonte and there is therefore, simply in his presence, some fleeting hint of masculine or at least boyish force. For the rest, Pearl Bailey is quite dark and she plays, in effect, a floozie. The

92 BLACK FILMS AND FILM-MAKERS

wicked sergeant who causes Joe to desert the army—in one of many wildly improbable scenes—and who has evil designs on Carmen is very dark indeed; and so is Husky Miller's trainer, who is, one is given to suppose, Miss Bailey's sugar daddy. It is quite clear that these people do not live in the same world with Carmen, or Joe, or Cindy Lou. All three of the leads are presented as indefinably complex and tragic, not after money or rhinestones but something else which causes them to be misunderstood by the more earthy types around them. This something else is love, of course, and it is with the handling of this love story that the movie really goes to town.

It is true that no one in the original *Carmen*, least of all Carmen and her lover, are very clearly motivated; but there it scarcely matters because the opera is able to get by on a purely theatrical excitement, a sort of papier-mâché violence, and the intense, if finally incredible, sexuality of its heroine. The movie does not have any of this to work with, since here excitement or violence could only blow the movie to bits, and while the movie certainly indicates that Carmen is a luscious lollipop, it is on rather more uncertain ground when confronted with the notion of how at-tractive *she* finds men, and it cannot, in any case, use this as a motivating factor. Carmen is thus robbed at a stroke of even her fake vitality and all her cohesiveness and has become, instead, a nice girl, if a little fiery, whose great fault—and since this is a tragedy, also her triumph—is that she looks at "life," as her final aria states it, "straight in de eye." In lieu of sexuality the movie makers have dreamed up some mumbo jumbo involving buzzards' wings, signs of the zodiac, and death-dealing cards, so that, it appears, Carmen ruins Joe because she loves him and decides to leave him because the cards tell her she is going to die. The fact that between the time she leaves him and the time he kills her she acquires some new clothes, and drinks—as one of her arias rather violently indicates she intends to—a great deal of champagne is simply a sign of her intense inner suffering.

Carmen has come a long way from the auction block, but Joe, of course, cannot be far behind. This Joe is a good, fine-looking boy who loves his Maw, has studied hard, and is going to be sent to flying school, and who is engaged to a girl who rather resembles his Maw, named Cindy Lou. His indifference to Carmen, who has all the other males in sight quivering with a passion never seen on land or sea, sets her ablaze; in a series of scenes which it is difficult to call erotic without adding that they are also infantile, she goes after him and and he falls. Here the technicolored bodies of Dandridge and Belafonte, while the movie is being glum about the ruin of Joe's career and impending doom, are used for the maximum erotic effect. It is a sterile and distressing eroticism, however, because it is occurring in a vacuum between two mannequins who clearly are not involved in anything more serious than giving the customers a run for their money. One is not watching either tenderness or love, and one is certainly not watching the complex and consuming passion that leads to life or death—one is watching a timorous and vulgar misrepresentation of these things.

And it must be said that one of the reasons for this is that, while the movie makers are pleased to have Miss Dandridge flouncing about in tight skirts and plunging necklines—which is not exactly sexuality, either—the Negro male is still too loaded a quantity for them to know quite how to handle. The result is that Mr. Belafonte is really not allowed to do anything more than walk around looking like a spaniel: *his* sexuality is really taken as given because Miss Dandridge wants him. It does not, otherwise, exist, and he is not destroyed by his own sexual aggressiveness, which he is not allowed to have, but by the sexual aggressiveness of the girl—or, as it turns out, not even really by that, but by tea leaves. The only reason, finally, that the eroticism of *Carmen Jones* is more potent than, say, the eroticism of a Lana Turner vehicle is that *Carmen Jones* has Negro bodies before the camera and Negroes are associated in the public mind with sex. Since darker races always seem to have for lighter races an aura of sexuality, this fact is not distressing in itself. What is distressing is the conjecture this movie leaves one with as to what Americans take sex to be.

The most important thing about this movie—and the reason that, despite itself, it is one of the most important all-Negro movies

Hollywood has yet produced—is that the questions it leaves in the mind relate less to Negroes than to the interior life of Americans. One wonders, it is true, if Negroes are really going to become the ciphers this movies makes them out to be; but, since they have until now survived public images even more appalling, one is encouraged to hope, for their sake and the sake of the Republic, that they will continue to prove themselves incorrigible. Besides, life does not produce ciphers like these: when people have become this empty they are not ciphers any longer, but monsters. The creation of such ciphers proves, however, that Americans are far from empty; they are, on the contrary, very deeply disturbed. And this disturbance is not the kind that can be eased by the doing of good works, but seems to have turned inward and shows every sign of becoming personal. This is one of the best things that can possibly happen. It can be taken to mean—among a great many other things—that the ferment which has resulted in as odd a brew as *Carmen Jones* can now be expected to produce something which will be more bitter on the tongue but sweeter in the stomach.

Lindsay Patterson

4 It's Gonna Blow Whitey's Mind

[1968]

Thank God there's no frock-coat Lawd thundering earthly plati-
tudes ("How de fish fry goin'?"), or Catfish Row nonsense, or
hallelujah singing for the benefit of the KKK, happening in Cleveland and Hollywood these days. It's kind of surprising. Some black
folks—for a change—are getting a chance to tell it *somewhat* like it
is, in, of all things, a multimillion-dollar Technicolor Hollywood
movie. What began as an updated, all-black Harlem version of *The
Informer,* John Ford's 1935 classic about the secret Irish Repub-
lican Brotherhood, is now *Uptight!* a sometimes ferocious story of
today's black militants and nonviolence advocates, set in the Hough
area of Cleveland—as shabby and dilapidated a black ghetto as is
likely to be found anywhere.

But before anyone gets the wonderful idea that Hollywood has
a guilty conscience and has finally conceded a racial crisis does
exist in our country, it should be explained that Paramount Pictures originally wanted director Jules Dassin to remake *The Informer* with an all-white cast. Failing that, the studio settled for
Dassin and an all-black cast. Of course, it never occurred to anyone
that a backlog of black material by black American writers exists,
or that two of the greatest American novels, *Invisible Man* and
Native Son, have never been made into major motion pictures. So,
instead of starting from scratch with young black writers or using
existing black materials, *Uptight!*—as so much else in our society
concerning the black man—neatly compromises, by employing two

of its stars, Ruby Dee and Julian Mayfield, along with Dassin, as coauthors.

Nevertheless, *Uptight!* by Hollywood's feeble standards is probably the most "daring" [1] film ever to be in production, certainly in its admission that there is more to the racial crisis than one manicured black man pining to become acceptable to the white establishment, and that there are some blacks in the ghetto who are tired of whitey's "junk" ("He ain't never gonna change"), and are doing something about it in the only terms that whitey seemingly understands.

Structurally, the film follows rather straightforwardly the situation and plot lines of Liam O'Flaherty's *The Informer* and the movie John Ford made from it. Tank Williams (Julian Mayfield), a bumbling, weak-minded, strong-as-an-ox alcoholic, is expelled by a black militant organization for refusing to assist three members in stealing guns the night Martin Luther King is murdered (Tank is devastated by King's death and has taken to the bottle). One member of the trio kills a guard, and Tank is more or less persuaded by a brilliant, cynical homosexual and paid police informer (Roscoe Lee Browne) to finger the gunman. Also, Tank feels deeply inadequate in not being able to support his girl friend (Ruby Dee), who, to make ends meet, resorts to part-time prostitution and welfare. After he informs, Tank's free spending of the reward money causes suspicion and the members of the militant organization elicit from him a confession of guilt. The ending—a departure from the original, in which the informer is shot down by his former comrades—has Tank atoning for his guilt by jumping to his death from a bridge. Apparently, Dassin did not want to conclude *Uptight!* with blacks killing other blacks.

Perhaps the most important moments in the film are the confrontations between the leader of the militant group, Raymond St. Jacques, and the leader of the moderate group, Frank Silvera, when each presents his case, the militant for guns and the moderate for education. The film avoids drawing a conclusion as to

---

[1] *Uptight!* turned out not to be "daring" at all. From most major critics it received less than favorable reviews and was seemingly a box-office disappointment. The film's mentality seemed more rooted in the liberalness of the 1940s than the direct action of the 1960s.

which program is more feasible (a mistake, I feel), but endeavors to dramatize what it sees as the two approaches open to blacks in white America.

Although the film does not wish to illustrate by concrete examples what either group can or cannot accomplish, the production unit, during five weeks in Cleveland, found out what a local militant group can achieve through unilateral action. When filming began in the streets of the ghetto, the group demanded that a black policeman—whom they charged with brutality and the indiscriminate use of firepower in previous encounters—be removed from escort duty on the movie. Their demand ignored by city authorities, they initiated a campaign of "harassment" by systematically marching in circles around the policeman. The situation became tense, and the predominantly white, middle-class production crew panicked, walked off their jobs, threatening to return to Hollywood. After a highly charged meeting between the blacks and the whites of the production, it was agreed that the whites had "reacted excessively" to an internal ghetto affair. Raymond St. Jacques and other actors went on television and radio to ask the ghetto community to "keep cool." St. Jacques explained what the film was about, and pointed out that it had the "blessing" of Carl Stokes, the black mayor of Cleveland. To many militants, however, the production was another example of the "establishment" locking them out, denying them a "piece of the action." It was not until someone got the "bright" idea of employing a few members of the militant group that production resumed in another location in the Hough area without incident and without the previous contingent of police escorts.

When I visited one shooting location recently—an abandoned Pennsylvania Railroad station of a bygone era at Fifty-fifth and Euclid—everything seemed, on the surface at least, to be going smoothly. There was a lively audience of ghetto residents (no police in sight) attentively watching a "black militant" fervently addressing a small crowd huddled in the rain at the edge of the station's promenade: "We got to get our own thing going, our own program. . . ." The same scene had been tried unsuccessfully in heavy rain the previous night. This was a clear and cloudless night, and water sprinklers had been placed on the northeast corner of the station's roof and in other strategic spots to provide just enough rain. After nearly three hours, the scene was finally wrapped up. The actors (mostly real militants from the area), were drenched, yet ebullient. Julian Mayfield was part of the crowd.

A big, broad, confident man, Mayfield is known primarily as a novelist (*The Hit, The Grand Parade*), but he did some stage acting "years ago," once as an understudy to a then fledgling young actor named Sidney Poitier in the Broadway musical *Lost in the Stars*. Mayfield has been in a kind of "exile" from the United States because of his intensely militant political activity. He has spent the years since 1961 in Ghana (he was a speech writer for Nkrumah) and Spain, and only returned to this country in June of last year.

"I didn't lose touch by being away so long," insists Mayfield, when asked if his absence had handicapped him in working on a script about today's young militants. "Instead, I gained more of a perspective. People like Muhammad Ali and Malcolm X were constantly passing through Ghana, and I got from them firsthand what was going on back here. If I had been here, I would've only gotten my information from the newspapers."

While the younger actors in *Uptight!* have great expectations for the movie (both in terms of their own careers and the impact it will make: "It's gonna blow whitey's mind"), the older generation is adopting a "wait and see" attitude. For the veteran black actor it is a too familiar scene, where hopes are raised only to be dashed cruelly by an indifferent white America. Ruby Dee offers perhaps the most sober view when she describes the film "as a good drop of water into that ocean."

Miss Dee—along with her husband, Ossie Davis—has, for about two decades, led the fight for integration in the theater, and she is probably the only black actress to have worked with any degree of consistency in nonstereotyped, dramatic roles (*A Raisin in the Sun, Purlie Victorious*). Being a black performer in America, she feels, limits not only opportunities, but the ability to perform at full capacity.

"My own career," she says, "has not been as flourishing as I'd like because of things inside me which make me wary of experimenting with roles. Many black people have hurdles within themselves which they have to overcome before they can function at top efficiency. Thank God my own children are seemingly free of any restrictions."

Unlike many middle-class blacks and whites Miss Dee does not put down the rebellious younger generation, but lays its unrest squarely at the door of the "old folks." "Our young people have sensed that there is something lacking in *us*. They have gotten the short end of the stick. They are rebelling against things they don't want. Too bad we live in a time when people have to destroy in order for us to listen. We seemingly can only listen under pain. The only time we move is after a tragedy."

Raymond St. Jacques, who has a mild reputation for flamboyant living (he likes to drive fast cars fast and serve brunches in flowing African robes in his $100,000 California house), will in all probability be the next black matinee idol. He has worked impressively as villains in *The Pawnbroker* and *The Comedians*, and is being described as a "black Lee Marvin." ("I want to be a black Raymond St. Jacques!") Currently in *The Green Berets*, he will get star billing for the first time in *Uptight!*. Off screen, he is an advocate of both black power and the status quo.

"I am not interested in wrecking the establishment," he says. "I am only interested in building. I want to contribute to the social revolution in my own limited way. I tried to get black money when I started my picture corporation, but you know how impossible that was."

Nevertheless, the 6-foot-3-inch, former Yale drama student is clearly pleased about his healthy film career. Max Julien, a young Broadway actor (he plays the militant who shoots the guard while stealing guns), is also working like hell in Hollywood and determined to make it. But if he is optimistic about his own career, he's pessimistic about the future of the black actor in Hollywood. "The door is open now," he says, "but will close after the elections [1968 presidential election] in November. What we got to do now is swell the ranks so they can't close it all the way."

Some attitudes among black members of *Uptight!* indicate something of the wide gulf separating blacks and whites. Many of the blacks suspect the technical crew (which includes three blacks) of "subconsciously" trying to sabotage the production, since "white hatred for the black man is so deep he can't help it." This has led to the conclusion by some that the film will never be released, because "it tries to deal too honestly with the black man, and whitey ain't never going to accept that."

Producer-director Dassin (*Never on Sunday*, *Rififi*, *He Who Must Die*) says that upon his return to Hollywood for interior filming he will try to persuade other producers and directors to push for more enrollment of blacks into the craft unions. But Dassin, who has not made a movie in Hollywood since he was blacklisted there during the McCarthy era, does not consider this production as marking his return to the film capital. "I will not make another movie in America," he declares.

Dassin has discovered (or rediscovered) that America is a maze of small bureaucratic minds that like nothing better than to exclude on the false issues of race, creed, or religion. *Uptight!* clearly is a hopeful step toward a broader vision. If there is any courage at all in Hollywood, it will be followed quickly by other steps, even bolder, so that more movies will tell it like it really is, without fear, for the good of us all.

Lindsay Patterson

5   In Harlem, a James Bond with Soul?

[1969]

Believe it or not, Harlem is going to get its own soul version of James Bond. There won't be Agent 007 himself, however, or any of those fancy gadgets and blonde playthings, just two hard-working Harlem detectives trying to recover $87,000 stolen at a "Back to Africa" rally. But don't get the notion *Cotton Comes to Harlem* will be serious because it takes place in the ghetto. Its director, actor-playwright Ossie Davis, is out to capture an aspect of the black man rarely exhibited in movies these days—his humor.

This is Davis's first assignment as a film director (he also co-authored the screenplay with Arnold Perl), and he aims to "show there is something different going on up in Harlem" that other film makers have missed, "the community's colorful, exciting life-style and wit." Davis regards the movie as basically an entertainment. This is not to say, however, there won't be a "residual message" of sorts; the film will attempt to treat honestly (and humorously) the way "black people outwit the establishment and stay one step ahead of the wolf's teeth."

Davis, a sometimes dazzling actor (*Jeb, Purlie Victorious, The Scalphunters* and *Teacher, Teacher,* for which he recently earned an Emmy nomination), has often put his own career on the line by speaking out forcefully for black causes (he delivered an eloquent eulogy at the funeral of Malcolm X). And he realizes that in this present tense climate in the ghettoes, there are dangers in

101

making a movie about ghetto residents, comic style. But "criticism," Davis says, "is to be expected. No man can be everything to everybody. No matter what you try to do, there is always some negative aspect to it. You pick your shots and take your chances. You hope that what you achieve outweighs in its good effects some of the bad effects. I see what I'm doing as an important contribution to the cultural life of my community. Somewhere down the line I might step on toes. I might have to make concessions so fundamental that they will cut the gut and heart out of what we are trying to say to black people. If I come up with a picture that black people don't like, then they'll just kick me out of the community and say don't come back again. I would have had my fair chance and failed. I don't hope to lose. I don't think I will."

The film is an updated version of Chester Himes's 1964 novel *Cotton Comes to Harlem*, about two detectives, Coffin Ed Johnson (Raymond St. Jacques) and Grave Digger Jones (Godfrey Cambridge), and their search for the missing money, which the organizer of the "Back to Africa" rally, a self-styled minister and con man (Calvin Lockhart), is after, too. Like the 007 epics, the movie will not overlook girls: Judy Pace will be the minister's tough cookie of a girl friend and Emily Yancy a sweet member of his tabernacle.

Davis is working like hell to perfect his directorial skills and "getting stronger everyday," beams *Cotton*'s producer, Samuel Goldwyn, Jr. Except for a junkyard sequence, the film is being shot entirely on location in Harlem and in the Filmways Studio there. Recently, the "Back to Africa" rally scene was staged outdoors, on the site of an abandoned gas station at 128th Street and Lexington Avenue. Weather conditions had slowed production somewhat, and on the first day I visited the location site, the sun continued to play hide and seek. About two hundred extras, recruited mainly from local theater groups and from the neighborhood, were being used. Watching the filming were many Harlem residents, most of them curious, some puzzled, and a few hostile. ("They should be doing something militant!")

The production, if not quite an armed camp, was well protected by members of the New York City Tactical Patrol Force, and the

Harlem-based Black Citizens Patrol, whose members (some in their black paramilitary uniforms and others in street clothes) were stationed with walkie-talkies on rooftops and at ground-level command posts. The preceding week, the white script girl had been hit on the head with a bottle thrown from a roof at 153d Street and Eighth Avenue (Godfrey Cambridge sent her a note with flowers, saying: "Some people throw flowers"), but thus far, there has been little in the way of overt hostility.

More hostility toward the production, however, has been exhibited within the apprenticeship program funded by the Ford Foundation for the purpose of providing on-the-job training for young technicians from black and other ethnic groups. The program, initiated recently with Harry Belafonte's *The Angel Levine*, has come under heavy attack on *Cotton*, especially from those apprentices who have some professional or educational experience. They feel the program suffers, like most black youth programs, from a lack of sound organization, from a lack of preproduction planning that would assign them genuine responsibilities rather than leave them to stand around aimlessly watching. Those in charge agree that the program could have done more and better planning on *Cotton*. There, however, agreement stops, and charges are aired, on the one hand, about the quality of some apprentices and their willingness to work, and on the other hand, about disinterest by the production unit, and the middle-class values of those in charge.

Sam Bennerson, a black second assistant director who "came up the hard way" and "slid in the back door of the Screen Directors Guild" ("I had to back my way in. They'd taken money from me for a good while before they realized I was black and there was nothing they could do"), has four apprentices under his supervision. "They got the attitude," he says, "like so many young people today, that the world owes them a living. They come when they want to and leave when they want to. There has only been one who has reported on time and showed any initiative toward some work. When I was breaking into this game, I was what you call a do-body—do this, do that—and I hustle."

The dissenters call it "go-for" (go for coffee, etc.), and reject the running of petty errands as not fulfilling the program's objectives. The acceleration and sharpening of skills with each film assignment, they feel, should be the main objective. But some of the dissatisfaction goes deeper, having to do with the apprentices' frustration in not being able to make the kind of movies they feel black people should be making. "Black people," says one dissenter, "are not interested in being entertained anymore. Black audiences have become sophisticated enough so that the film must give them some substance, something which they can relate to and can apply to their own problems in life to help bring about change.

"*Cotton*," the dissenter concedes, "is good black folklore, but it does not represent or project the black concept, or the black mind, or what black people are really trying to say or strive for today. It is another Hollywood fantasy of what they think Harlem really is."

That dissenter feels, too, that there is a generation gap between young black film aspirants and Hollywood and director Davis, and that the black revolution "is nothing more than an instrument for Davis and others like him to use as a weapon in dealing with the establishment—to get those concessions that they as a group want." Nonetheless, the dissenter admires and respects Davis as "a decent man" and acknowledges that Davis himself has helped the apprentices in all the ways that he can.

Not all of the seven apprentices are actually dissatisfied with the program; some have worked out well. One is now the production publicist, and another is casting director. The greatest barrier in implementing the program fully seems to be resistance and restrictions from the craft unions.

For Godfrey Cambridge, who has gone from 310 pounds to a streamlined 203 within the past year, *Cotton Comes to Harlem* represents a "shifting image" from the stand-up comic to the actor, with "the laughs coming out of the character." In preparation for his role as Detective Grave Digger Jones he made the rounds with the Twenty-eighth Detective Squad in Harlem. What he witnessed, he says, "reaffirmed" the squalor and the degradation of Harlem, but Cambridge does not believe in message films. "Message pictures," he asserts, "I'm not going to do. They operate on a basic fallacy that you are going to get a bigot into the theater and convince him. Can't do it. What banks are concerned with and why they back pictures is to make money. Why people go to the theater is to get entertainment. A residual message, of course. There is a residual message in anything."

The fact is that there should be every kind of film, message and nonmessage. Everyone should be allowed to do his own thing, and Ossie Davis is obviously having fun doing his. "Black film," says Davis, "must first present the black man so that he and the world will understand who he is. Right now the black man is too much, in Ralph Ellison's words, the 'invisible man.' To bring the cameras to Harlem and to establish the truth of us and our existence is a tremendous step forward, and you don't have to have the cameras become soapboxes or lecture platforms. You can tell fascinating stories about fascinating people who are black, who enjoy their blackness, who are striving to control communities and themselves. That's where I'd like to head.

"In twenty-five years Harlem is going to be the film capital of the world. I've run across some very outstanding young production groups since I've been up here that I didn't know existed. People who have produced things for television and film. These people are standing by, ready to roll right now. One of the things I'd like to do when I finish *Cotton* is to do something with the young film companies here, to give them a push forward up the ladder. There is a greater degree of readiness to take over, to be prepared, than I anticipated."

Lindsay Patterson

6 *Sounder*—A Hollywood Fantasy?

[1972]

I grew up in a small Louisiana town surrounded by plantations heavily populated with black sharecroppers, and the story told in *Sounder* of one such family's adversities during the 1930s is, at its best, fanciful. It bears no resemblance whatsoever to reality as I observed it, and sometimes lived it, among black sharecroppers.

Sounder catalogues the difficulties the Morgan family supposedly undergoes during 1933, in one of the most fertile farming regions in Louisiana or the world—a region also outstanding for its wild game. The father, a conscientious worker, is unable to provide sufficient food for his family in spite of the arable land at his doorstep and the large bayous close by (which at that time were certainly unpolluted and brimming full of catfish, perch, and bass). He steals meat, and is sentenced to one year in a work camp. While he is incarcerated, the mother, assisted by her three young children, harvests a bumper crop of sugarcane.

It is the mother in the film, as played by Cicely Tyson, who has been focused upon in reviews and singled out as the epitome of black female "strength and dignity," a new high in the screen portrayal of black women. Strength and dignity the character has in abundance but, as the faithful and dutiful wife of a black farmer in Louisiana, she is strangely remiss in the care and feeding of her family. Food in the arid, red clay hills of Georgia may have been difficult to grow or obtain during the Depression, but certainly not in the fertile lowlands and watery marshes of Louisiana where the story of *Sounder* takes place.

In reality, every black woman who had access to any good-sized plot of land planted her own vegetable garden. It was mandatory if she wanted to feed her family properly, for at that time it was unthinkable to purchase canned foods when you could easily grow and home-preserve your own.

As for meat, every farm family that I knew had at least one hog, or owned a portion of one with another family. The men would slaughter it in late fall and salt and smoke the ham and fatback portions for winter consumption. No part of the hog was thrown away. The intestines were used to make chitlins and the skin, to the delight of us kids, would be fried in its own fat to make crackling. And everybody always had a few egg-laying chickens running loosely around.

However, if for some reason a crop had been ruined by natural causes, or a mysterious blight, a plantation owner would simply not permit a conscientious sharecropping family to go hungry. His "Christian conscience" ("Jesus knows I help my good niggers") and his acute business sense wouldn't allow him, for experience would tell him that "hungry niggers" do not work well, or at all. Nor would a plantation owner allow a conscientious sharecropper to be imprisoned for stealing as little as a couple of joints of meat, since most whites inherently believed that male "darkies" were "natural born thieves" anyway, and the black man was simply executing a bodily function that he had no earthly control over.

But in all my years of growing up in Louisiana, I never witnessed—as in *Sounder*—a sheriff, or any other law enforcement official, handcuff a black man, then lead him peacefully away. The black man would be beaten, punched, and kicked until blood flowed, in order "to teach the black bastard a lesson."

But any black family which understood as well as the family in *Sounder*, and could articulate as perfectly, some of the reasons for their impoverished condition, would not have hesitated to pack up in the dead of night and start out for Chicago, St. Louis, or Los Angeles, for the promise of a better and a freer life.

There are many other incidents in *Sounder* which do not ring true to me. It is unlikely, for example, that a black teacher in a one-room rural school near a backwater town in Louisiana in the 1930s would have owned or even read a book by William E. B.

Du Bois, or any other black author. My mother, who was born and reared on a farm, also taught in a one-room rural school, and she considered herself highly informed and well read. But it was not until after I had left Louisiana and settled in a large city in North Carolina that I discovered black people wrote books. In Louisiana, Joe Louis was our only hero.

Sharecropping was, indeed, a harsh and bitter life and in Louisiana, at least, a family was kept in a cycle of poverty because the plantation owner juggled the financial records of each year's crop to his own advantage, a practice that white merchants in Northern black ghettos have since refined into a high art.

Within the last decade, there have been so many easy hypotheses and generalities bandied around by just about everyone about the whole of black life that it is hard for anyone to separate fact from fiction any more. But perhaps the saddest spectacle of all is the hasty and unquestioning embrace of *Sounder* (and projects like it) by the black establishment, simply because it is unoffendingly "positive." It points up the depressing fact that blacks still know too little about each other and their own regional and diverse histories in this country. But then, too many black *leaders* and critics have shown a much greater penchant for condemning, rather than actively constructing. Meanwhile, white film makers are laughing their heads off all the way to the bank, and with millions of black dollars crammed securely in their pockets.

Editor's Note: Among reviewers this was a minority opinion of *Sounder*. It was nominated for an Academy Award as Best Picture of the year; its two stars, Paul Winfield and Cicely Tyson, were nominated as Best Actor and Actress, and Lonne Elder III was nominated for his script.

Maurice Peterson

7 Book of Numbers

[1973]

It was a sizzling hot July day in an old vacated bar, somewhere on the outskirts of Dallas, and I was about to witness what many considered a major event. I felt almost as though I had stepped into the past. A group of black people were gathered at the bar close to a huge radio. They were listening intently to a countdown. "Five! . . . Six! . . . Seven! . . ." shouted a voice from the radio, while the people cringed with the hope that a black man soon would be the heavyweight champion of the world. "Eight! . . . Nine! . . ." and the tension grew almost unbearable. Men and women in their antique, Sunday best crowded closer to the radio, as if to be the first to hear the final number, "TEN!" The bar instantly exploded with cries of jubilation. Music and screams filled the hot, heavy air as the people joyously danced the Lindy and drank toasts to their new hero.

The scene was wonderfully cathartic and authentic; a chapter from black history, beautifully recreated for the film, *Book of Numbers*. Raymond St. Jacques, the highly acclaimed actor, was directing the scene. He mounted a platform to prepare the cast for a retake. "That was fantastic!" he told the company. "Now let's see if we can do it again, but much better. More important than getting to your positions, is achieving the exultation of the triumph of the Great Black Hope—Joe Louis. Remember, as bad as things seem today, there was almost no hope at all in the thirties. Any kind of hope was like the second coming! If he had lost,

109

everybody in this bar would have just laid right down and died! All right, I think we're ready to do it!" The crowd was silent. "Action!"

While black communities across the nation were being outraged by the wave of exploitive and negative influences of current black-oriented movies, the St. Jacques Company was hard at work in an effort to prove black films can be made with integrity, by black talent. With a million-dollar budget, Raymond St. Jacques was cutting no corners in bringing an authentic picture of old black lifestyles to the screen. Using the numbers racket as a focal point, *Book of Numbers* was planned to illustrate realistically the way our parents and grandparents dealt with the intense pressures of racism and poverty that were prevalent during the Depression. And, from what I saw happening before the cameras in that old bar, it should be quite a success.

After hours of shooting in the sweltering bar-turned-studio, the cast and crew broke for lunch. Philip Thomas, Hope Clarke, D'Urville Martin, Raymond's son Sterling St. Jacques, and others walked in the scorching Texas sun to a vacant lot for a meal and some rest. Not having had much opportunity to appear in previous films, most of the principals in the cast were unknown. However, the actors' names were especially exciting because of their potential, since this production is bound to start many of them on world-famous careers.

Freda Payne was the only cast member other than Raymond who had already achieved widespread recognition as a performer, although her success has been in recordings. Singing the songs, "Band of Gold," and "Bring the Boys Home," Freda earned two gold records and a chance to move into film acting. The movies have rarely had a luckier break. Freda Payne's physical beauty is as captivating as that of any screen goddess. She has a nearly flawless "Garboesque" photogenic quality that makes her a natural for films.

"I had always dreamt of being a film actress, but the roles offered to me were too narrow to accept until now," she revealed—a frequent complaint from irate black women that their image has been scandalously distorted. "That's why I turned down the title role in *Melinda*. I also objected to the nude scene in the film that involved several men. I have a love scene in *Book of Numbers*, but it's not completely nude, and it's with only one man! I considered the scene in *Melinda* obscene."

As we talked, Freda expressed pride in playing the role of Kelly Sims. "In *Book of Numbers*, I'm not being used as an object, I'm an actress with the image they desire. Black movies have stereotyped our women. There are so many kinds of women in the black race that you can't put a certified stamp on one image. Kelly is set off from the rest of characters. She's of middle-class background, which, at the time, was an oddity. Her father is a professor at Fisk University, and she is a college student. She's not connected with the way of living in the ward, which today we call the ghetto, but she is interested in finding a man to whom she can relate in terms of blackness and getting ahead in life. She's very aggressive, but not frighteningly so. She thinks about the well-being of herself and her man in the present and future. Unlike many women in black films, she isn't so dumb that she falls into a trap with her man. She has the strength and self-awareness to look out for herself. I think that she projects a good image for the black woman of today."

Not all the female characters have Kelly's background, but it seems that they are all treated with respect. Irma Hall, a local Texas teacher and newspaper columnist, was spotted by St. Jacques and cast in the role of Georgia Brown, a "madam." Before shooting recommenced, Ms. Hall commented on Georgia Brown's characterization.

"I can't moralize on whether it's right or wrong to be a 'madam,'" said Irma, a real life mother of three, "but as far as Georgia is concerned, I can understand her reason for it. The film shows that it was a way this black woman could provide for herself. She regards it as a business. Her women had also lived through certain unfortunate incidents that had left them in hard situations. So they considered prostitution the best way to keep from walking the streets. We're trying to show things as they really were, and it's important that all facets of black life be portrayed."

Evidently the enthusiasm displayed in the Joe Louis victory

celebration scene had been maintained since shooting had begun six weeks previously. Philip Thomas, who starred in *Stigma*, had thrown himself into his leading role of David Green a bit too hard. When he and Hope Clarke filmed a car crash scene—they used no doubles—Philip got a whiplash and spent the rest of his off-camera time wearing a neck brace.

Hope, who was taking time off from her role in the Broadway show, *Don't Bother Me, I Can't Cope*, had created quite a bit of good talk by giving so much humor and spunk to her character, Pigmeat Goins. Everybody agreed that Hope had the most devotion and guts in the cast—although one cast member believed she had "more guts than brains." "I had a marvelous time filming the car crash," she said, "but I hope the Stuntman's Association doesn't come down on me. In the scene we were sideswiped, and then I drove the car into a tree. Philip got hurt, but I loved it!"

Hope also expressed her love for the costumes by Gertha Brock and hair styles by Rudel Briscoe. Both designers are black and on their first film assignment. The designers did extensive research into the black styles of the thirties, and Rudel had the additional task of discovering the styling methods as well. He insisted that all the women wear their own hair instead of wigs, for the sake of authenticity. The same went for the men, who resented being authentic from the minute he cut off their Afros and began slicking on the pomade.

D'Urville Martin, who recently had begun to display his acting talents in such films as *The Legend of Nigger Charlie*, *The Final Comedown*, and *Hammer*, disliked his barber as much as any of the others. "I hate having my hair straightened. I've had to have it done at least once and sometimes twice a day. There's something about my hair, it just won't lay down," he said. As Billy Bowlegs, D'Urville brings comic moments to the action drama. In addition to acting, he was also Raymond's directional assistant, aiding him when he had to make the switch from director to actor.

After the day's work was completed, I was taken to dinner with Raymond St. Jacques and his handsome son, Sterling, who also plays a major role in the *Book of Numbers*. We met in one of the very best restaurants in Dallas—and Raymond knew them all. He admits to loving good food "to death," just as he does clothing and traveling. He ordered our dinners with the same authority that he used to direct the cast earlier that day.

I remarked favorably on the insight and forcefulness I saw him employ to evoke such extraordinary reactions from his actors. "I have to be forceful," he explains with his finely polished elocution. "However, I have not tried to be brutish just to manipulate the people. I meant every word of what I said about Joe Louis. I want it to be a moment of tribute to him because he was a hero then. All our characters are heroes, because to be black and simply survive was a challenge in the thirties.

"I play an Uncle Tom, and I show that even he was heroic in his actions. More Uncle Toms saved black people from hanging than the NAACP, CORE or anybody else. Of course Tomming is by no means necessary or excusable in the seventies, but I think there was a justification for it during the extreme racism of the times.

"The film documents a colored lifestyle—and notice I say 'colored'—I want to put the old thirties lifestyle up on the screen and show people the way it was. In this way, young black people may have a more visual understanding of their past." Raymond, therefore, doubts that his film will be charged with glorifying the numbers racket, as *Super Fly* was attacked for allegedly glorifying dope dealing. "In the thirties, the numbers were the only thing black people had to put hope in."

Raymond St. Jacques is a veteran motion picture actor, having starred in such films as *The Pawnbroker, Uptight, Cotton Comes to Harlem,* and *Come Back Charleston Blue.* The character of Blueboy Harris, the man who opens the numbers bank, was a special challenge to Raymond because Blueboy was twenty years Raymond's senior. But more challenging than using the "aging" makeup and body padding were Raymond's additional roles of director and producer, both of which he was playing for the first time. He raised the money for the projects from Fabergé, a white-owned cologne company. It seems that no black businessmen were willing to take a gamble and invest.

"I originally went to black people to get the money. However,

I found that when blacks have been able to override all the barriers in this country and make money, that they aren't about to part with it—especially to another black. Black people themselves are becoming prejudiced and don't think their brothers are ready to handle funds. They'd much rather give their money to a white. I went to the heads of magazines, insurance companies, and so on, and I didn't get a quarter. When they see the picture, I'm going to sit back and say 'too bad,' because it is going to be a success. I was originally sorry I had to go to a white company to get the money, but actually it was fortunate because they gave me a million dollars."

What did he think of a black director who would make a film on a white subject? "If somebody asked me to do a picture on the Queen of England or the Archduke Ferdinand, I'd be delighted. But I think at the time, that if I have some expertise as an artistic director and can lend myself to orienting people to the contributions blacks have made, I'm going to hang in there and make pictures about it. I'm trying to present a film for a human audience, which will give black heroes to my brothers and sisters who need them, as God knows *I* did."

SECTION III

THE BLACK ACTOR:
THE EARLY YEARS — Part I

Geraldyn Dismond

1   The Negro Actor and the American Movies

[1929]

The Negro actor and the part he has played in the development of the American movie is one of the most interesting phases of what is now one of America's greatest industries. Because no true picture of American life can be drawn without the Negro, his advent into the movies was inevitable; but also because of the prejudices that have hampered and retarded him since his coming to America, his debut was delayed. To be perfectly frank, the Negro entered the movies through a back door, labelled "servants' entrance." However, beggars cannot be choosers, and it is to his credit that he accepted the parts assigned to him, made good, and opened the door for bigger things.

In order better to appreciate the attitude of the white producer toward Negro talent, we must keep in mind the change in the social status of the group. To put it briefly, at the time of the Civil War, the Northern white man considered the Negro a black angel without wings, about whom he must busy himself in spirit and deed. On the other hand, the Southern white man detested Negroes in general and liked his particular blacks. After the Negro had been given his freedom, there soon arose the feeling that he was an economic and social menace and we find him depicted everywhere as a rapist. Then the white dilettante, exhausted with trying to find new thrills, stumbled over the Negro and exclaimed, "See what we have overlooked! These beloved vagabonds! Our own Negroes, right here at home!" And voila! Black became the fad.

These types of thinking have influenced the development of the Negro as part of the moving picture game. Within the remembrance of all of us, and still in some pictures and stage productions, we find whites blacked up for indifferent imitations of their dark brothers. But more and more is the practice falling into disrepute. The old cry that Negroes with ability cannot be found has not held water. In fact, it has been conclusively proven that under the proper director, the Negro turns out some of the best acting on the American screen and stage. A people of many emotions, with an inherent sense of humor and a love for play, they do not find it difficult to express themselves in action, or to bring to that expression the genuineness and enjoyment they feel. Nevertheless, excuse after excuse has been made to keep the Negro off the silver sheet, and it was the servants of white stars, who as individuals first got the breaks.

For example, Oscar Smith, who came to the Paramount Studios nine years ago [1920] as the personal servant of Wallace Reid, and at present owns the bootblack stand at the studio, has worked in two hundred pictures and has recently received a contract exclusively for Paramount talking pictures. Stepin Fetchit, who is billed as the star in the William Fox all-talkie *Hearts in Dixie* was the porter on the Fox lots. Carolyn Snowden, who played opposite Fetchit in *In Old Kentucky* was also a lady's maid for a prominent star. And so it went. Another point is also true. They worked in the early days in character. By that I mean, often the star's maid went on as her maid, provided she could be made to look homely and black enough. And all Negroes, perhaps with one or two exceptions, were cast as menials and as comedy characters.

As for the exceptions, they were for the most part African chiefs and the members of their tribes. One, however, I do recall from my first experiences with movies. He is Noble Johnson, of whom practically nothing is heard now in connection with Negroes. The last time I saw him, he was playing the part of a Mexican bandit, and rumor has it that he owns considerable stock in the company for which he works and is used for all parts calling for a swarthy skin. The other two unusual individuals are Sunshine Sammy and Farina, the two juvenile favorites of the Hal Roach-*Our Gang* comedies.

Negroes in any great numbers were first used for atmosphere—for mobs, levee and plantation, native African jungle, and popular black-belt cabaret scenes. Griffith's *Birth of a Nation,* which, by the way, employed the old rape idea, and for that reason was so distasteful to Negroes, is an excellent example of the Negro as atmosphere. *West of Zanzibar,* a popular Lon Chaney film, and the *Stanley in Africa* pictures used large groups of Negroes for the jungle scenes.

The next move on the part of producers was evident. Isolated Negro characters and Negroes as atmosphere were combined for the Universal feature production, *Uncle Tom's Cabin,* with James B. Lowe as Uncle Tom. Not all Negro parts, however, even in this picture, were assigned to Negroes. Topsy, Liza, her husband, and baby were played by whites, but up to the introduction of the "talkies," *Uncle Tom's Cabin* was the outstanding accomplishment of the Negro in the movie world.

It is significant that with the coming of talkies, the first all-Negro feature pictures were attempted by the big companies. White America has always made much of the fact that all Negroes can sing and dance. Moreover, it is supposed to get particular pleasure out of the Negro's dialect, his queer colloquialisms, and his quaint humor. The movie of yesterday, to be sure, let him dance, but his greatest charm was lost by silence. With the talkie, the Negro is at his best. Now he can be heard in song and speech. And no one who has seen the William Fox *Hearts in Dixie,* featuring Stepin Fetchit, Clarence Muse, and Eugene Jackson, or Al Christie's *Melancholy Dame,* an Octavius Roy Cohen all-talking comedy with Evelyn Preer, Eddie Thompson, and Spencer Williams, will disagree with the fact that the Negro's voice can be a thing of beauty in spite of the mechanics of this new venture in the art of the movies.

Of these two Negro all-talkies, *Hearts in Dixie* is by far the most pretentious. The story, as such, is nil. Here indeed, we have the "beloved vagabond." It does embody the idea, however, that some Negroes are not superstitious and are anxious to better themselves, and is a rather entertaining picture of plantation life; but it lacks substance. You were ever conscious of the fact that the producers were not interested in the plot, but rather in the talking and sing-

ing sequences. The ensemble singing and the voice of Clarence
Muse were decided contributions and well worth the price of
admission. *The Melancholy Dame*, a short comedy with little
music or dancing, depends principally upon its comic dialogue,
which is given in the best Octavius Roy Cohen dialect, for its
interest. Incidentally, Mr. Cohen himself directed the picture.

Of course, it is generally believed that the Metro-Goldwyn-
Mayer production, *Hallelujah*, will be the ace of the all-Negro
talking pictures. King Vidor is directing. Daniel Haynes, formerly
of *Show Boat*, has the principal role and is supported by Nina May
McKenney of the Blackbirds of 1929; Victoria Spivey, a blues
recording artist; Fannie DeKnight, who played in *Lula Belle*;
Langdon Grey, a nonprofessional, and 375 extras. There are forty
singing sequences, including folk songs, spirituals, work songs, and
blues. Eva Jessye, a Negro, who has compiled a book of spirituals
and trained the original "Dixie Jubilee Choir," is directing the
music. The story, which is devoid of propaganda, is that of a country boy who temporarily succumbs to the wiles of a woman, is
beset with tragedy, and ultimately finds peace. It is a known fact
that several studios are holding up all-Negro productions until the
fate of *Hallelujah* has been pronounced.

In the meantime, *Show Boat*, a talkie using the present Ameri-
can *Show Boat* company of both blacks and whites, has been made
by Universal and had its première at Miami and Palm Beach,
March 17; Ethel Waters, greatest comedienne of her race, and
Mamie Smith, blues singer of note, have been signed up by
Warner Brothers for Vitaphone comedies; Sissle and Blake, inter-
nationally famous kings of syncopation, have been released by
Warner Brothers; Christie Studio is preparing another Negro film;
Eric Von Stroheim is working on the Negro sequence of *The
Swamp*, and John Ford's *Strong Boy* is using a large number of
Negroes.

Three by-products have resulted from this slow recognition of
the Negro as movie material—Negro film corporations, Negro and
white film corporations, and white corporations, all for the production of Negro pictures. They have the same motives; namely,
to present Negro films about and for Negroes, showing them not

as fools and servants, but as human beings with the same emotions, desires, and weaknesses as other people's; and to share in the profits of this great industry. Of this group, perhaps the three best known companies are The Micheaux Pictures Company of New York City, an all-colored concern whose latest releases are *The Wages of Sin* and *The Broken Violin*; The Colored Players Film Corporation of Philadelphia, a white concern, which produced three favorites—*A Prince of His People, Ten Nights in a Barroom*, starring Charles Gilpin, and *Children of Fate*; and The Liberty Photoplay, Inc., of Boston, a mixed company, no picture of which I have seen. There is rumor of the formation in New York City of The Tono-Film, an all-Negro corporation, for exclusive Negro talking pictures, and that its officers and directors will include Paul Robeson, Noble Sissle, Maceo Pinkard, Earl and Maurice Dancer, J. C. Johnson, F. E. Miller, and Will Vodery, all of whom are known in America and abroad. So far, the pictures released by this group have been second rate in subject matter, direction, and photography, but they do keep before the public the great possibilities of the Negro in movies.

In conclusion, it must be conceded by the most skeptical that the Negro has at last become an integral part of the motion picture industry. And his benefits will be more than monetary. Because of the Negro movie, many a prejudiced white who would not accept a Negro unless as a servant, will be compelled to admit that at least he can be something else; many an indifferent white will be beguiled into a positive attitude of friendliness; many a Negro will have his race consciousness and self-respect stimulated. In short, the Negro movie actor is a means of getting acquainted with Negroes and under proper direction and sympathetic treatment can easily become a potent factor in our great struggle for better race relations. And the talkie, which is being despised in certain artistic circles, is giving him the great opportunity to prove his right to a place on the screen.

Floyd C. Covington

2   The Negro Invades Hollywood

[1929]

What part, if any, does the Negro play in the motion picture industry of California? Behind the walls of the legion studios that festoon the Hollywood district, what place has the Negro taken in the cinematographic world? These questions are, no doubt, in the minds of the casual observers who live outside the environs of "Filmland."

When one attempts to catalogue the information that might answer these questions, one is apt to find enthusiasm more abundant than figures. However, it is apparent from observation and available statistics that Negroes have been employed in the motion picture industry in various capacities for a period of years. The major portion of these have been (and are) employed as "extras" to create atmosphere in jungle, South Sea Island, and African scenes as natives, warriors, and the like. In scenes requiring domestics of color the Negro is employed to do these "bits." Others are employed to do individual roles or "parts" such as mammy types and other character sketches that receive camera close-ups and remain prominent throughout the picture. Many within this latter group are exceptionally talented, and their names are included with the other principals in the respective pictures.

In previous years the custom has been for each studio to operate its own casting office and hire those who applied at its gates for employment. In January 1926 the fourteen leading picture corporations of California, namely, Metropolitan, United Artists, Hal Roach, Christie, F. B. O., Mack Sennett, Educational, Universal, Pathe, Warner Bros., William Fox, First National, Paramount, and Metro-Goldwyn-Mayer organized the Central Casting Corporation at Hollywood. This agency acts as a clearing house for "extras" of all types for the fourteen named studios. Approximately eleven thousand adult applicants are registered according to type at the Central Casting and are available for immediate call from any of the studios.

The Casting Agency has among its personnel a Negro casting director who is one of the salaried employees of the company. The director, Mr. Chas. E. Butler,[1] has been with the organization for about two years. He has been engaged in casting work for more than five years and was formerly with the Cinema-Auxiliary. Mr. Butler is responsible for the collecting, classifying, and distributing of the Negro "extras." His job is not an easy one. During the staging of the all-Negro talking picture *Hallelujah* he was responsible for more than 340 "extras" to report at the studio one Sunday morning. The particular scene—a camp meeting service—required types who could both sing and act. Interestingly enough, the church choirs of the city were practically empty for the day.

Those individuals who do "parts" are employed usually under contract by the individual studios. The records of these employees are not kept by the Central Casting but by the casting offices of the various companies. It is very difficult to get definite figures concerning this group, as the offices are reluctant to give any information concerning salaries or length of contracts. Each company may have on its list various Negro types that are used in its pictures. On the other hand, these types are interchangeable. When a picture con-

---

[1] In an article, "Your Future in Hollywood" (*Our World*, 1946), Carlton Moss declares that during World War II black talent was in short demand and hardly any was used in war stories despite the fact that there were a million Negro servicemen and servicewomen in our armd forces, and millions in the war industries. He quotes Charles Butler as saying that ". . . you don't need maids and porters when you're making mostly war pictures." Butler further states: "At present there are 78 Negro men and 67 Negro women on the rolls, a total of 145 against the 300 that were carried before the war." Carlton also reports actor-agent Ben Carter as saying that "during the last two years there have been no calls for any of the 100 Negro singers or 60 dancers."

tract expires at one studio the company releases the individual, who is then free to offer his services to any other having need of his type. For example, Mr. Zack Williams, recently roled as "Deacon" in Fox's all-Negro talking picture *Hearts in Dixie*, has been doing "parts" in pictures for the past eighteen years. He is an unusually large physical type, which enables him to enjoy quite a wide range of parts.

It is interesting to note that Negroes have been employed in large numbers in many of Lon Chaney's pictures. In *West of Zanzibar* more than one hundred were used as natives. In *Big City* eighty were used in the Harlem Nite Club scene. In the *Road to Mandalay* and *Diamond Handcuffs* more than two hundred were used as natives for atmosphere. In the latter picture one hundred men of picked physical type, measuring six feet upwards, were used in the Kimberly diamond mines scene. In Mr. Chaney's current picture *East Is East* Negroes are being used with a few Chinese and Filipinoes as natives of Siam. Lon Chaney has been willing to demonstrate the racial versatility of the Negro by using them in his pictures for Eskimos, Chinese, Malays, Africans, and many other types of Oriental character. Mr. Locan, Mr. Chaney's assistant, stated that Negroes had been more successful doing Oriental parts than the actual racial types. He expressed the opinion that Negroes are natural actors and easier to handle before the camera. He gives Mr. Chaney's opinion in the matter by saying, "You can pull any one of them out of the mob and they can act. It is only a matter of makeup and costume to create anything from a Chinaman to an Eskimo. They require no interpreters and are always available in large numbers."

The approximate number of Negroes employed through the Central Casting is available for the years 1924 (3,464); 1925 (3,559); 1926 (6,816), and 1927 (3,754). The table on page 128 shows the number of Negroes employed through the Central Casting for the year 1928. The total amount paid in wages includes those employed by the day and receiving a standard wage of $5.00 to $15.00 per day. The average is $7.50 per day for "extras." The amounts given in the table do not include the number of Negroes employed under contract or the amount of money paid to them. In general the wage scale of the contract group ranges from $25 per day to $300 per week and above. Perhaps the largest salaries paid to Negroes in the industry were those paid to the principals of the two all-Negro talking pictures, *Hearts in Dixie,* produced by William Fox Company, and *Hallelujah* by the Metro-Goldwyn-Mayer Company. The salaries in some instances approximated $1,250 per week and above. If the total amount paid to those working under contract in the above pictures and those in which Negroes have figured prominently, prior to this date, could be added to the total amount given in the table, it would be even more striking.

No charge is made by the Central Casting to the individuals it places through its offices. In fact the Agency makes every effort to prevent exploitation of the workers in the industry. Its attempts have gone far to reduce the number of sporadic organizations that rear their heads from time to time, supposedly to make "everyone's face their fortune." The Casting is anxious that everyone should know that no worker—colored or white—has to pay for the employment he receives in the motion picture industry.

The total number of placements for 1927 was 3,754. The total amount paid in wages for that year was $30,036. The increase in the number of Negroes used and the wages received by them is striking in comparison. The year 1928 shows an approximate increase in placement of 345 percent; and an increase of 335 percent in wages received.

According to Mr. Butler, the Negro "extra" receives more money than any other "extra" in the industry except Chinese. In other words, they are next to the highest paid in the industry. It must be remembered that the number of placements for the month do not represent that number of different individuals. The motion picture industry is, as far as "extras" are concerned, a seasonal industry. Some individuals may be used dozens of times within the month, depending upon the various needs of the companies. Those individuals who are temporarily employed or who may leave their jobs at will are the ones who enjoy a monopoly of the industry.

The question has been continually raised whether there has been or will be a Negro star in Hollywood. The first part of the question may be disposed of by saying that there has been no Negro star to date. There have been many outstanding Negroes in pictures, but none rated as stars. The reason for that is obvious. Negroes have been employed principally for *atmosphere* in large numbers and disposed of chiefly *en masse*. Those who have reached places of importance are those who by sheer force of ability or because of the value of their distinctive type have outstripped their fellows. James B. Lowe of *Uncle Tom's Cabin* and Lincoln Peary, known as Stepin Fetchit, have reached places of importance and have, no doubt, a great future in pictures. Such names as Mattie Peters, Madam Sultewan, Gertrude Howard, George Reed, Louise Beavers, Oscar Smith, Mildred Washington, Clif Ingram, Noble Johnson, Jim Blackwell, and many others have gained places of importance and have a long-standing record of merit around the studios. We have already cited the distinctive work of Zack Williams.

With the introduction and improvement of talking pictures, comes, perhaps, the Negro's real opportunity to produce stars in his own right. That opportunity will largely depend upon the work of such artists as Mr. Clarence Muse taking the role of "Nappus" in the Fox production *Hearts in Dixie*; and the work of Mr. Daniel Haynes and Miss Nina Mae McKenny in the Metro-Goldwyn-Mayer production of *Hallelujah*. King Vidor, famous director of the *Big Parade*, who is responsible for the all-Negro picture *Hallelujah* ventures an opinion: "It will either be one of the greatest successes in pictures or one of the greatest flops. Frankly, I don't know which—but believe that when colored drama succeeds as it does on the stage, it must also be good for the screen. At any rate it has injected some new ideas into pictures. . . . The Negro is one of the greatest actors by nature principally because he really doesn't act at all, but actually feels and experiences the emotions he seeks to portray."

The director, author, and assistants of the Fox picture *Hearts in Dixie* are also counting the pulse beats of the Negro's dramatic possibilities. Mr. Walter Weems, author of the scenario, and Mr. Paul Sloan, director, are exceedingly enthusiastic over the group with whom they have worked. They expressed the opinion that in all their experience in pictures they have never worked with a finer group of people—colored or white. They believe that such a group has unlimited possibilities for all phases of motion picture work.

Apparently, then, with the current venture of all-Negro talking pictures, the Negro emerges from a somewhat obscure place in the industry to take a place in the center of the stage. It is hoped that with the increase of all-Negro pictures, the Negro will also develop directors and technicians who may aid in a large way to improve the technique of the pictures being staged around them. The time is ripe for Negro scenarists to produce stories from the rich fields— still virgin—of their folk life. It is interesting to note here that at the MGM studio a young Negro who has been formerly employed as a shoe-shine around the studio has made quite a rapid stride. Known as "Slick-'em" on the lot because of his ability to give a brilliant shine, Harold Garrison is now acting in the capacity of second assistant to King Vidor in the production of *Hallelujah*.

The Negro's place in the motion picture industry in California depends largely upon himself. The future is provocative of greater possibilities. A Culver City writer expresses a view somewhat naïvely, "It's the day of the dark star in Hollywood. . . . Perhaps there will be more Negro pictures—perhaps there will be many colored stars in the future. No one can tell yet. But the colored troupe isn't worrying much about this. They want to tell their story—the story of their race—just this once."

In the wake of this new experiment in all-Negro pictures comes the Negro's chance to be articulate in his own behalf. Greater still, the success of these pictures shall erect the foundation of the Negro's permanent place in the cinematographic industry in California.

Placements of Colored People by Central Casting Corporation from January 1, 1928 to December 31, 1928

Month	Placements	Aggregate Wages
January	308	$ 2,906.65
February	240	2,268.38
March	773	6,690.17
April	152	1,546.78
May	212	2,075.75
June	272	2,343.27
July	1,270	11,859.38
August	278	2,915.00
September	748	5,692.50
October	4,502	34,054.38
November	882	8,188.00
December	1,279	9,162.63
	10,916	$89,702.89

William Harrison

3   The Negro and the Cinema

[1939]

It is universally recognized that the Negro possesses considerable and unusual histrionic ability, and that this talent has imperfectly revealed itself in the cinema. The reason for this deficiency in utilizing an admitted reservoir of talent must be sought in the fact that the roles usually assigned to Negro actors have had only two stops: farce and pathos. To be so "cabin'd, cribb'd, and confin'd" is to be without the means of interpreting all the emotional nuances between those two extremes. Hence the Negro's dramatic genius has been curtailed, and the cinema as an art has suffered from its failure fully to exploit the talent which the life of the Negro people, in Africa, in the West Indies, or in the United States, so amply provides, as even casual travelers, with no intimate knowledge of Negroes, can bear witness.

There was nearly universal satisfaction with Mr. Paul Robeson's acting in the title role in the cinema version of Mr. Eugene O'Neill's *Emperor Jones*, but it is certainly not unjust to say that this satisfaction was prompted by Mr. Robeson's magnetic personality as a singer rather than by any severely critical appraisal of his talents as an actor. For not even the cognoscenti will deny that Mr. Robeson has never been an "actor's actor," despite the host of imitative Hamlets who have endeavored to follow in the wake of his success. He is manifestly not an artist so finished in his command of the technique of acting that he has made a genuine and lasting contribution to that most ephemeral of all arts, while, as

Mr. Max Beerbohm has reminded us, "theatrical reminiscence is the most awful weapon in the armoury of old age." Mr. Robeson's acting is limited to the spontaneous impression, the winning acquiescence obtained by a personal idiosyncrasy, such as his smile. His interpretation of a role is, in no disparaging sense, profoundly superficial by its reduction of all attributes of character to the lowest common denominator; in being bereft of subtlety, however, it has the virtue of imparting a ready understanding, and this merit is not to be despised in an age when many arts are ingrown, afflicted with intellectual paralysis and spiritual anaemia, unstimulated by any flow of common values commonly understood. Mr. Robeson is not, therefore, in the great tradition of Negro acting, to which actors like the late Richard B. Harrison (the original "De Lawd" of *Green Pastures*) or the late Charles Gilpin (the earliest Emperor Jones) belonged, or an earlier Shakespearean actor like Ira Aldridge, who played Aaron the Moor and Othello in the nineteenth century. Whatever his ultimate evaluation as an artist, Mr. Robeson undoubtedly broke new ground with his Emperor Jones, though this innovation was not fully appreciated by all Negroes. Indeed, he was harshly berated by American and West African Negroes of the educated classes for his acting as Bosambo in *Sanders of the River*, and he was accused of selling his racial birthright for a mess of Hollywood pottage. Nor has the thunder of outraged disapproval abated altogether, as is evident from the rumbling of a leading article in *The West African Pilot*, the native daily newspaper published at Lagos, Nigeria (January 12th, 1939):

In *Big Fella*, which is a recent production featuring Paul Robeson and three really good coloured actors and actresses, he is the leading star of the picture, and although his assignment is the usual one depicting him as a scum and a renegade, yet he portrays the type of virtues which any race on earth would be glad to emulate. His love and devotion to a white boy is the theme of this story, and the acting and singing of Robeson, in particular, are very impressive and convincing, despite obvious flaws in the technique of the film and the plots of the story.

Apparently conscious that he is at the crossroads of his career, Mr. Robeson has publicly announced, on several occasions, that it is his ambition to enact roles which, at any rate, do not bring discredit on the Negro people. He has signified his desire to play the part of Joe Louis in a film based upon his career. In this way he hopes to make amends to his sensitive Negro public, who have all too readily identified him with the often discreditable roles which he has enacted. His ambition offers a challenge to Negro playwrights, who have lagged considerably behind the demand for plays of Negro life.

Mr. Robeson's hitherto indisputable preeminence in important roles has now been contested by various people, among whom the most considerable appears to be Mr. Robert Adams, who is Bosambo in *Old Bones of the River* (Gainsborough), another cinema version of an Edgar Wallace thriller. Mr. Adams is less spontaneous, less the "original genius" in the romantic connotation of the term, and more the controlled, systematic artist in his acting, and in these respects, with proper vehicles for his powers of interpretation, he may prove himself a worthy continuator of the great tradition of Negro acting.

It is precisely the dearth of proper vehicles that has thwarted the Negro dramatic artist. The roles in which such actors as the inimitable Stepin Fetchit are cast have created and perpetuated racial stereotypes that are patently false. Thus Stepin Fetchit affects the lazy languor of the Negro roustabout in the South at an epoch when the plantation Negro has disappeared, since industrialization has transformed the American Negro into an urban dweller or a very much urbanized agricultural laborer, thereby uprooting his African traditions and almost totally destroying them. It has been difficult for playwrights to depict fully the changes in Negro life and all that they imply since the war. Many an attempt to record the difference in tempo and consciousness has failed. For example, the appearance of Miss Fannie Hurst's *Imitation of Life* evoked much controversy, because of its subplot with the time-worn theme of the tragic mulatto. A leading literary critic among the American Negroes, Professor Sterling Brown of Howard University, recorded his objection to a line uttered by a minor character: "Once a pancake, always a pancake," for he held that this particular line, in its context, was a slur cast upon the Negro race. In rebuttal Miss Hurst countered that all her Negro characters were serious and so afforded scope for Negro actors and actresses wider than that previously enjoyed by them. She felt that Negroes owed her a debt of gratitude for this service, but her statement aroused even further resentment from a notoriously sensitive people, as her knowledge of the nuance of interracial relations in the United States is not equal to her sympathy. Yet the Negro spokesman had to realize that without financial resources for large-scale production the Negro community is dependent, and will be so for a long time, upon the Hollywood industry, despite the formation in 1937 of a Negro film company which produced a film, *Spirit of Youth*, with Joe Louis in the leading role. This was a typical and hence banal "success story" of the poor man who fights his way up to the pugilistic Valhalla, after many melodramatic obstacles in his path are hurdled in the nick of time and with the intervention of his Guardian Angel, with whom he clenches in the final fade-out. To assess its worth one has only to compare it with *Golden Boy*, and to become fully aware of the dramatic possibilities inherent in the life story of a prizefighter one has merely to recall the vivid contrasts among the characters of Mr. Clifford Odets's play.

It can be stated candidly that so far the Negro-controlled cinemas have not improved the artistic status of the Negro actor, for they have taken the line of easiest resistance: they have fostered stereotyped melodramas patterned after the models of "gangster" and "success" films. Their only and dubious gain has been the portrayal of Negroes as heroes and heroines, and not exclusively in minor roles. They have wrought no fundamental change in the Negro's position in the cinema. In fact, when Mr. Clarence Muse acted as the Negro physician in *Arrowsmith*, though his part was small, more was done to remove racial stereotypes from the minds of the general public. Of course, neither in Africa nor in America has the Negro been other than a consumer, and it is only very recently that his efforts at being a producer have achieved any degree of permanency. A gangster film, *Dark Manhattan*, produced by Messrs. George Randol and Ralph Cooper, had its Los Angeles premiere in 1937. Mr. Cooper is the head of Million Dollar Productions, as this Negro company is called. *Bargain with Bullets* and *Life Goes On* are other films produced.

It may be interesting to interpose the remark that like other small independent producers Negro companies rent their equipment from the larger studios. As they also pay at least the minimum wage scales set by the Screen Actors' Guild, they command technical resources of no mean order. Only artistically mediocre scripts with hackneyed plots have hampered their usefulness. One cannot repeat too often that the casting of the Negro, in America especially, has not kept abreast of his social, political, and economic development since the emancipation of the Negro people from chattel slavery. Life in Harlem has not been sufficiently exploited, and of course the life of the Southern Negro workers and peasants, along the lines defined by Mexican cinema art, for example, has been rather cavalierly neglected, though the films of the Hall Johnson choir, to be sure, do something to promote a wider knowledge of Negro folk music such as the "Spirituals."

The conclusion is inescapable that independent Negro producers have lacked the social vision needed if the Negro is to be represented fully and truly in the cinema today, if the stereotypes in which he is cast are to be discarded. The dramatic possibilities of Negro life, which is so rich and varied, and the potentialities of the Negro actor, already demonstrated in even the poor media accessible to him now, will reveal themselves fully when this social vision arrives. When a good documentary film can be made at a cost of as little as $5,000 there is no valid excuse why Negro producers, even if they are without the resources to produce feature films, should retail the old stereotypes of film art, those debased pictures with canned emotions and boxed social situations. For there is a great ignorance everywhere about Negroes, and it is their duty to help to dispel it.

William Thomas Smith

4   Hollywood Report

[1945]

Because of the war, Hollywood does not glitter quite as brightly as of yore, yet the films continue to be made, and with emphasis on social overtones.

This is worthy of our close attention. Despite almost frantic effort at democratic preachment, as exemplified in the film crop of the past few years, Hollywood's attitude toward the Negro actor, the Negro worker, and the Negro race remains unchanged; the democracy it preaches is as usual "For White Only."

While it is true that the war has to some extent curtailed film production, the earnings of Negroes in pictures have declined in a manner which cannot be explained by the film curtailment. Fewer Negro extras are now used than in the past decade. Only the most deeply rooted, and well-connected bit players have managed to survive. Jesse Graves, whose face is familiar to millions of film fans as a portrayer of butler roles, played in forty-eight pictures last year, but earned only seven thousand dollars. Ernest Whitman, an actor of undoubted talent, landed on the film payrolls but twice.

The biggest news of recent years is the signing of Miss Lena Horne to a seven-year contract by the Metro-Goldwyn-Mayer company. Miss Horne is definitely a lovely girl, and heretofore lovely colored girls have not been given any sort of chance in Hollywood. Miss Horne's first appearance before the cameras was in *The Duke Is Tops*, one of the best of the all-Negro pictures of the period prior to 1940, which starred Ralph Cooper, and was made by Million Dollar Productions. Her fortunes rose sharply when she was taken on by MGM a few years later. She appeared in *Cabin in the Sky* and *Stormy Weather*, on loans to the Fox studio and in *Right About Face, As Thousands Cheer, I Dood It*, and other films for her own studio. Miss Horne again broke all sorts of precedents when the entire cover of a nationally famous motion picture magazine carried her picture in color last year; and articles about her have been written in other national periodicals.

However, despite Miss Horne's success, no other film maker has sought to emulate MGM in featuring other beautiful colored girls. And no satisfactory picture for Miss Horne has yet been found which would fully realize her potentialities and her proven box-office allure.

Eddie "Rochester" Anderson continues as a unique person in that his parts in the Jack Benny pictures are not only large and hilarious but do not show him in a racially unfavorable light.

Veteran Clarence Muse, as fine an actor as has ever been in Hollywood, and whose rich talents have never been given an opportunity before the cameras, still remains a bit player. This is significant, because few producers in Hollywood would even bother to deny the fact of this player's ability.

A few brighter spots of recent years would include the part given Rex Ingram, and his performance of it in *Sahara*, a Columbia picture in which Mr. Ingram played a Sudanese soldier of courage, intelligence, and dignity. This was likewise true of Leigh Whipper, who as Hailie Selassie in *Mission to Moscow* scored impressively. Ben Carter was given a fairly good part in *Crash Dive*, a Fox production in which he played a heroic messman, à la Dorrie Miller, a real life naval hero.

Harry Levette, nationally known Hollywood commentator and West Coast Associated Press correspondent, brings to mind other small gains. One of these is the abandonment by the studios of the word "nigger" when speaking of a black electrical screen. The word for this apparatus is now "gobo." This seems a small thing, but it has unnerved many a Negro player awaiting preparation of a set upon which he was to appear. Another gain is that Warner

Brothers studio now employs two hundred Negro custodians, and has made a Negro the superintendent of this force.

Despite the war and the crying need for skilled technical help, the door is still barred against the Negro in this Hollywood field. One very bright exception is Ralph Vaughn, skilled architect and artist, who for two and one-half years has held a post as a scene or set designer on the MGM lot. Mr. Vaughn, formerly of the staff of Paul Williams, noted Negro architect, is one of the seven persons admitted to membership in the Union of Set Designers, Local 1421, A. F. of L., since Pearl Harbor.

One other such exception is Calvin Jackson, who for the past year has won laurels as an assistant in the MGM music department.

Negro newsmen and publicists have for years tried to batter down the Hollywood bars against them, but until young Phil Carter landed with a major film company, none had succeeded. However, Mr. Carter's assignment was but for a single, all-Negro picture, and when that was well launched, so was Mr. Carter— right out of the studio.

Until very recently motion picture companies have discriminated brazenly against the advertising columns of Negro publications. Publications of every other minority group carried heavy advertising from the film industry. This was not only to advertise the film product, but to assure the goodwill of these groups. Apparently Negroes, as a racial group, were unimportant, judging from their treatment by the film makers. Yet along came Billy Rowe, shrewd motion picture and theatrical editor of the *Pittsburgh Courier* a few years ago, and when he returned east the advertising bar had been broken. Now many Negro papers carry some motion picture advertising in every issue.

This brings to mind what many friends in the film industry have told me over a period of years: The colored man is treated as he is by Hollywood because of all the racial minorities touched by the films, his is the only one that has never made organized protest against ill-treatment, or organized demands for better treatment.

To me that seems highly significant. Walter White, chief fighting man of the NAACP, in recent years made a trip to Hollywood to register the protest of his organization against the light in which Negroes were invaribly shown in the films.

Although this was but one man, representing but one organization, his protest had almost immediate effect in that the Hayes office issued a directive to all studios to cease casting the Negro in an unfavorable light.

Unfortunately, no directive could be issued to show the Negro in a *favorable* light. Many studios resented the directive at first, and struck back by simply not using Negroes in their pictures at all. And many actors who had eked out a most precarious existence on the bits thrown them by the film makers took strong issue with any movement that would take away their means of livelihood.

There are many truly liberal individuals in Hollywood who, if they had the power, would begin making powerful documentary and dramatic pictures of the Negro at once—*if* they had the power. But the power rests with those who head the studios, and these groups naturally regard the work in which they are engaged as a hard, cold, highly competitive business, whose end and aim is to make money.

Some of the studio heads have been extremely frank about the situation. It is their claim that if a picture offends the South, then the profits shown by that picture slump deeply. So that the way to make profits is, among other things, not to offend the South. Also, they must not offend the Catholics, nor the Jews, nor the Mexicans. To offend the Negro apparently isn't a matter to be considered.

Unfortunately, what the studio heads mean is not what they say. Those whom they seek not to offend are the exhibitors, the censors, and a few scraggly politicians who suffer acutely from Negrophobia. It is in the hands of these few that the determination rests as to what pictures shall be shown the South. The censors and the exhibitors of the South do not hesitate to use their shears on any scene in any picture which they may consider objectionable. A recent survey showed that those things "most objectionable" were those in which Negroes were shown "acting, or talking, or dressing

like white folks . . . acting smart-alecky and talking back to white
folks . . . shooting or striking white folks . . . or in any manner
committing any breach of the code which would by implication or
otherwise create an equality between the two races . . ."

To those who realize that a majority of Southern white people
are not Negrophobists, the case is not without hope. However,
Hollywood, whatever its attitude, past or present, is quick to
jump aboard any movement that seems popular. There are a few
really important men in Hollywood who would, as they say, "take
a gamble" on producing worthwhile Negro pictures if they were
sure that Negroes themselves would be solidly behind them. And
there are many great Hollywood stars who would aid such a move
in every way possible.

Perhaps the matter is squarely up to Negroes.

Lena Horne and Richard Schickel

5 Lena

[1965]

I was discovered for the movies by a man named Roger Edens. The truth of the matter is that he had heard me at Café Society, and one night he came into the Little Troc to hear me sing. At one time he had been Ethel Merman's accompanist. He had come to Hollywood to work on special material and had written stuff for the Andy Hardy pictures and had done "Dear Mr. Gable"— the song Judy Garland sang at an MGM party and which served to bring her to the attention of the studio bosses after she had been under contract for months and had received no parts. Now he was working mainly for Arthur Freed's unit at Metro-Goldwyn-Mayer that produced most of the big musicals there. Apparently Roger liked my work at the Little Troc and he got in touch with Harold Gumm, who was in Hollywood following my fortunes at this time. Harold was not licensed to handle movie deals, so he in turn got in touch with the large agency run by Louis Shurr and they agreed to handle any negotiations that might develop.

In a few days Harold and Al Melnick from the Shurr office accompanied me to Culver City to talk about my being in the movies. I suppose I was excited, but I could not seriously believe anything would come of it. I remembered what Barney Josephson had said to me when I talked to him about going to the Coast. So my hopes were not exactly high.

Roger Edens met us and escorted us to Arthur Freed's office. I could tell from his voice that he was a Southerner, but for some reason I didn't feel that instant distrust a Southern accent usually creates in me. I felt that he was a gentleman.

"I heard you sing and liked it so much," he said. "Would you sing for us?"

With that, he ushered us into Freed's office. Roger played and I sang "More Than You Know." There was some artfulness in my choice of a song, because my agents knew Freed was anxious to produce a movie version of Vincent Youmans's *Great Day*, the score of which contained this song. Apparently the stratagem worked, because Freed asked me to stay and sing for Louis B. Mayer, the head of the studio.

While we were waiting to go see him, Vincente Minnelli, the director (and Judy Garland's second husband), walked in. I had met him in New York when he had been associated with Vinton Freedley in musical productions. They had briefly toyed with the curious notion of having me play Serena Blandish in a musical. He was terribly cordial to me. "Wouldn't it be wonderful if we could finally do something together," he said. Among all these strangers, sitting in Arthur Freed's big, impressive office, it was good to get such a greeting from Vincente. We seemed to be the "New York group," a little bit at bay, making a sort of informal, unspoken compact of friendship among the Hollywood crowd nervously awaiting to see whether the great man, Louis B. Mayer, would deign to see us.

In a little while there came a cryptic-sounding phone call and then we were excitedly informed that Mr. Mayer would see us. Off to his office we went.

He was a short, chubby man and by now everyone is familiar with the tales of his temperament. But on this occasion—as upon most of the very few others that I dealt personally with him—he seemed very genial and fatherly to me. I sang for him and I remember him just sitting there, beaming at me through his round glasses. After I had done a couple of songs he disappeared into some inner sanctum and reappeared with Marion Davies on his arm. She was just visiting, but I had to sing for her, too. It was kind of funny. But not funny, too. By this time everyone was all charged up, excited by some possibility that I could not see.

It turned out that MGM had bought *Cabin in the Sky*, the all-Negro musical, a fact I discovered as the afternoon wore on. But I also learned that it would be some time before they could put it into production. There was obviously a part in it for me, but what would they do with me until they were ready to shoot?

The question did not seem to bother any of my companions. In the car on the way back to my apartment they were all absolutely certain that I would be signed by the studio. By the time we got back to Horn Avenue they had convinced me that the possibility was a real one. I decided I needed someone I could absolutely trust to talk all this over with, someone who had no interest in the business except my interest. It was not that I distrusted Gumm or the Shurr office but in my dealings with them I carried with me my habitual distrust of white men.

Now, just before the possibility of this contract had been presented to me, my father and I had had the most wonderful renewal of our life together. He had come to Los Angeles to visit with me and we did everything together. After I finished at the Little Troc in the evening we would go to the Negro night spots together. We danced, we ate all the foods we liked, we drank champagne. In the daytime we went sightseeing. Later, he rented a bungalow at Lake Elsinore, a Negro spa outside the city, and took Teddy and Gail there to stay with him a few weeks (I visited on weekends). I loved it when people said things like, "You look like sweethearts" or "You're such a handsome couple." I hoped it would be like that always and I was very sorry when he had to go back to Pittsburgh to attend to his business. We talked often by phone. Now, when it began to look as if MGM were serious about hiring me I called him and said, "I'm alone and don't trust any of these people. Come to me." He quickly agreed.

At the same time Walter White happened to be on the Coast and I consulted him, too. He had a personal interest in my welfare, since he had advised me to come to California. But he also saw the dangers and opportunities that would be presented to me.

At the time there were no Negroes under long-term contract at any of the studios. All the Negro actors in town were free-lancers, hired for a job here and a job there as the need arose. Walter's concern, and mine too, was that in the period while I was waiting for *Cabin in the Sky* they would force me to play roles as a maid or maybe even as some jungle type. Now these were the roles, as I have said, that most Negroes were forced to play in the movies at that time. It was not that I felt I was too good or too proud to play them. But Walter felt, and I agreed with him, that since I had no history in the movies and therefore had not been typecast as anything so far, it would be essential for me to try to establish a different kind of image for Negro women.

A few days later I went back to Freed, this time with my father along, as well as the agents. My father was great at that meeting. His basic mistrust of white men is so deep he was able to be very cool with the studio people. Flattery and empty promises get you absolutely nowhere with my father. I know those MGM executives had had to deal with the parents of child stars at the start of their careers, but I'm sure this was the first time a grown Negro woman ever arrived with a handsome, articulate, and unimpressed father who proceeded to show them the many disadvantages, spiritually and emotionally, that his daughter might suffer should she be foolish enough to sign with them. It was marvelous for me to watch them listening to him. Since neither one of us believed in the damn thing, we must have been infuriating.

"I don't want my daughter to work, I want to take care of her myself," my father said. "Now many people are telling her how wonderful it is to be a movie star. But the only colored movie stars I've seen so far have been waiting on some white star in the picture. I can pay for someone to wait on my daughter if she wants that."

Well, they assured him they had given a great deal of thought to all the problems he raised, they appreciated his sense of dignity. To make a long story short, if they had filmed that interview it would have made a great movie scene, but in a sense they were as good as their word. They didn't make me into a maid, but they didn't make me anything else, either. I became a butterfly pinned to a column singing away in Movieland.

The agents took care of the money—which was something like two hundred dollars a week to start—but, as I had occasion to discover in later years, agents are interested in very little besides money. For a Negro performer, that is frequently the least serious problem. Generally, every actor should have written into his contract all kinds of special protections. This was especially true in my early days working alone on the road, when I had to have it spelled out in writing that I could have room service, or use the front door of the hotel, or the swimming pool. Actually, I had no trouble of this kind on the MGM lot. Arthur Freed and Roger Edens were men of a certain sensitivity, and as long as I worked with them I was treated with great decency and respect.

Even so, my first screen test, which came after the signing of the contract, was a farce. They were planning a picture costarring Jeanette MacDonald and Robert Young and were thinking of Eddie Anderson (Rochester) and me to play their servants and, I guess, to have a romance in the film too. It was a good role—the maid was to be just as flippant and fresh as anyone. She was a human being, not a stereotype. They asked Rochester and me to do a test together. They wanted me to match Rochester's color so they kept smearing dark makeup on me. And then they had a problem in lighting and photographing me because, they said, my features were too small. Meantime, poor Rochester had to stand around and wait while they fussed over me. It was embarrassing to me, though he was very pleasant about it. In the end, the test was a disaster. I looked as if I were some white person trying to do a part in blackface. I did not do the picture; Ethel Waters got the part.

My friends thought it was all nonsense. Roger Edens said, "It's ridiculous; they should photograph you as you are. That's why they hired you in the first place." My father just laughed, and so did Billy Strayhorn and Vincente Minnelli. It was even funny to me.

But the consequences were't funny at all. For one thing, they set the makeup department to work on creating a kind of pancake that would make me look as dark as they thought I should without turning me into a grotesque. Eventually they came up with a shade that they called "Light Egyptian," which had an unfortunate side effect. They used it on white actresses they wanted to play Negro or mulatto parts; which meant there was even less work for the Negro actors, with whom I was already in trouble.

They were afraid of what they called "my attitude," by which they meant the terms I had insisted upon in my contract. They feared the studios might think it was the beginning of a large-scale campaign on the part of Negro actors to raise their status, or that it might be thought the beginning of a revolt against roles as menials. They also suspected that the NAACP was taking an official interest in me, since the signing of the contract had made me the NAACP's first available guinea pig. My friendship with Walter White was suspect.

My chief interest was in protecting my opportunity to sing. Though Walter White did take an interest in my career, he was also a family friend. And most important of all, I was not trying to embarrass anyone or show up my colleagues. I was only trying to see if I could avoid in my career some of the traps they had been forced into. It was no crusade, though of course I hoped that if I could set my own terms in the movies and also be successful, then others might be able to follow. But, I must admit, that was not my main motive.

There was talk about me for many months in Hollywood, and it finally culminated in a protest meeting. I was called "an Eastern upstart" and a tool of the NAACP and I was forced to get up and try to explain that I was not trying to start a revolt or steal work from anyone and that the NAACP was not using me for any ulterior purpose. Only one person among the Negro actors went out of her way to be understanding about the whole situation. That was Hattie McDaniel, who was, I suppose, the original stereotype of the Negro maid in the white public mind. Actually, she was an extremely gracious, intelligent, and gentle lady. She called me up and asked me to visit her. I went to her beautiful home and she explained how difficult it had been for Negroes in the movies, which helped give me some perspective on the whole situation. She was extremely realistic and had no misconception of the role she was allowed to play in the white movie world. She also told me she sympathized with my position and that she thought it was the right one if I chose it. I was very confused at the time; the one thing I had not expected was to get into trouble with my own race. Miss McDaniel's act of grace helped tide me over a very awkward and difficult moment, and after that the public tension eased somewhat.

But never completely. In a large part of the Hollywood Negro community I was never warmly received.

Here again was a new lesson. I had not been brought up to think that racial solidarity was the way to get a job and to protect it. I had known two kinds of Negroes—those who worked at low-level jobs that no one else would take, and those who were educated enough to break out of the pattern, or had a unique talent like athletes or musicians. In a sense, each group was protected; one because no one wanted their jobs, the others because no one else could do them as well. But the Negro actors in Hollywood were not in either category. Plenty of people wanted their jobs, irregular as they were, and the kind of acting they did was not beyond the power of almost anyone. They were mainly extras and it was not difficult to strip down to a loincloth and run around Tarzan's jungle or put on a bandanna and play one of the slaves in *Gone With the Wind*. It seems significant to me that the people who had real talent—like Miss McDaniel or Eddie Anderson or the musicians—did not join in the attacks on me.

The terrible irony, I came to realize, was that the people who did attack me were upholding a continuation of a status quo that was corrupt, and that they were stirred up by the handful who profited most from that status quo. The system for casting Negroes as extras and bit players in those days, before the formation of a strong union, was something like the system of hiring dock workers through the shape-up. There was a small group of leaders in Los Angeles who acted as captains. The studios would call them and ask for a certain number of extras for a certain number of days for a certain picture. They would tell them how many of each physical type they needed and leave it to the actor to provide them with warm bodies, the identities of which they did not care about. In return for this service the leader would be guaranteed the most days' work or the largest part. So if you wanted to work you had to stay in with these gentlemen. You had no personal leverage with the studios. To borrow a phrase from Jimmy Baldwin, nobody knew your name—but nobody. I guess it's not surprising that these so-called leaders were my most vocal adversaries. They stirred things up because they feared I might want to be a potential leader myself or, more likely, that I might establish a precedent that would, in the end, undermine their position. Finally, in the 1950s, more and more talented Negroes came into the movies. They were people with whom the studios had to deal as individuals, and the extras themselves got sick of having to toady to the hiring bosses.

But the full implications of all this became clear to me only after some time had passed.

* * *

I started to work on *Cabin in the Sky* the minute I returned to Hollywood when the Savoy-Plaza engagement ended. This was not only the first picture in which I was to play a real part, it was also to be the first completely directed by Vincente Minnelli, who up to that time had been employed by MGM only as a director of musical sequences.

I was very glad about that, because Vincente and I had drawn close in the months since I ran into him in Arthur Freed's office. It was a completely undemanding relationship, with no pressure of any kind on either side. We did not go out at all. He had a beautifully run house with a wonderful library and fine paintings on the wall and we spent most of our time together there. Occasionally he would come over to my place and Edwina and I would cook dinner for him. He was living like a displaced New Yorker, just as I was, and we shared a dislike at that time for Hollywood life. It gave me a great deal of confidence that he was going to direct this picture; I knew I could trust him and lean upon him.

I knew I was going to need all the support I could get, because Ethel Waters was to be one of the stars of the picture. Long before we met I began hearing rumors around the lot that she was—to put it mildly—a rather difficult person to work with. We had only a couple of scenes together, and they were not scheduled to be shot until we were well along in production. The kids who were working in her scenes told me she was violently prejudiced against me. Miss Waters was not notably gentle toward women and she was particularly tough on other singers. Billie Holiday had told me she cost her a job once, when she desperately needed it, by refusing to go on with the show if Billie was hired. I suppose she had all the normal feminine reactions toward another woman who might be a potential rival.

Besides that, she was very unhappy with the studio. Ethel Waters had spent many hard years playing small and unpleasant clubs before she achieved stardom, and had been terribly exploited.

In my own career, I had been aware of this kind of exploitation but I had not been too hurt by it. When I did encounter it, I was well enough established to be able to fight it or ignore it. Miss Waters had not been so lucky and she was, therefore, chronically suspicious of her employers and somehow she got the idea that I was in league with them in some way. So as the day approached when we were to work together I knew I would encounter a good deal of antipathy from her, taking place against a background of extreme distrust of the studio which had, I heard, already led to many minor incidents in the course of shooting.

Up to then, *Cabin* had been heaven. The story, of a good woman (Miss Waters) contending with a bad one (me) for the soul of a man (Rochester) was warm and funny, despite its underlying seriousness. There were wonderful songs, some from the original Broadway version by Vernon Duke, John Latouche, and Ted Fetter, some written especially for the movie version by Harold Arlen and Yip Harburg, among them "Happiness Is a Thing Called Joe," Miss Waters's song, destined to become a standard, and a big show-stopper for Rochester and me, "Life's Full of Consequences."

Unlike Miss Waters, I was enjoying myself hugely on this picture. For the first time I had a real role to play and for the first time I felt myself to be an important part of the whole enterprise, not just a stranger who came in for a few days to do a song or two. By this time I had made quite a few friends around the studio. The makeup men and cameramen were basically friendly people and more inclined to be democratic with me than with some of the big stars. Also, I think they respected me because I always showed up on time and knew my songs and my lines and therefore was a "pro" in their eyes. And they were interested by the challenge I presented. The cameramen finally decided they liked the way I photographed and the makeup people finally invented a shade for me that didn't make me look like Al Jolson doing "Mammy," and Sidney Guilaroff, the head of the hairdressing department, did great things with my hairdos. Mostly I did not have characters to play, so there were no restrictions on what he could do—I was only supposed to look beautiful leaning against my pillar. He would invent Victorian hairdos or coronet braids or whatever his fancy dictated and there was no one to say, "No, that's not right for her character."

For quite a while all these people kept reporting to me about how difficult Miss Waters was in general and that, in particular, she resented my appearing in the picture. She thought others deserved the part more and that I was part of the plot against her that she was sure the studio bosses had concocted. Maybe they were unhappy with her, but it seemed to me that it would be out of character for them to hire her and spend the money to do the picture and then turn around and make trouble for her on the set. And I just couldn't believe that she would dislike me without knowing me at all.

Miss Waters did have one legitimate complaint against me. She was supposed to do a parody of me doing the "Honey in the Honeycomb" number. In it, she drops her righteousness, her good-woman attitude, and sings a steamy hot version of the song in an attempt to show up the hollowness of our values. Of course, I had recorded the song before we started production, as we always did, so it could be played back on the set when it came time to stage the number. Miss Waters went up to the sound department and heard my version of the song. She claimed that I had imitated her and that it would be impossible for her now to parody the song.

If I had imitated her, it was completely unconscious. She was a great singer, someone to be admired, and of course some of her style had come into that number. I'd worked hard to get it there so her parody would come off. Still, sometimes it's hard to see things that way. I'm always being told that some young singer is doing me nowadays and I'm not complimented, though my husband tells me I should be.

With all this tension building up, I was prepared to be very, very careful when we finally started working together. While the picture was shooting, I did not see much of Vincente. Like most directors at work on a picture he used the nights to prepare for the next day's shooting. But we did talk occasionally about how I should play my scenes with Miss Waters. Up until then I had done nothing but fun comedy stuff with Rochester and Louis Armstrong. Now Vincente suggested that the only way to compete against Miss Waters's intensity was to be terribly helpless, almost babyish, when I confronted her. He thought it would make a good contrast with the hoydenish way I had played the comedy and musical scenes and that since she had the basically sympathetic part—the good woman trying to protect her marriage—this would be the best way to give my part a bit of complexity.

It might have worked—except for an accident. The day before our scene was scheduled I was rehearsing a big, dancing entrance into a night club with Rochester. We were to arrive in a Cadillac and make our way through a big crowd and then do this production number involving a huge number of people. Just as we started to do a full rehearsal with the music, I twisted my ankle and I heard a snapping sound. Rochester made a joke about it later; he said Ethel had put a hex on me. Hex or not, they carried me down to the studio infirmary and the doctors there sent me downtown to a bone man. He discovered that I had chipped a bone in my instep and he put me into a cast. It was painful and cumbersome and, of course, it meant extra trouble for everyone, restaging musical numbers, setting up difficult camera angles so my plaster cast wouldn't show and so on. For example, "Honey in the Honeycomb" now had to be done with me perched on a bar instead of moving through the set.

This caused a certain amount of the attention to be focused on me, which was just exactly what I did not want to happen when I was working with Miss Waters. The atmosphere was very tense and it exploded when a prop man brought a pillow for me to put under my sore ankle. Miss Waters started to blow like a hurricane. It was an all-encompassing outburst, touching everyone and everything that got in its way. Though I (or my ankle) may have been the immediate cause of it, it was actually directed at everything that had made her life miserable, the whole system that had held her back and exploited her.

We had to shut down the set for the rest of the day. During the evening, apparently, some of the people at the studio were able to talk to her and calm her down, because the next day we were able to go on with the picture. We finished it without speaking. The silence was not sullen. It was just that there was nothing to say after that, nothing that could make things right between us.

When the picture was released in the spring of that year I went to New York to appear with Duke Ellington's band at the premiere showing at the Capitol Theater. That was a wonderful time. It was a Negro picture—a Negro movie—and the people were lined up all around the block waiting to get in and see it. Even Duke, who had been feted by the crowned heads of Europe and who's normally so cool—he has the artist's need to wrap a protective wall around himself so he can do his work without distractions—even Duke was impressed. I had an arrangement of songs from *Cabin* that Phil Moore made and it was just a fantastic engagement.

I went back to Hollywood to find a couple of pictures waiting for me to do. The first was a little segment in a Red Skelton picture, *I Dood It*, at MGM, the second was a loan-out to Fox to do *Stormy Weather*, another all-Negro picture. *I Dood It* was a silly little thing about the romance of a pants-presser and a movie star. It was of no importance to anyone and I doubt if I would even remember being in it if it were not for the fact that while we were shooting the picture my life began to take a new course.

SECTION IV

THE BLACK ACTOR:
A NEW STATUS—Part II

Albert Johnson

1   The Negro in American Films:
Some Recent Works

[1965]

Nowadays, it seems that a majority of Americans are committed, one way or another, to accepting the social revolution of the American Negro, as well as the demands for total recognition on the part of Negroes in other parts of the world. Fourteen years ago, film critics thought it brave to acknowledge the "daring" racial themes handled in Hollywood films. But when seen in the light of today's violences, how very tame and naïvely well intentioned those films seem! Actually, however, it is harder than ever before to dramatize truthfully the American Negro's dilemmas on stage or screen, because the angers are too intense. Even James Baldwin (heretofore the most eloquent literary spokesman for the Negro intellectual) created polemical stageplay in *Blues for Mister Charlie,* a work that manages to endow the Negro with an unintentionally mock-epic stature, and brings a hysterical sort of animosity to his heroic quest for political and social equality. Despite cries for "moderation" from the conservative elements in America, this quest goes on. Yet it seems impossible for writers and film makers to capture the essence of courage or dedication that drives many Negroes toward self-sacrificial death in the Southern states, or compels young white men and women into violent demonstrations for the Negro's cause.

Recently, the Negro poet and playwright LeRoi Jones has created a "revolutionary" theater, in which Negro characters articulate their grievances against white authority and social injustices with every nuance of spoken frustration and brutish malevolence, and it is his work that has emphasized the bold strides toward realism in dramatic images of the Negro and Negro attitudes. If one contrasts the allegorical subject matter of Jones's play *The Slave* with the film *The World, the Flesh and the Devil*, the distance between two decades' points of view is astonishingly clear.

In my article "Beige, Brown, or Black" (*Film Quarterly*, Fall, 1959) (*see* page 36), the plea for honest depiction of Negroes on the screen was based upon an exasperation with films that pretended to explore the Negro's social troubles, but only succeeded in exploiting the inflammable subject matter of Negro-white relationships. Since 1960, the gradual increase in racial demonstrations in American cities, the growing influence of such groups as the Congress of Racial Equality (CORE) and its more militant counterpart, the Student Non-Violent Coordinating Committee (SNCC), made it inevitable that Hollywood's film industry would be attacked by Negro leaders, and, at last, by Negro actors themselves. The bitterness against the industry's long-standing traditions of stereotyping minority groups finally exploded in 1963, when concerted pressure was put upon film and television producers to hire more Negro performers, with favorable results.

The 1963–64 period has indeed been an amazing one, in which television serials have included Negroes playing such unprecedented roles as doctors, nurses, lawyers, teachers, pilots, business executives, and in a stroke of wildly off-beat but authentic casting, *cowboys*. The emphasis, in such instances, has been directed toward changing the *image* of the average colored citizen. Moving determinedly away from the chitterling-child inanities of the Stepin Fetchit-Mantan Moreland-Willie Best era, American television has rather self-consciously embellished standard plots with glimpses of Negroes in everyday situations. This is a welcome if hardly revolutionary contribution to racial understanding. In films, however, some closer observation must be given to those works that best illustrate the American cinema's experiments with the Negro's dramatic encounters with white compatriots; and the word "experiment" is necessary to emphasize the uncertainties with which producers and scriptwriters have approached the material involved.

It must be remembered, at the outset, that miscegenation is still the *bête noire* of American cinema, and only very recently has an independently produced film (*One Potato, Two Potato*) caused some critical controversy in dealing with this theme. Until now, Hollywood studios have only flirted with miscegenative plots. In Paramount's *Paris Blues* (1961) the American expatriate jazzmen (Paul Newman and Sidney Poitier) are presented as "hip," articulate, interracial soulmates, but their romantic involvements with two American girls on the loose (Joanne Woodward and Diahann Carroll) only hint at attractions between members of opposite sexes and races. The promise of an affair between Newman and Carroll, for instance, soon shifts its direction, and suddenly the races are paired off in the conventional manner; the white and Negro couples jauntily walk the Paris streets, with Duke Ellington's score triumphantly playing in the background. Nonetheless, in certain respects *Paris Blues* is an excellent example of sophisticated racial understatement, and one guesses that Martin Ritt intended to say much more in this film than he did. The desire to present intelligent Negroes, with unaccented speech, fashionable clothes, and an attitude of contemplative pride about their racial heritage lies behind *Paris Blues*; its failure largely stems from an inability to allow the Negro couple to admit their own prejudices. Furthermore, the film unconvincingly tries to persuade an audience that it is basically the duty of expatriate Negro intellectuals to come back home and improve, or dedicate themselves to, the civil rights struggle. This sort of unforgivable naïveté reduces Poitier and Carroll to likable puppets quite unlike any Negroes one might meet in Europe or America. They are, ultimately, only figments of a white person's literary fancy, and once past the initial hint of miscegenative romance, the film loses its nerve. According to Hollywood tradition the Newman-Carroll liaison would be acceptable to audiences (after all, it *is* in a Parisian setting), but the Poitier-Woodward romance would have sown dismay.

Another major flaw in Hollywood's racial romanticism concerns the Negro male as sexual symbol. Hollywood's choice of Negro actors has, for the past thirty years, been limited to a specific type of Negro—one who is representative of all the anthropological characteristics associated with the term "Negroid" (lest there be any uncomfortable hint of genealogical interracialism)—and if these men were not subordinated to the leading white members of the cast, they were either stolid, humbly educated types embodied by Ernest Anderson, Canada Lee, or Juano Hernandez, or else postwar neurotics, embittered and jazz-maddened, like James Edwards. In any case, none of them were ever allowed to fall in love (unless the film had an all-Negro cast) or in any way intimate that they ever considered romance.

The change in the Negro image in American films within the last decade is illustrated by the robust, casually friendly personality of Sidney Poitier. Since this artist has recently won international distinction as the first Negro to win an Academy Award for Best Actor, it is indeed interesting, as is apparent, after rescreening all his films, to see how his roles have been written in order to eliminate any deliberate sexual overtones. It is a unique shock to see Poitier playing a love scene in *Paris Blues*—not only because he does not appear to believe the inconsistent motivations of his role, but because the film maker assumes that audiences accept Poitier as a romantic figure. Hollywood producers should, from time to time, watch their films in a theater with a predominantly Negro audience and learn that they, too, have been subjected to decades of the glamor image. This long exposure to the cosmetological gods and goddesses of the white race has very much contributed to the American Negro's desire to recreate himself in that image, no matter what the Black Muslims might think. It is a fact that Sidney Poitier does not fit the Negro ideal of the romantic hero, and his most successful roles have been those in which he is already married (*No Way Out, A Raisin in the Sun, Edge of the City*) and concerned with racial turmoils, or when he plays the carefree, humorous vagabond (*Virgin Island, Lilies of the Field*) without romantic involvements.

Of course, Poitier is a "star," and in the proper roles can be a tremendously moving performer; but in trick parts like the disastrous *Porgy and Bess* or *The Long Ships* he is ineffectual. It is clear that attention must finally be given to presenting different Negro actors on the American screen, *with a wider range* in types to populate the cautious world of the cinema. The visual stereotype was only temporarily jolted by Harry Belafonte's frustrated screen career; and by now there is something definitely artificial about the omnipresence of Poitier and Sammy Davis, Jr. as the sole major Negro actors on the screen. As long as art is secondary to star-billing, regardless of race, color, or creed, one can only shudder if Negroes are not allowed to choose their own cinematic gods. How can one help but feel apprehensive about future cinematic depictions of beautiful Billie Holiday, trapped by her lyric passions and the irresistible Mr. Levy, or the tragedy of Charlie "The Bird" Parker, his handsome face gleaming behind a blue-toned horn?

Ralph Nelson's second film, *Lilies of the Field*, is an example of the trend toward showing the American Negro "as he really is." Of course, this phrase is merely a generalized slogan, because actually the American Negro, educated or not, rich or poor, is actively engaged in trying to discover *what* he really is or should be in his own country—as a free, ordinary citizen. *Lilies of the Field* is an important landmark in the cinematic depiction of this kind of Negro free citizen, roaming across the country in an automobile and coming into serio-comic emotional struggles with a group of expatriate German nuns. It is important because the major character (Sidney Poitier) displays a subtlety and understanding by a Negro actor who is able to build his role with certain visual and intonational ironies and reactions that cannot be written into a script, but only improvised into it.

In other words, Poitier's intelligence and self-respect do not prevent him from playing a semieducated, good-natured "nigger"; his portrayal of Homer Smith is an acutely realized interpretation of the type of American Negro who can be thoroughly appreciated both by Negro spectators (because they will recognize the humor in his intonations, the smile *behind* the smile and the truth of Homer's reactions), and by non-Negro spectators (because Homer is not presented as a "problem," but as an ordinary human being). The audiences are thus not intimidated by the racial differences between the major characters, and the religious overtones of the story do not, as one might expect, turn the emotionalism into treacle. There have been charges of sugary sentimentality leveled against the film. However, this is a matter of one's personal acceptance or rejection of the emotional film as a genre. There are bound to be comparisons made with such films as *Come to the Stable* or *Heaven Knows, Mr. Allison,* but it would be unfair to imply that *Lilies of the Field* is similar to these, except of course that nuns are involved in each film. It is also obvious that the intention of the latter film is to make a positive statement about the Negro's ability to become amicably involved with white people in the United States. The relentless goodwill of the story makes *Lilies of the Field* a necessary opposite to the relentless angers of *The Cool World.* Both are necessary to the American cinema's gradual move toward a kind of neorealism—as well as to a motion picture contribution to racial understanding.

Nelson's directorial style is exceptionally personal in *Lilies of the Field* (even to the point of playing one of the roles); only in the nun's childlike responses to Homer's Negro hymn does the situation seem a trifle forced, despite the humor involved. In the nuns' obeisances to Poitier's grammar lesson, played entirely for laughs, the film indulges in an oversimplification of the nuns' intellectual curiosity about the mysteries of American linguistics. The incongruity of the situation does not keep the sequence away from vaudeville sketch levels, and one feels that although searching for subtlety, Nelson cannot resist the temptation to have Homer point out the difference in skin color between himself and the nuns—or to slyly add a "Sho' nuff" to his grammar lesson, which the sisters repeat with the guileless innocence of kindergarten babes.

The film is at its best when the theme is not made too obvious; the image of the nuns walking to Mass along the stiflingly hot, dusty New Mexican highway; their unspoken gratitude and joy when Homer's stationwagon comes along to rescue them from their stoical exhaustion; the nocturnal solitude as Homer lies in the back of his car, listening to the radio, while the Mother Superior watches him from the convent window, annoyed by the secular cacophony but restrained by her own compassion—these are two instances in which the element of racial understanding is strengthened by the sort of understatement that cinema is able to convey *visually.* There is also a sequence in which Homer begrudgingly accepts help from the Mexican townspeople in construction of the chapel. It is primarily a wordless episode, and Poitier plays it beautifully, but Nelson has allowed the musical score to emphasize the purely comic aspect of the situation rather than its sardonic overtones, so that the sequence is weakened unnecessarily. The Mexican tavern owner (Stanley Adams) and the patronizing construction boss (Ralph Nelson) are utilized as catalysts for the theme of the film; the former for humor and the latter for dramatic emphasis. There is a peculiarly elusive self-consciousness about the scenes in which these men talk to Homer, especially the biased construction boss. One knows, supposedly, that adult Negroes do not like to be called "boy" by white men, but one does not expect Homer to react with such indignation (without that Anatolian smile). For the first time, we wonder if Homer *is* from the South or not; suddenly it *does* make a difference. Homer as a symbolic Negro is rather annoying (again this may be linked to the position of Sidney Poitier as *the* symbolic Negro actor) because what the spectator really wants from him is human *unpredictability* in his reactions to white people, bigoted or otherwise. The construction boss if far more interesting because it could be that he represents an average New Mexican attitude, which is strange enough to most American film audiences, and one wishes that his moral turnabout from antagonist to friend had more point to it than the casual joke about getting one's foot in the door of heaven.

Lilies of the Field combines two compelling sociological issues (the Negro and Catholicism) in American life at the present time and it treats both with the sincerity of good intentions and scrupulous taste. One could have done without yet-another chorus of "Amen"; the point was made the first time, but when Nelson decides to close the film as if the entire story is akin to prayer, it is hard to deny that behind the film lie the director's deepest convictions about the growing interdependence of Americans, white and black, upon one another.

Hubert Cornfield's *Pressure Point* (1962) represents a more complex, more ambitious attempt to illustrate the ironies of racial prejudice. It presents us with an intellectual struggle between a Negro psychiatrist in a federal prison (Poitier) and a truculent, incipiently violent patient who has been arrested for sedition

(Bobby Darin). The period is 1942, and as soon as Darin walks into the psychiatrist's office, looks at Poitier and begins to laugh, the tensions of the film begin tightening. Poitier's physical appearance is slightly altered—he now has the intellectual's steel gray temples and steel-rimmed glasses, the resigned patience of those to whom irrational human behavior is tragically commonplace. Although Darin, as a member of the German-American Bund, is the central figure in *Pressure Point* (and in the initial source of Cornfield's screenplay, the psychiatrist was a Jew, not a Negro) the implications are extremely revelatory of certain Hollywood viewpoints. The contemporary problem-figure of the Negro (quite box-office in the sixties) was interwoven with the "period" (are the forties so far in the past?) problem of Nazi anti-Semitism.

The film grips the spectator because it was, and still is, the most outspoken cinematic presentation of racial feelings, openly spoken about between a white and a Negro character. "What have you got against us whites?" asks Darin, with craftiness in his eyes, and the effect of this line upon an American audience is nervous laughter. After studying reactions on four different occasions, with various types of audiences, I must admit that *Pressure Point*, despite its flaws, is one of the best of the American films dealing with racial encounters. It exemplifies many of the attitudes held by white Americans who have not lived around Negroes or who, for one reason or another, have not found it necessary to think about Negroes except as dream figures in a modern jazz fantasy. Despite the technical brilliance of *Pressure Point* (its photography by Ernest Haller is altogether extraordinary, and the film's subtle stylistic excellences, unfortunately, cannot be discussed in this article), it remains most absorbing to us here because of the dialogues between Darin and Poitier. As Darin derides the psychiatrist, the latter remains imperturbable—the detached professional doing his job. One waits impatiently for the explosion, especially when the prisoner points out the doctor's second-class citizenship: "They've got you singin' 'My Country 'Tis of Thee' and they're walkin' all over ya!" he jeers. At this line, a white audience mummurs its awareness, chuckling sardonically, while a Negro audience bursts into loud laughter and applause. For once, the Negro character was as much on the defensive as the white character, and if the entire problem of the home-grown Nazi became somewhat remote, so did the side issue of the psychiatrist's colleagues doubting his abilities to remain unprejudiced toward his patient's racial views. This latter aspect of the screenplay was worthy of a full-length film in itself and tended to make *Pressure Point* rather overloaded with intricate racial relationships on an intellectual level; in other words, too much subtlety marred the overall issue.

When Poitier's colleagues decide to release Darin from prison as "cured," despite the Negro's protestations, the mood is set for the emotional climax the audience has expected. The psychiatrist, disillusioned by the entire case, resigns his position. As he is packing his office belongings, Darin, now freed and in civilian clothes, comes by for a farewell and final bit of mockery. His words comprise an incisive, terrifyingly apt monologue on the inequality of man, and Poitier, finally impassioned, responds with an eloquent, stirringly delivered speech, heavily patriotic, containing such lines as: "Now you listen to *me*. . . . This is *my* country!" and ending with a violent "Get OUT!" The energy with which the speech is delivered is awe-inspiring. A white audience, dazed and moved by the unusual image of the symbolic Negro as a modern Patrick Henry, roars its spontaneous approval with deafening applause; the Negro audience is contemplative, tensely moved, and silent.

This duality of response to the crucial moments in *Pressure Point* is indicative of the ambivalent feelings in America about the position of intellectual Negroes in the civil rights movement. Patriotism is certainly not the proper approach, especially when the *cinéma-vérité* documentaries on television have supplied the country with truthful images of Southern bigotry and violence against Negroes. Besides, after all, Darin might have been correct in his assumptions regarding the Negro psychiatrist's status as an American. We never see the Negro's home or his life outside the prison, and one supposes that he went home to a comfortable part of the Negro ghetto, particularly in 1942. The gradual breakdown of the psychiatrist's control is also vaguely presented; after all, he should have been accustomed to racial attacks by psychopathic patients *before* his encounters with Darin, so that his patriotic explosion, engendered by the patient's Nazism, seems theatrically motivated. The American Negro intellectual of 1942 was not the same as his counterpart in 1962; the former would not have cared much (if at all) about the already disrupted malcontents in Fritz Kuhn's German-American Bund. Assuming that the Negro psychiatrist was an intellectual product of the Depression, he would have been too mutely disillusioned to spout patriotism to an unregenerated bigot. The deepest flaw in *Pressure Point* is thus its inability to give depth to the Negro psychiatrist in terms of his own racial outlook and his position as a "period figure." Unless the psychiatrist had a brother or close friend in the service, fighting the Nazi order to preserve the zoot-suited teenagers of wartime Harlem; unless he was particularly frustrated by long-repressed anguish as a racial pioneer in his field, continually misunderstood by his colleagues; or unless memories of a semiforgotten Dorie Miller or Jan Valtin's *Out of the Night* danced in his head, one found it difficult to accept him as a sepia version of Hollywood's familiar omniscient white head-shrinker. It is not possible to merely put Negro actors or actresses on-screen, endow them with accepted clichés of celluloid intellectualism, and have them emerge as human beings; and this also applies to Chinese, Japanese, Tibetans, Indians, and Eskimos.

Inevitably, there are always attempts to place the Negro character in his proper milieu of American urban life. New York film makers are particularly interested in breaking the barriers of stereotype, and the intelligentsia of that city, comprising some independent film directors, have mostly concerned themselves with the exasperating anonymity of Manhattan (an inescapable cliché made more annoying because it is a fact) and its accompanying boredom and intellectual inertia. In order to give verisimilitude to their stories, the directors of such independent works as Norman Chaitin's *The Small Hours* (1962) and Jack O'Connell's *Greenwich Village Story* (1963) will show Negroes as extras or bit players in party sequences, street or restaurant sequences—holding cocktails and in general being part of "the scene" of New York's semihighbrow literati or artistic underworld. John Cassavetes's *Shadows* (1960) brought attention to the rootlessness of

the city Negro in Greenwich Village, and established the beginning of a very tentative reevaluation of the Negro image, since
some interracialism was taken for granted in the plot of the
film. For a time, it appeared that the actor Ben Carruthers might
become a new and most interesting screen symbol of rebellious
Negro youth—someone to counterbalance the placidity of Poitier
and the matinee idolatry of Belafonte. However, we now know
that *Shadows* was a bit ahead of its time; its theme and interpretation were justly heralded, but the general public had not yet
been forced to realize the truths of the "Negro Revolution," which
was only beginning its first rumbles in 1960. The portrait of
Carruthers living the life of a white man, hustling doxies in a
café with his white buddies, and most of all, *resembling* a white
man in physical characteristics and color—this was still a bit too
discomfiting for audiences to accept. Carruthers's sullen, pessimistic
character, alternately charming or hostile, seemed to represent
something fearful and uncontrollable, someone that Hollywood
film makers would not wish to have imitated by the already restless Negro youth of America. It is indeed an unfortunate loss to
the cinema that Carruthers's talents have not been utilized more
often. He has been the most exciting new Negro *actor* (not personality) on the American screen since Henry Scott's brief debut—
also not encouraged because he was "dangerously" nonstereotyped
in *Anna Lucasta* (1959).

Occasionally, when film critics or screenwriters become involved
with the creation of a film, the resultant works are, according to film
distributors and reviewers, too abstract or surrealistic for popular
tastes. Jonas Mekas, editor of *Film Culture*, and Ben Maddow, the
famous scriptwriter (*The Asphalt Jungle* and *The Unforgiven*)
have both made unusual, intelligent features, extremely avant-
garde examples of the New York school of American cinema, and
important to us because of their presentation of the Negro in
urban society. The critical reaction to Mekas's *Guns of the Trees*
(1961) has been rather hostile because Mekas is an avowed "revolutionary" in his aesthetic tastes and because of his antagonism
toward the more obvious aspects of conformity in American social
and intellectual life. Mekas's view of America is symbolized by

his treatment of New York City as the epitome of the *Angst* of the sixties, an impassive and unyielding fortress of complacent efficiencies against which his characters struggle to thrive. Here we have the cinema of the disturbed intellectual, one that coldly observes an American milieu with the subjectivity of a European emigré. In the world of Greenwich Village's watered-down Bohemianism (yes, the environment still exists: bearded young men linked with serious-faced young girls; loose-limbed and attractive Negroes of indeterminate, vague talent or pretensions toward art) Mekas indulges in petulant attacks upon day-to-day routine, police authority, atomic-bomb fears, and human noncommunication. Mekas's view of humanity is troubled, too. He juxtaposes the lives of two couples, one white, the other Negro. The relationship of the white couple is sterilized by their inability to transcend the wastelandish world around them, and their spiritual self-exile is based too much upon self-pity. The Negro couple, however, played by Ben Carruthers and Argus Speare Juillard, are amusing odalisques, exotic and undisciplined; if one were not certain of Mekas's good intentions, his depiction of these two could be termed patronizing. Again, oversimplification of contrasts between viewpoints (racial or otherwise) destroys the cinematic power of *Guns of the Trees* as a protest film. When one sees the Negroes wandering somewhat incongruously around a railroad yard, reading the names of various routes on the sides of boxcars (this bizarre piece of Americana went out with Dos Passos and Wolfe, one thought), or clowning aimlessly through a fish market, it is impossible to believe that Ben and Argus could ever be responsible to any single pursuit. Is it to be assumed that they have resigned themselves to being social outcasts, and, if so, is their status the result of racial prejudice? Mekas does not tell us. When Ben seeks a job, the sequence becomes a comic pastiche of endless corridors, with a shifty-eyed applicant who races with Ben to apply for the same position. This touch of cinematic expressionism is contrasted to an image of Argus sitting forlornly at her office typewriter in what seems to be a large municipal building, gazing out the window at the clear, sunny skies. We are asked to admire the overwhelming inner impulse toward freedom inherent in Ben and Argus; Mekas admires their childishness, their simple rejection of responsibility. Yet for all of their sensuality, the Negro couple seem oddly sex-less—as if they respond to each other physically because of bio-logical fact rather than from any sense of the responsibilities of *love*; they dress alike and respond alike, and are free to leave one another at will. Ben, representing the cynical city-Negro, hand-some and semiandrogynous, is a character who treads a very thin line between mockery and despair; he refuses to take anything very seriously. Ironically, Ben is the major figure in the film's most singularly moving episode: the rainy-day café sequence. The four protagonists sit in a booth with nothing to do and Ben comments upon the world as he reacts to it. For the only time in its telling, the narrative and characters in *Guns of the Trees* merge into meaning. The quest for self-discovery in New York is captured in this moment of rain-provoked solitude, and the atmosphere is absolutely authentic. Mekas has remembered most clearly in this instance that the outcries of isolated human beings are most telling in the anonymity of big-city bars and cafés, whether white or black.

The Negro as "free spirit" in the New York jungle of cultural malaise also appears in Ben Maddow's *An Affair of the Skin* (1963). The film has been almost unanimously denounced as pretentious, but actually it is a very honest and compelling attempt to dramatize the frustrated love affairs of overly sophisticated New Yorkers. It is an urbane fantasy, really, and if one looks at the film in this light, its truths are more evident. Maddow presupposes a certain chicness on the part of the spectator, and since the major characters are wholly unsympathetic, wallowing rather grandly in self-pity, he expects the audience to be able to discern the interweavings of exposed needs and the subterfuges of manner that people adopt in order to protect their emotions. In *An Affair of the Skin*, the dis-oriented lovers are represented by two couples—the married squab-blers, Allen and Katherine (Kevin McCarthy and Lee Grant), and a glamorous model, Victoria, and her middle-aged lover, Max (Viveca Lindfors and Herbert Berghof). When Allen becomes at-tracted to Victoria, Max tries to interest him in another young woman named Janice Cluny (Diana Sands), a commercial photog-rapher. In contrast to the other characters, Janice is not dominated by her need for physical love (or so she says) and Maddow presents her as a sarcastic, lonely, often volatile Negro on the periphery of New York's social world.

Janice lives in picturesque splendor in a Village duplex, implying financial security and an enviable freedom of artistic expression. She sleeps as late as she likes, works at random, and is by implication promiscuous. Remembering Diana Sands's performance in *A Raisin in the Sun* (1961), one sees the dominance of her personality over the characterization. She personifies the hip, sagacious Negro woman who is already disappointed in her experiences with men, white or Negro, and who pretends to be emotionally detached from the love throes of those around her. The part of Janice could have been played by an actress of any race, which makes Diana Sands's work in *An Affair of the Skin* of chief interest here. It is because she is a Negro that her behavior breaks all stereotypes established from the days of Madame Sul-Te-Wan through Dorothy Dandridge. Sands's character is also the most *alive* in the entire film; we first see her in a rhythmic succession of sequences where she wanders through Harlem, snapping photographs and thinking to herself "Oh, God, I wish I were Michelangelo, but I don't think I'm gonna make it." When she shows Allen some of her work and he describes it as illustrating "the sad dance of ordinary life," she replies, *"Bull!"*

Maddow as writer-director is so intent upon having his audience think for themselves that he never tells us very much about Janice. From all that we observe, however, it is apparent that she is ashamed and resentful about her parents and her background. When her mother (Osceola Archer) comes to stay with her, Janice behaves abominably, rudely attacking her father's birthday cake (the mother insists upon having a requiem cake for the deceased) and arguing violently about the older woman's bourgeois standards of morality. Then, in a surprisingly tender dialogue, Janice quietly admits her immoral behavior. The relationship between mother and daughter is odd, unnatural, and almost "absurd" in the Brechtian sense. Osceola Archer (the *grande dame* of the American Negro theater) is hardly representative of the old-fashioned Negro mother, and her sense of grandiose comedy is beautifully exhibited in a sequence of haughty outrage as she sententiously plays Beethoven on the piano in order to drown out a risqué conversation between Janice and her friends. Mrs. Cluny recognizes Janice's neuroticism and fears it enormously; regrettably, Maddow's script is so dependent upon the activities of his four major protagonists, and his determinedly "artistic" style of European cinematographics, that Janice and Mrs. Cluny are left stranded, blazingly memorable in a cobwebby narrative.

One of the film's strangest sequences occurs when Janice pretends to be having sexual intercourse with Allen on the upper level of her apartment, within full hearing of her mother. Mrs. Cluny, a plate of cupcakes in her hand, is unable to restrain her disbelief and sense of maternal outrage, and fearfully climbs the stairway in order to peek. She discovers Janice and Allen awaiting her appearance, mockingly amused at the deception; Janice had only simulated cries of sexual ecstasy and Mrs. Cluny, defeated by her daughter's triumphant stroke of dismissal, collapses in tears. It is a moving example of grotesque behavior in a love-hate relationship between parent and child; and how far removed it is from the same sort of conflict in *Imitation of Life!* How strange it was to see Negroes enacting a kind of psychodrama previously withheld from them on the American screen. At any rate, the Negro heroine in *An Affair of the Skin* remains the major positive creative force in that Antonioni-like world of cinematic New Yorkers, all trying to rework a suitable living-pattern for themselves in an atmosphere of wealth, existential death wishes, and impotent love affairs. We finally see Janice encouraging Allen, as she stands like a phoenix amidst the rubble of a building site—quite free, the ghetto girl escaped; and we wonder what is ever to become of her.

The Negro and his struggle for freedom and personal integrity in the American South is the most obviously urgent area for cinematic involvement today, but so far, only two television surveys have captured these turmoils (*Sit-In* and *Crisis*). It is not difficult for us to understand why. The members of the Motion Picture Producers Association, and practically every film exhibitor in the United States, would hesitate to release a fiction film based upon the true-life horrors experienced by white and Negro civil rights workers in the backward counties of Mississippi, Georgia, and Alabama. To make such films today would be inflammatory and raise cries of anarchy. So far, only four American feature films have tried to analyze the Southern Negro's dilemma, and all in an undisturbing fashion. Roger Corman's *The Intruder* (1961) is the most daring; and as of this writing the film has not yet been shown commercially throughout America. The story, based upon a novel by Charles Beaumont, concerns an anti-integrationist, Adam Cramer (William Shatner)—an opportunistic white Northerner who comes to a small Southern town to arouse the townspeople against integration in the local schools. The film, as a whole, is a study in satanic demagoguery, but its best qualities may be seen in a sequence in which a Negro adolescent, Joey Green (Charles Barnes), is getting ready to go to school on the first day of integration. He is silently troubled and his mother anxiously prepares his clothes, while his old grandfather mutters his disapproval; this is excellent, perceptively authentic material. Another sequence dramatically describes a courageous white newspaper editor (Frank Maxwell) leading a group of Negro high-schoolers along the dusty street on their first day at an all-white school. For these moments alone, *The Intruder* is distinguished, because these simple acts encompass a major dramatic fact which was faced by hundreds of Negro schoolchildren in the South and is still being enacted in real life. *The Intruder* was actually filmed in a Southern town, too, so that the atmosphere is real, and several townspeople (unaware of the nature of the film) participated. The Negro characters are peculiarly one-dimensional in their roles, however, and in the film's climax Corman grossly underestimates the wisdom of a typical Negro adolescent regarding the ways of Southern whites: he asks us to believe that Joey would innocently allow himself to be caught in a compromising situation with a white girl, particularly during a period of racial tensions in the area.

The characterization of the intruder himself ultimately became the center of the film; the integration theme was still a very taboo subject at this time. Nevertheless, Corman is to be commended for being the only producer-director who would venture to make such a film, and despite its melodramatic plot *The Intruder* is historically important as part of the American cinema's commitment to the civil rights movement.

Ossie Davis, the notable Negro stage actor, transposed his comedy *Purlie Victorious* to the screen, and in 1963 it appeared as *Gone Are the Days*, directed by Nicholas Webster. Most of the original cast appeared in the film, with Davis again playing the leading role of an oracular preacher who craftily overthrows a racist plantation owner, Cap'n Cotchipee (Sorrell Booke) in order to turn an old barn into an integrated church. The style of the film is entirely farcical; it is not very far removed from a prolonged vaudeville sketch. Davis's intention was to make audiences laugh, from a sophisticated distance, at the stereotyped image of the Negro held by the white Southerner. There are many amusing lines, indeed, but the film is not very laughable. There is too much self-consciousness about this deliberate attempt at parody. *Gone Are the Days* only intensifies the Negro spectator's reluctance to laugh at himself *on the screen*, even when he is trying very hard to do so. Subtlety is the essence of true comedy. For instance, there is a sequence in *Stand Up and Cheer* (1934), in which Stepin Fetchit does a slow, brilliantly ineffectual soft-shoe dance while muttering nonsense that recently sent an audience of white and Negro university students into orbits of laughter unmatched by any single sequence from *Gone Are the Days*. But Davis and his cast are guilty of overplaying their farce, and considering circumstances in the South in 1963, it was extremely difficult to accept the film as satire. It is a Northern intellectual's amusement at the expense of what is considered to be funny in the Southerner's ignorance about Negro guile. The appearance in the theatrical world of such Negro comedians as Dick Gregory, Bill Cosby, Nipsey Russell, and Godfrey Cambridge sets a new standard and makes it imperative for Negroes who appear in film comedy today to maintain a high level of subtlety and sophistication, which before now was not expected of them. At long last, one can realize that Stepin Fetchit was *acting*, and no matter how many dreadful lines and actions he had to interpret, there were instances in which he revealed an artistry and style that transcends time, embarrassment, and popular tastes and which remain irrevocably comic.

Godfrey Cambridge's performances in the off-Broadway production of Genet's *The Blacks* and as a fire inspector with an Irish brogue in the film, *The Troublemaker*, exhibit his wide range of dramatic talent; since *Gone Are the Days* was made before Cambridge's rise in comic popularity, it is acknowledged that his scene with Cap'n Cotchipee, in which he is called upon to swear his allegiance to his master, is the film's most inspired and successful moment of comedy. In his performance as Gitlow, the epitome of the old-time darky, Cambridge underlined the nuances of bitter satire that are only beginning to be defined in a comic approach to the American Negro's search for self-identity.

An unusual amount of praise has been given to Michael Roemer's first film, *Nothing But a Man* (1964), because it tells a calm, dignified story about an average "undramatic" Negro railway laborer, Duff Anderson (Ivan Dixon), who struggles to live decently and peacefully in a small Alabama town of today. The film is, however, exceptionally tame, chiefly because Duff's commitments to his race are entirely self-centered, and the civil rights movement has not really affected him personally. He falls in love with a fairly prim but attractive young schoolteacher, Josie (Abbey Lincoln), and despite the disapproval of her family, he marries her. Roemer keeps his film focused upon the casual, understated sequences of Duff and Josie's relationship, and vignettes of Southern life meant to jolt the non-Southern spectator with the realities of prejudice and racial distrust in that part of America. These moments appear and disappear suddenly, like images of evil seen briefly in a dream. During their courtship, for instance, Duff and Josie are approached by two white youths while parked on a country road. The romantic charm of the Negroes' conversation and Josie's "twenty-ninth" kiss is disturbed by a charged air of danger which hangs in the silence; the youths drive away, but only after one of them recognizes Josie as a probable source of trouble if a rape is attempted (her father is a respected minister in the town). As their wild, taunting cries ring out over the motor noise, the lovers sit, inwardly troubled: "They don't sound *human*, do they?" Duff murmurs.

This statement might be taken as a keynote to the film: this awareness of the *humanity* of the Southern Negro's stoicism in a world of discrimination. Just as Renoir brought dignity to his poverty-stricken couple in *The Southerner*, so does Roemer concentrate his narrative upon those heartbreakingly commonplace situations of married couples everywhere: the courtship, marriage, new home (or shack), the quarrel, separation and reunion, and the imminent baby. This is familiar "Americana," though with a sympathy that strains for significance. Duff and Josie are likable characters; but their environment is, in reality, much worse than Roemer has pictured it. In order to avoid making a preachment, thus, *Nothing But a Man* falls into the category of mere domestic tragedy (along with *From This Day Forward, Dust Be My Destiny, Made for Each Other*, and the sadder moments of *Mr. and Mrs. Smith*). The only freshness about all the adversity here is that two young, attractive Negroes are involved. Ivan Dixon is noble and persuasive at all times, and Abbey Lincoln's look of controlled satisfaction is so unusual that she seems a contemporary Sibyl of the deep South. Yet all around them lie many more vivid things to behold, and in comparison to the conviction of the players, the atmosphere is somehow more lively.

There is squalor and deprivation, photographed with semidocumentary brilliance (by Robert Young), especially in the street ramblings; the workers' ginmill; the bar where Duff goes with his disconsolate father, Will (Julius Harris) and Will's common-law wife, Lee (Gloria Foster); and in the spattered, unkempt house where Duff's abandoned young son (by a previous marriage) is tended by a slatternly worn-out girl. In the little church, Roemer captures the fervent hysteria and emotional religious frustration of the singing congregation (though not as memorable as Reichenbach did in *L'Amérique Insolite*), and he is not too engrossed in streets and faces to miss a detailed glimpse of a flying cockroach or bottletops on a broken checkerboard. All of these are fine humanistic cinema, part of a traditional sense of storytelling.

As in most films where white directors are dealing with Negro themes, there is some awkwardness; the prostitute in the ginmill sequence and Josie's father (the acquiescent "Uncle Tomish" minister) are not properly handled. In these instances, Roemer needed

a technical advisor, preferably Negro, to instruct him on the modes
and subterfuges of such types. Also, the unguarded, bunkhouse
raillery between Duff and his Negro coworkers often sounds a bit
too literary and un-hip to be totally acceptable. It is a fact that
Southern Negroes speak a different kind of slang than Northern
Negroes, particularly inhabitants of a small Alabama town.

For all the vigor and fascination of *Nothing But a Man*, one cannot deny its major flaw of not being truly Southern in feeling; I
am not sure where the film was actually made, but the absence of
the tension of the contemporary South gives the film an air of
unreality. One is confounded by Josie's lack of involvement with
the civil rights issue; and Duff, feeling that one cannot live without trouble, finally deciding to remain in the South after suffering
one indignity after another, never mentions the upheaval which
has torn the South apart.

It is impossible to make a timeless film about Southern Negroes
at present. To accept Duff and Josie as figures in a tragic vacuum
might be a relief from the "problem" category of Negro films, but
by its very nature and locale, *Nothing But a Man* must be a problem film; only the Negroes are good and the whites are bad. It
was Lee, finally, who seemed to illustrate best the Southerner's
attitude toward her environment; she had set her indomitable features into a defiant mask, and all that she uttered had the ring of
tragedy, truth, and a fatigued rebelliousness that would linger
long after death.

The national image of the Northern Negro in the United States
is not centered upon the "free" bohemians of Greenwich Village,
but upon our country's most famous ghetto, Harlem. Nonetheless,
films about life in Harlem are still rare, and fourteen years after
the sad, memorable images of Lenox Avenue in Alfred Werker's
Lost Boundaries (1949), or James Agee-Helen Leavitt's *The Quiet
One* (1947), the imaginative and courageous director, Shirley
Clarke, made a film version of Warren Miller's novel *The Cool
World* (1963).

For all its brusque cutting, disjointed narrative, and frustrating
half-glances at its characters, this is the most important film document about Negro life in Harlem to have been made so far. It is

a steadfast perusal of a group of adolescents, members of a gang calling themselves the "Royal Pythons"; but Clarke is as interested in the streets, buildings, backyards, and faces of Harlem as she is in her misguided young hero, Duke Custis (Hampton Clanton). With the aid of two extremely perceptive cameramen, Baird Bryant and Leroy McLucas, the director manages to seize upon those details that make *The Cool World* a work of visual poetry, and in sound, a tone poem of the slums. There is little humor in the film, although an early sequence, in which an anguished high-school teacher leads his unruly class of Negro boys through the Wall Street district, has a wild, improbable sort of inanity about it. Most of one's attention is drawn to the routine of the gang as they quarrel, fight, and disperse in Harlem's pattern of violence and moral corruption. We are shown a close-up of a Muslim's face, spouting black supremacy, and Duke's association with a "cool" racketeer, Priest (Carl Lee), gives us limited insight into two areas of accepted Harlem resistance to the white man. The former's hatred is explicit; Priest's personal war with his white colleagues from "downtown" is implicitly waged, but ends with his execution at their hands.

In the novel form, *The Cool World* was easier to tell; in the film version, every character is so vivid that each one struggles (because we are able to see him in many varying and fascinating situations) to have his story told. The film is so totally alive with the desperation of the dark, of being black and ignored, that Duke is often the least interesting person in the story. As we look at *The Cool World*, its restless air gradually works itself into a whirlwind of themes: Duke's desire to purchase his own "piece" (gun); the tragic obliteration of healthy childhood, exemplified by "Little Man" (Gary Bolling), a teenage drug addict, and LuAnne (Yolanda Rodriguez), the boys' exclusively owned, fourteen-year-old harlot; the desolation of Duke's home life, and finally, the gang fight and arrest of Duke.

It is amazing that Shirley Clarke was able to compress as much into the film as she did, because it is fairly bursting with questions to unresolved problems and unresolved people. The cry of displacement is sounded by Duke's grandmother (Georgia Burke), an offshoot of the familiar, oh-lawdy matriarch from the screen lineage of Louise Beavers to Claudia McNeil. ("I'm sorry we left Alabama! Nothin's been right since!") His mother (Gloria Foster), a deeply disillusioned, hip scuffler, knows too well that Harlem usually gets to be "too much" for its men to endure; they run away to a less stultifying oblivion. Most denizens of Harlem are not overtly aware of their isolation, because when one is born into a ghetto, it becomes a refuge, and disturbingly enough, a comfortable retreat from the vast anonymity of white life "downtown." The social crudeness of Harlem's youth and their unruffled acceptance of death, sex, and narcotics as necessary parts of human existence makes the film appear shocking to those white spectators who are familiar only with juvenile delinquency in suburbia. Duke has his dream reveries of death and his coveted "piece," and when he makes love to LuAnne in the Pythons' cluttered den, he is still enough of a boy to imitate his mother's lover, repeating an endearment he had overheard earlier in the film. One has to adjust to the terrifying maturity of the children, each of them a trapped human being who is incapable of fighting his artificial exile.

We do not get close enough to Duke and his gang; Priest remains a mystery, a further extension of actor Carl Lee's mastery of restrained malevolence and simulated indifference, not very far removed from the world of "Cowboy" in *The Connection*. Priest's white mistress, Miss Dewpont (Marilyn Cox) has a touching scene with Duke as she describes her loneliness in the Hotel Theresa. Half-inebriated, influenced in acting style by the work of Monroe, Barbara Nichols, and Toby Wing, her caricature of a call-girl is rather moving. However, the character of Miss Dewpont is so fragmentary that one is not certain whether to be sympathetic or horrified by her advances to Duke, or to accept her as a serio-comic floozie. In reality, she would be a tragic figure, in much the same way that boxer Jack Johnson's white wife was—misunderstood by white and black in the hostile, fear-ridden atmosphere of miscegenation among the lower classes.

In the Mount Morris Park sequence, where the displaced, drug-ridden "Blood" (Clarence Williams), the Pythons' former leader,

Farina in Hal Roach's *Our Gang*

Bill Robinson in *The Littlest Rebel* with Shirley Temple

Ethel Waters, Eddie "Rochester" Anderson, and Paul Robeson in *Tales of Manhattan*

Starts Thursday, June 24th, 8:30 P. M.

GALA WORLD PREMIER

MANSFIELD THEATRE

47th St. West of Broadway — Phone Circle 6-9056

Adm. Opening Night, $1.80 to $2.40, Incl. Tax TWICE DAILY Thereafter,
2:30 and 8:30 P. M. Adm. 90c. to $1.80 — ALL SEATS RESERVED

The Season's **DRAMATIC THUNDERBOLT** and

THE GREATEST NEGRO PHOTOPLAY OF ALL TIMES!

OSCAR MICHEAUX'S
Thrilling Motion Picture Epic

LEROY COLLINS
as "Martin Eden"

GLADYS WILLIAMS
as "Mrs. Dewey"

The Betrayal

THE STRANGEST LOVE STORY EVER TOLD!

Based on the immortal novel
"THE WIND FROM NOWHERE"

Please Show This To Others In The Apt.

THANK YOU

They plan to steal
her away before
her husband returns.

Introducing and Featuring

LEROY COLLINS · MYRA STANTON · VERLIE COWAN
HARRIS GAINES · YVONNE MACHEN · ALICE B. RUSSELL

and a Carefully Selected Colored Supporting Cast

ASTOR PICTURES CORP.

Produced and Directed by OSCAR MICHEAUX, Distributed by ASTOR PICTURES CORP. 130 WEST 46th STREET N. Y.

Tickets on Sale at Mansfield Theatre
Box-Office 47th St. West of Broadway
Commencing Mon. June 21st

Sidney Poitier with Tony Curtis in
The Defiant Ones

BELOW: Lena Horne in a publicity
photograph from MGM

OPPOSITE: A broadside advertising *The Betrayal*

Johnny Nash in *Take a Giant Step*

Hattie McDaniel with Vivien Leigh in *Gone With the Wind*

Butterfly McQueen as Prissy in *Gone With the Wind*

Ossie Davis in *The Scalphunters*

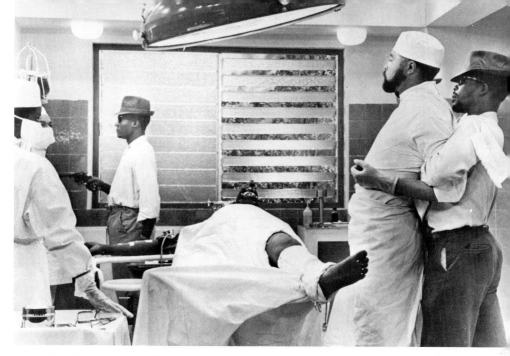

James Earl Jones in *The Comedians*

Mantan Moreland in the Charlie Chan series

Sammy Davis, Jr. with Peter Lawford in *Salt and Pepper*

Godfrey Cambridge and Judy Pace in *Cotton Comes to Harlem*

Vionetta McGee and Richard Roundtree in *Shaft*

Moses Gunn and Richard Roundtree in *Shaft*

Fred Williamson and Vionetta McGee in *Hammer*

Yaphet Kotto with Anthony Quinn in *Across 110th Street*

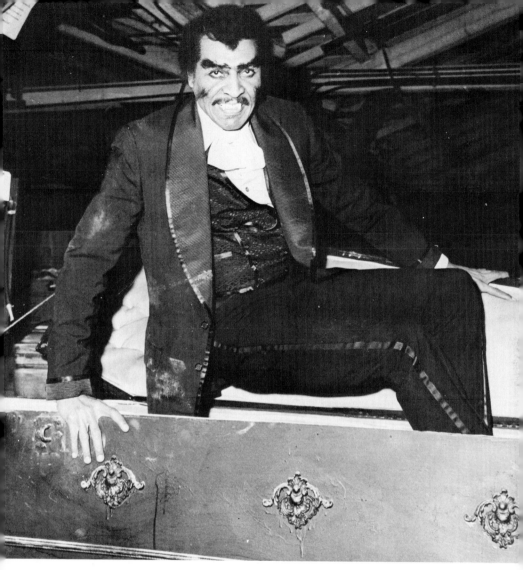

William Marshall in *Blacula*

Rosland Cash and Calvin Lockhart in *Melinda*

Raymond St. Jacques *(left)* and Godfrey Cambridge *(right)* in *Come Back Charleston Blue*

Cicely Tyson in *Sounder*

Paul Winfield and Kevin Hooks
in *Sounder*

Ron O'Neal in *Super Fly*

argues with his brother, the theme of rejection is brought to our attention. The older brother is well dressed, handsome, and socially adjusted; he is carrying some books, but seems to be more of a Manhattan dilettante than a dedicated intellectual—a symbolic contrast to the dishevelled, wild-eyed "Blood," who slumps against a wall in a narcotized haze. The-brother-who-wants-to-help is also a typical, tragic Harlem figure to whom his beleaguered sibling is forced to shout: "I fought your battles for you, baby! Go back to your white world! Leave me alone!"

In *The Cool World*, the white world is rejected: its codes and standards, its well-meaning visitor, its curious stares from Sunday bus riders, its storekeepers, its landlords, its *everything* is rejected. Harlem's dependence upon the white world around it is not explored in this film, adding to the peculiar incompleteness of the story. For example, there had been some episodes in the book (and, I believe, in the initial cut of the film) describing the boys' hustling of white homosexuals in Central Park for spending money; and one of the boys, Chester, became the kept lover of a wealthy patron in a swank Manhattan penthouse. However, probably because of the taboo subject matter and contemporary concern with "the image" of racial characterizations, these aspects of the narrative were eliminated. Only a passing snide reference to Central Park, leading to a sporadic fight between two of the Pythons, remains as an allusion to the boys' acceptance of profitable inversion.

The struggle for self-improvement is made to appear a hopeless one for these Harlemites. When Duke stops in a playground to talk to Hardy, a neighborhood basketball player, it becomes clear that Hardy's skills are aimed toward athletic success that will surpass all similar accomplishments by "those half-assed little grey boys": At the basis of every motivation in *The Cool World*, there is an undercurrent of antiwhite anger. The "coolness" that *must* be maintained is an emotional control, repressed in turmoil, camouflaging the Negro's realizaton that the white world, no matter how "uncool," is one in which he *needs* a place; a desirable world with which he is not yet able to cope.

Shirley Clarke's contributions to the American cinema are honest, extremely personal works, and *The Connection*'s portraits of Negroes in the narcotics underworld and *The Cool World*'s violent Negro juveniles illustrate the background of that urban demoralization which ultimately destroys whatever might possibly flower in American Negro culture. To Negro audiences, these lessons and images are not new; the works of Richard Wright and Ann Petry, for instance, long ago dramatized the ghetto-as-battleground in American literature. But to white audiences, wherever *The Cool World* is shown, the beautifully observed vignettes of Negroes living calmly in an unnatural habitat—the baking, narrow streets and tenements, the sidewalk conversations, the gambling, a tight-suited girl waiting for a bus—these are etchings of cinematic truthfulness. Naturally, there are jazz trumpets in the air; after all the decades of history-with-myth, the linkage of dark people and jazz music is inescapable, an accepted cultural cliché. But Shirley Clarke is very much aware of all these matters and in Harlem the muses do hum the blues.

One would like to think of America as a vaster place than the American cinema permits us to see. We have read of Negroes rioting in such unheralded places as Rochester, New York, or Cleveland, Ohio; if such dramatic conflicts break out there, what is the plight of Negroes in South Dakota or Firebaugh, California? Are there Nostromos arising in such settled, typical American communities to change the emotional and social patterns of their towns in some irrevocable way? The deepest and most interesting dramas of American Negro life have yet to be told; these will be stories about people who have become "accepted" by the white community and whose personal embattlements are totally emotional—in that struggle to reach another person's inner self and to find security in the torture garden of human love. In 1965 there are still far too many ignorant people to bring about an integration of intelligences; the physical side of American life has too dominant a hold on our society, which can only become concerned with "toplessness" or the cacophony of much popular song-and-dance. The possibility of interracial love is additionally distorted by this routine vulgarity; held apart by a century of racial ignorance and hostility, the races in American life are also imprisoned by a strong undercurrent of puritanism in our social behavior. Today young men and women dance the Monkey, Swim, Jerk, and Frug, watched by their elders with the same dismay as their parents watched the Bunny Hug or the Shimmy; yet many whites believe that so-called "Negro music" is a chief contribution to the "moral decadence" of the younger generation, and conveniently forget their own earlier discoveries of Dixieland, ragtime, or swing.

The quest for intelligent integration of Americans on a simple, humane level, outside the South, is the concern of *One Potato, Two Potato* (1964), directed by Larry Peerce. The importance of the film lies in its sensitive treatment of a love affair and marriage between Frank (Bernie Hamilton) a Negro man, and a white divorcée, Julie (Barbara Barrie). The locality is a small town—Painesville, Ohio, replete with the cycle of the seasons and the nostalgia associated with the reveries of Wolfe or Agee. The screenplay, by Rafael Hayes, is honest in its dialogue and emotional understatement. The shock intrusion of racial antagonism on the part of the white man is presented joltingly, as in *Nothing But a Man*: Here, a policeman insults Julie (believing she must be a prostitute) as she strolls along the street with Frank. The two films inevitably resemble each other in a certain tendency to become symbolic. Peerce's difficulty lies in his overwhelming dedication to making Frank and Julie an "average" couple—so that he applies the average sentimentalities to this highly *unusual* couple. Frank is urbane (much too much so for Painesville) but Peerce makes him behave with what he believes is wholesomely appealing faunishness; his clowning is interesting but odd. The innate decency of Frank and Julie is cleverly emphasized, however; they attain a remarkable innocence. Their lovemaking is filled with a tentative sense of wonder, and their affair is respectably lustless. If the spectator relaxes and accepts *One Potato, Two Potato* as in imperfect breakthrough in the dramatization of interracial marriage, its successful episodes remain memorable, and the parable overtones are less disturbing. The sequence in which Julie wins Frank's confidence as they sit in an automobile is very poignant. The emotional disillusionments of the Negro are engraved upon Frank's face; and if one begins to believe that he *could* have remained in Painesville so long without a deep attachment to anyone, this very fact reveals something of the Negro's enforced neuroticism in America. When Julie's former husband, Joe (Richard Miller), appears on the scene, the antimiscegenative feelings of white Americans are displayed in a highly melodramatic sequence. "You know how *they* feel about white women!" he tells her in an excellently played hotel bedroom argument. Once touched by the reality of a Negro, a white man's intuitive inclination is to think the worst of him. The idea of serious emotional relationships between Negro men and white women is incomprehensible to Joe; and in an inept fury of self-righteousness he attempts forcibly to seduce his former wife. This particularly horrifying episode is a subtle dramatization of the age-old bugaboo supposed to underlie the competitive, masculine ego-struggle between black and white. Convinced that segregation has intensified the black man's lust (possibly true, and possibly also a projection of the white man's own intensified lust), the white fears that the Negro male is more sexually satisfying to woman-kind. This ancient piece of cultural mythology is, unfortunately, as indigenous to the Western world as Santa Claus; and one grows weary of having it dramatized and articulated as if it were truth— in the work of Baldwin and the "irreverent" Mr. Jones, for example. When Frank hears about Joe's mistreatment of Julie, he cries out, "They won't let me be a *man!*" He is unable to thrash Joe, and *any* assertion of his natural virility will be misunderstood. Frank's parents are initially hostile to an interracial marriage; their veiled glances and awkward silences represent a sense of shame, as if their son had heard the call of the lorelei and fallen under the curse of miscegenation—still linked in the Negro mind with the demoralizations of slavery. Frank tragically tries to resist the spiritual impotence that racial prejudice creates and maintains in American life, to escape being taken for granted, and for the wrong reasons. *One Potato, Two Potato* sympathetically portrays Frank's isolation. Before the marriage, he is seen wandering alone in the town square, reliving his games and chases with Julie, reading a Civil War monument inscription in silent misery. His symbolic self-exile is perfectly imaged in one of the film's most powerful moments: as he tearfully watches Indians charging cavalrymen in a drive-in movie, unable to control his dammed-up feelings, he screams within the isolated prison of his auto, "Kill him! Kill those white bastards!"

One is certainly moved to compassion for Frank and Julie when the court gives custody of her daughter to the biological father. The action is staged with cold simplicity, adding to an excruciating sense of injustice felt because Peerce has already proven that Joe is an insensitive blackguard, unworthy of his daughter. He takes her away as much out of spitefulness as racial prejudice, and if one's credulities are strained a bit, it is because the film implies that where interracial marriages are concerned, social position, love, intelligence, economic security, a home in the country, and preference of a child for her Negro foster father have no force whatsoever against American society's condemnation of miscegenation. *One Potato, Two Potato* bravely takes a position of racial tolerance but fails to eliminate the spectator's doubts concerning the "Why?" of the court's decision. When interracialism becomes too heroic, the machinery of theatrical maneuvering begins to creak very loudly. One is left closer to disbelief than complete, honest sympathy.

There are further steps being taken to emancipate the Negro from his cinematic stereotype, some faltering, some bold: Ford's *Sergeant Rutledge*, in which Woody Strode's epic stoicism set the pattern for assimilating outstanding Negro athletes like Rafer Johnson and James Brown into the image of either noble savage or stalwart nineteenth-century cavalryman; Sammy Davis, Jr.'s stylized performances in *Convicts Four* and *Sergeants Three* (in which he plays a Negro Gunga Din!); Samuel Fuller's *Shook Corridor*, in which Hari Rhodes plays a Negro student driven to paranoid schizophrenia by the strain of being at an all-white college in the South; and Eartha Kitt's strikingly mannered portrayal of cynical heroinistics in Richard Quine's *Synanon*. There are well-intentioned failures in *Black Like Me* (1964), directed by Carl Lerner, a potentially notable film marred by a weak script and overcautious ineptitude in the dramatic approach; or successful mock-heroics as in Ossie Davis's splendid performance as a West Indian soldier-prisoner in Sidney Lumet's *The Hill* (1965); and

Sidney Poitier as Simon of Cyrene steps forth in a spotless white-cowled robe to lift the cross from Christ's shoulders in *The Greatest Story Ever Told*—with obvious sociological implications.

An all-Negro film, *Living Between Two Worlds* (1964), directed by Robert Johnson, has not been widely shown; it deals with a mother-son conflict in Los Angeles, and it illustrates the growing desire among Negro artists to put together their own cinematic works. However, there are specific needs which must be attended to in future involvements of the cinema with the American Negro.

First of all, the drama of the intellectual Negro, isolated by the uniqueness of being ahead of his time or environment in American culture, must be illustrated, perhaps through depictions of the lives of such brilliant men as W. E. B. Du Bois, Alain Locke, and Bert Williams. Negro screenwriters must be encouraged, as well as Negro directors; despite the brilliance of the Englishman Tony Richardson, one is disturbed that he intends to film Baldwin's novel, *Another Country*, when the talented Negro director, Lloyd Richards, has yet to make his film debut in this category.

Documentary approaches such as Haskell Wexler's *The Bus* (1963), and independent short works such as *We'll Never Turn Back, The Streets of Greenwood* or *Ivanhoe Donaldson* (1964), a feature-length documentary directed by Harold Becker, vividly illustrate the civil rights struggle; but the paradox of white-Negro relationships throughout the world must be dramatized in the narrative film, and the works of Nadine Gordimer and Shirley Ann Grau, for instance, are rich in elements from which great films could be made.

There must also be a more sophisticated role for Negroes in American lyric cinema, with the creation of a new style far removed from the *Carmen Jones* myths. This might happen through a merging of foreign and domestic talents: if Jacques Demy, Michel Legrand, and Duke Ellington collaborated on a Harlem musical, in color, with choreography by Alvin Ailey, including new, outstanding talent like Barbara McNair, Leslie Uggams, Lou Rawls, and Charles Louther, the brown Nureyev of modern dance —with these and established veterans from the world of Negro entertainers, an unqualified masterpiece could be created.

But finally, the strength and humanity of American Negroes, embodying the immigrant power, grit, and the struggle of thwarted hopes should be encompassed in the comedies and dramas to be visualized on film. Hopefully, a latter-day Aristophanes will emerge and create a new point of view about white and black Americans interrelating in a tragicomic world. For much too long now, we have grown weary of unvaried Sophoclean cries from the world of the darker brother.

Catherine Sugy

2   Black Men or Good Niggers?

[1970]

"Hit him again, man!" The shout comes from somewhere in the predominantly black audience at a Forty-second Street theater. And Kirk Douglas's black servant lashes him some more; a close-up shows tears streaming down a face that is very gentle, very black.

The film is *The Way West*, the date Spring 1967. By November there's a change. The black man still belts Douglas, but for a shorter time, without a profile close-up. And without any tears. This time there is no response from the audience.

Why the cut? Who knows? We live in jittery times. But either way, does it really matter? The black man is a servant; he strikes only when he's been ordered to. And as he obeys, he cries. Tearful or tearless, the beating understraps and strengthens, not the old Adam, but the old Uncle Tom.

Race, the uses and abuses of, is back in the public eye. The *New York Times, passim*, tries to find where we're all at, racewise, in movies and plays. Mr. Walter Kerr, that most honest of brokers, calls for a "less realistic, more stylized theater in which color is irrelevant" (*N.Y. Times Magazine*, October 15, 1970). He is not to be blamed if some see this as mere nit-picking. *Ebony*, organ of black commerce and hair-straightening, exults in the Leslie Uggams hoop-la. *The Teachers' Guide to Media and Methods* has Professor Manchel of the University of Vermont put the finger on the "new stereotype image of the Negro." The same issue (April 1967) has a Mr. Ned Hoopes, who looks after TV at Hunter College, lauding Bill Cosby's characterization of Alex Scott, black *wunderkind* of NBC's *I Spy*:

Scott is the antithesis of the Negro school dropout. A Rhodes scholar and a graduate of an impressive Ivy League College, he provides proof of the benefit to someone from a minority group who takes advantage of school.

And that, somewhere between P.S. 105 and the Harvard Yacht Club, is where Mr. Hoopes is at.

Black People as Extras

"I shall try to look like a small black cloud. That will deceive them."—Winnie-the-Pooh

The sincerity of white middle-class support for black civil rights has often been questioned. But that such support is sincere is indicated by the near universality of black extras in films produced in and around the first half of 1965, that is, at the height of the civil rights drive. In fact, apart from Grade B potboilers and teen-age surf-rock films, the only all-white film to open in New York City between March and May of 1966 was *Inside Daisy Clover*.

For the most part these black extras appear almost exclusively in middle-class roles: members of a jury (*Madame X*), nightclub guests (*Harper*), attending elaborate parties (*Do Not Disturb*), even a Western saloonkeeper (*Gunpoint*). We may assume that an audience is pleased to see blacks in positions of implied social prestige; whether it would be pleased to see them as laboring men or as protagonists in more mundane middle-class situations is something else again.

However, the black extra serves a more immediately political role than the straightforward one of underlining support for civil rights. The extras were included in the first place, not only to capitalize on civil rights support, but also to answer the very real need to think that the racial issue is being absorbed successfully.

Were this not so, these extras would have vanished with the movement's collapse—as of course it has collapsed, under the weight of the Vietnam-induced, violence-oriented domestic crisis in the cities.

Has the older use of extras changed in any way? As of the fall of 1967 they appear less frequently and in different situations—although in early '67 that particular use was spreading even to conventional teen-age films (Elvis Presley's *Spinout*, Troy Dona-hue's *Come Spy With Me*). What change there has been may be credited to the increasing politicization of movies, for it is becoming best either to leave blacks out altogether or to represent them with a small role rather than an extra appearance. Even so, the extra still turns up, often lighter skinned, discreetly middle class, the very model of the "spook" figure satirized by black activists.

A brief word on the old Uncle Tom role in its straight form: Till the end of the forties, a popular black role was that of loving servant, a role that has since been extensively adapted, even though it still shows up undiluted. The Devoted Servant is of course an international figure, tending to appear in the literature of countries with an acute class struggle—the Russian *muzhik* or French *confidante* maid. Admittedly such figures may be useful in the plot of a play or book, but their appeal remains sociological. Often they will point up the hero's goodness—he is kind "even to a servant." And while servants are working-class figures, their devotion is proof that "they aren't all dangerous." Uncle Tom, by his love, gives the dominant classes the certainty both of their virtue and of their survival. He reassures them.

Thus, while the traditional approach would be too much for this hyped-up age, the gimmick remains wonderfully alive. At the beginning of *The Trouble with Angels*, Hayley Mills's girl companion bumps into a black train-conductor and excuses herself shyly; he smiles and nods. Or in *Come Blow Your Horn* and *A Guide for the Married Man*, Frank Sinatra or Walter Matthau stops to pay a black delivery man or flower vendor. The blacks say "Thank you."

Everybody's just doing their thing.

Black Supporting Roles

"A Whiter Shade of Pale"—New Song

These could equally well be filled by whites—but this would miss out on the sociopolitics. What is most interesting about black support roles is what they are not: male parts follow a rigid formula. And there are few female roles.

To take the second one first: that there should be few roles for black actresses is the result of the stereotyping of women in the general run of American movies. Women are for decoration and sex. This can pass with white actresses; with black women it's more difficult. The folklore that white American men are uncomfortable about black women would seem to be borne out by the emphatic unsexiness of black movie actresses.

As for black male support roles, at first glance the sky's the limit. A Western trapper *(The Professionals)*, soldier-convict *(The Dirty Dozen)*, gladiator *(Spartacus)*, football star *(The Fortune Cookie)*, Harlem gangster *(The Pawnbroker)*, and a detective *(Penelope)*. Social mobility everywhere.

The servant role has changed. Or has it just expanded? Does it, despite the change, actually continue to conform with an image that has supposedly been rejected?

World War Two comes into play here. The servant of the forties became the war-buddy of the fifties and early sixties *(Oceans 11; The Manchurian Candidate)*. There was the added convenience of credibility; servility was, apparently, left behind in Europe or Guadalcanal. And the old war-buddy could be a sentimental figure, while at the same time not being all that close. In other words he fulfilled what seem to be the three absolutes for contemporary black roles: that he not come too close to whites, that he love them, and that he be entirely positive.

Every subsequent part has met these criteria. Like the extra who is a nightclub guest but misses out on the barbecue, the role of detective, athlete, underworld boss, schoolteacher tells the audience that this black man has made it, without, in the plot, bringing him too near.

And every role shows the black helping whites. In *The Professionals,* the trapper is one of four horsemen sent on a mission to Mexico. There's a lot of fighting and dying, but the only killing our man does is to save his white friends. In *The Dirty Dozen,* the black convict acts with special bravery, kills the villain, and dies. Conspicuously. In *Spartacus* only the black gladiator likes Kirk Douglas (except of course for the heroine). In *The Fortune Cookie,* the football player voluntarily comes close to becoming Jack Lemmon's servant. He calls Lemmon "my buddy."

And finally, black roles are wholly positive. No bad, or even complex, black people is the rule.

To sum up: These films adapt the "Negro" formula. They present a view meant to be honestly opposed to previous stereotypes. But the formula remains: Sexual guilt is sidestepped by turning black women into the most puritanical figures in Hollywood. And the men must be excessively good, in order to calm a fear which, though unformulated, is real.

The Black Star

"Pale hands I loved beside the Shalimar"—Old song.

The most famous black movie star is Sidney Poitier. He is handsome, sophisticated, gentlemanly, cultured; his occupation—student, bank employee, reporter, detective, teacher—shows him to be boss. He automatically fulfills the first demand on the currently acceptable black, that he help whites feel that their society accepts him. Moreover, in his help to whites, his image again is Uncle Tom refurbished; and his films, although with some elaboration, again emphasize remoteness and victimization.

Poitier has no worries of his own. The plot of each film hinges on white problems and his success in solving them. He is the Black Knight on Westchester Avenue. In *A Slender Thread* he saves a woman from suicide and reconciles her with her husband. In *To Sir, with Love* he teaches teen-agers the middle-class proprieties. In *Lilies of the Field* he helps build a church for German nuns. In *In the Heat of the Night* he solves a murder case. And in *A Patch of Blue* he rescues a blind girl from her slum home.

In every picture he is far more wise than the whites. And in every picture, by gentleness and tact, he helps.

But what about the criterion of closeness? Here we may distinguish between black support role and black star role. In the former, particularly if the role is a short one, the black may enter the film in some professional capacity—second detective in *Penelope*, secretary in *Doctor, You've Got to Be Kidding*. This is called the natural, or casual entry. But in more substantial support roles, and emphatically in star-billing, the black must enter by accident. This is known as the accidental entry—literally true in *The Fortune Cookie*, in which our football player becomes involved by injuring Jack Lemmon during the game.

In the case of Poitier, his lack of substantial ties with the white world is established at the beginning and end of each film. In *In the Heat of the Night* his involvement becomes almost a parody of the accidental formula. He was just visiting his sick mother in Mississippi.

The last scene in a Poitier film does two things: It shows black-white contact coming to an end; it further shows the divorce to be a result of black decision. In *A Slender Thread*, he is invited by a policeman to meet a woman he's saved. "Oh, no," he replies, gently smiling. In *A Patch of Blue*, he puts Elizabeth Hartmann into the car taking her to the institution. Again gently smiling and with much shaking of the head and sighing, we infer, as she does not, that it's the last time. And so on. *To Sir, with Love* does have him stay on teaching. But his students have graduated and as the theme song says: "The time has come for closing books/ and long last looks must end/ and as I leave I know that I/ am leaving my best friend." In any event the good teacher image is ideal here, since traditionally this is the person of whom one retains a sentimental memory, without any lasting connection. Rather, in fact, like a servant. Or a war-buddy.

Thus the separation theme is further elaborated in the Poitier films by the act of refusal. This is particularly apposite when there's a romantic angle. (Why, incidentally, are the female leads in Poitier films all previously unknown actresses? Elizabeth Hartmann, Katharine Houghton? Very odd.)

The Poitier image, then, is the most recent version of the

American knight-errant. He appears unexpectedly, solves problems, is always unmarried, has no personal worries, and his background is a mystery. The climax, if that is the word, is reached in
Lilies of the Field, in which he drives away into the evening, still
leading the nuns in song.

The Everywhere Threat

"Every Heffalump that he counted was making straight
for a pot of Pooh's honey, *and eating it all.*"
                    —Winnie-the-Pooh [emphasis in the original.]

It should not perhaps be necessary to underline the fact that the
films under discussion are made by white men, with white money,
for white audiences. And they will reflect in varying degrees the
fears, hopes, and wishes of these audiences. What, then, is the connection between racial and class animosity? And if there is such a
connection, how does it express itself?

One Potato, Two Potato provides something of a text. Here
the black lead is middle-class. He works for a corporation, his
family resemble solid New England farmers. Like Poitier, in *A
Patch of Blue*, he falls in love with a white woman. Unlike Poitier,
he marries her and they have a baby; Poitier doesn't even kiss his
girl friend. His wife is his social equal; black militancy—the acid
test—is portrayed through his father's pride. There is some sense
of the existence of a black collectivity even if it is more or less
ignored. *One Potato, Two Potato* was an independent film.

A Patch of Blue changes all that. It was released in the spring
of 1966, about a year and a half after *Potato*. Poitier's girl friend
is blind, lives in a slum; her grandfather is a terrible drinker, her
mother is a whore and a waitress. This is not Poitier's scene.
Black militancy this time is represented by his brother, probably
since *Birth of a Nation* the first black who is shown to be really
rotten and awful. But then: "We don't agree on race or politics,"
says Poitier.

The extraordinary performance of Shelley Winters is crucial
here. She plays the mother with a rare vulgarity. No heart of gold
lurking underneath her whore's chatter, this is the underclass as

the middle class really sees it. Naturally she hates blacks, as the underclass is supposed to. Naturally the middle-class whites in the film are seen to ignore her "racial" outbursts. Naturally Poitier will be beautiful to her daughter and teach her to say "aren't" instead of "ain't," Mozart instead of jazz. Rarely has a film provided such a feast to the bourgeois sensibility: On the one hand, it is positively invited to indulge its hatred of its own underclass —you just love to hate Shelley Winters; on the other hand it is titillated at the prospect of being told once more that it, at least, is not racist—you just love to love Sidney Poitier; and on the third hand, it is invited to join the consensus of the beautiful people—itself, nice Negroes, deserving poor like winsome, blind Elizabeth Hartmann—against the uglies, the Shelley Winterses, and the militants and the things that go bang in the ghettos. And the trick is turned by adopting a "liberal" attitude to the secondary problem of race.

On this reading, then, politics is seen as a hardy annual in American films. The image of the Old Tom refurbished as knight-errant provides political sanction for a white middle-class attitude that admits a black man with proper credentials to a share in power. It helps to continue the tradition of ignoring the real roots of violence in the ghettos while allaying fears of that violence. As the white problem becomes more critical, the Poitier films become more popular. *To Sir, with Love* and *In the Heat of the Night* were released into the heat of the '67 summer, while the older films, particularly *A Patch of Blue,* are regularly trotted out for reruns.

However, it is probable that ghetto explosions may not be the deepest source of racial anxiety, since, in the last resort, one-tenth of the population is held to be containable. The real sense of menace comes from foreign revolution. This, accurately, is seen to be nonwhite. It would require another study to delineate some of the twists and turns that are accompanying the portrayal of orientals in movies—a critical eye might be cast on the early James Coburn efforts, for example. It may be the return of Fu Manchu is upon us. And the connection between the sociopolitical use of black people and these new substitute-blacks might provide further insight into the heart of darkness that is American racism.

Michael Mattox

3　The Day Black Movie Stars Got Militant

[1973]

The *Black Artists Alliance* is an organization composed of Black people in the film, television and theater industry who have come together to confront the image-makers of America. B.A.A. will act as a pressure group from within the industry; it will set up an atmosphere of critical artistic self-evaluation in an effort to encourage artistic excellence and experimentation among Black people in media; it will seek community support and set up training programs and scholarships for Black students of media.

—Gilbert Moses

Hollywood America. Black folks in the Hollywoodland of sunshine-smog. Made-it brothers live on the Hill (Laurel Canyon-Mulholland Drive, etc.) above the smog line with views of pools. Brothers and sisters trying to make it hustle round the flatlands below the hills looking for a foothold. There is work in Hollywood for black folks this season; black is selling right in through here and the big studios are shopping.

If you hang around Hollywood long enough you can learn something about what it does to people, to brothers and sisters looking for work in film or television, and a chance to stretch out. It's a very competitive environment and it's hard for black artists to get together when there are only a few jobs this week and everybody is trying to get them. It's an environment that generates divisiveness in the face of the tremendous need for collective action by the black artists and film makers. I'm an outsider, on an extended

190

vacation in Hollywood, looking in on the scene trying to see what's goin' on.

So, I went to a meeting at Maverick's Flat, a black disco in the Crenshaw district of Los Angeles. It was to be a panel discussion with a dual purpose: first, to discuss the question, "The Current Rash of New Black Films; A Blessing or a Curse?" and second, to raise money for and publicize the Kilpatrick Cambridge School of Acting. Lonne Elder, playwright, screen writer, and friend of the school, worked to organize the panel discussion. He contacted Ossie Davis, Gil Moses, Oscar Williams, Hugh Robertson, Chris Kaiser, Denise Nicholas, and Terry Carter, all of whom agreed to participate as panel members with Lonne.

The folks really turned out. We got together, summoned by handbills and word of mouth. Everyone I had ever seen in a "black movie" was there, as well as many whose names were familiar from the credit lists that roll by before and after the "black" film and television program. Members of the larger black community of Los Angeles were conspicuous by their absence. The audience was composed of black movie makers, not black movie watchers.

The joint was jumping with egos and superficial conversation until Lonne Elder, acting as moderator, opened the proceedings. It was apparent shortly after he turned the discussion over to the panel that this was not to be merely an event in style. There were strong feelings among the panel members and the audience, and very soon there was a high level of emotional involvement. Once the panel members had made their opening statements, the audience of actors and actresses took over. There followed a parade of cathartic statements and stances all of which amounted to a collective repudiation of the negative black exploitation films in which many of the audience and panel had been involved: i.e., *Cool Breeze, Shaft* (1 and 2), *Cotton Comes to Harlem*, and others. The other collective statement that came across through all the rhetoric was the common recognition of the desperate need for something that would cause change, that would loosen the stranglehold of white control on black artistic development in the film and television mediums.

Although this gathering was not conceived as an organizational

meeting, efforts were made before the meeting broke up to formu-
late some on-going program to bring about change. Many present
responded favorably to these efforts, while others continued to
pursue that American myth of individualism.

Following the Maverick's Flat meeting, on August 3, 1972, a
group of black women consisting of Wilma Moses, Cicely Tyson,
Judy Ann Elder, Violet Jones, Tracey Lyles, Nancy Carter, Gertha
Brock, and Susan Robertson got together again at the home of
Lonne and Judy Ann Elder. The sisters were serious. They met to
capture the energy and frustration generated at Maverick's Flat
before it evaporated in the sunshine. Their purpose was to facili-
tate an organization that could be used to draft a letter to be published in *Variety* in answer to a letter written by the Reverend
Jessie Jackson in the *New York Times* of Sunday, July 30, 1972,
which letter had dealt with the exploitative nature of Hollywood's
"black" films. The sisters felt that it was time a group composed
of black artists involved in the film industry entered the raging
controversy. Already groups composed of black people outside the
film industry were organizing to protest black exploitation in films
and TV; groups like CORE's Blackploitation and the Beverly Hills
chapter of the NAACP's Rating Committee for Black Films. Unfortunately these groups were approaching the problem from the
position of black censorship; i.e., only the positive aspects of blackness are acceptable, and we must not look at the negative side,
and so forth.

The letter to the Reverend Mr. Jackson provided the needed
vehicle for organizing black artists in Hollywood. The sisters
spread the word and a third meeting was held at the home of the
Elders on August 9, 1972. This time it was an open meeting including the brothers and people who had not previously been
involved. The purpose of this meeting was to acquaint everyone
with the incipient organization that had been formed around the
task of writing the letter. Ideas and energy flowed freely at this
gathering. Everyone present felt the pressing need for a collective
statement on how the black artist views the current tend in Hollywood and television's exploitation of the black experience. It was
decided that a committee of three, Gil Moses, Ed Cambridge, and

Walter Burrell, would take the ideas expressed in the first draft, as well as material discussed in the meeting, and work on a second draft to be presented at the next meeting of the as yet unnamed group.

The committee of three met within a few days to begin work on the letter to the Reverend Mr. Jackson. I was present at this meeting. There was a great deal of discussion about how best to say what needed to be said, but little actual writing was accomplished. The next time the committee got together, the composition of the committee had changed to include Gil Moses, Cynthia McPherson, and myself, due to the lack of participation by Ed Cambridge and Walter Burrell. The three of us spent the good part of three straight days in intensive examination of what it actually means to challenge the institutional racism of the film industry and media (TV, radio, news services, etc.) in general. We talked, taped, and wrote down everything for two days and on the third day Gil and Cynthia refined all our thoughts into an open-letter format suitable for publication in the trade papers. The final product was brought to the larger group at the next meeting and there it underwent further editing and was accepted. The specific task that had brought everyone together was now complete, and an organization had been created in the process: *The Black Artists Alliance.* The letter appeared in *Variety* on August 18, 1972, under the heading of Black Artists Alliance:

Dear Reverend Jackson:

On July 23rd, 1972, a group of 400 Black actresses, actors, directors, writers, producers, announcers and technical people working in film and theatre met in Los Angeles to express common outrage at the gross and deliberate distortion of Black life in motion pictures, television, radio and commercials. Out of this coming together the Black Artists Alliance was formed.

We will no longer tolerate the cheap movies about us. Cheap in terms of the range of human emotions expressed, and cheap in their one dimensional investigations of human problems.

We will no longer tolerate the visual images of Black people that are paraded across the screen as little more than reincarnations of racist stereotypes which demean our women and make ludicrous caricatures of our men.

Your statement of July 29th as published by the "New York Times" indicates that you share our concern:

"We will take on those films . . . that project into the minds of our children the images of killers rather than healers, of dope pushers in the vein rather than hope in the brain."

The men here, Reverend Jackson, who control the film industry, dictate to the Black artist what is indigenous and vital to his own life. Every day they deny the Black artist the right to work at his craft with a sense of dignity. We will change these conditions.

Our fight to open up corporate fists and minds to Black people, Reverend Jackson, is your fight. We are in the middle of the problem, and we as Black artists cannot and will not neglect our responsibility to Black people and to ourselves.

We invite the support of all Black people and organizations in our struggle for self realization and liberation as people and as artists.

PEACE BE WITH YOU,
BLACK ARTISTS ALLIANCE

The letter generated so much attention that the *Hollywood Reporter*, thinking they had missed something, began calling around to find out who the Black Artists Alliance was and how come they hadn't run an ad with the *Hollywood Reporter*? One of the brothers they contacted advised them to run the ad also, even though he was not affiliated with BAA and they did. In their haste to catch *Variety*, the *Hollywood Reporter* gave BAA unsolicited ad space.

Following the publication of the letter in the trades, there was a pause in the momentum of BAA due to election of officers. On September 10, 1972, Lonne Elder, Judy Ann Elder, and Gilbert Moses were elected to serve as commissioners. Beverly Hope Atkinson was elected as recording secretary. Ms. Teddy Stewart, Susan Robertson, Cynthia McPherson, and Walter Burrell were elected to the Public Relations Committee. Al Cook, Lynn Hamilton, and Reuben Cannon were elected to the Community Relations Committee, which is designed to deal directly with the wants and needs of the black community in relation to black images in media. Tracey Lyles was elected to the Finance and Laws Committee and Cynthia McPherson was elected chairwoman of the Monitoring and Research Committee. New elections for all positions will be held after January 1, 1973. People elected at this time will serve for one year.

Black artists coming together is not a new concept.[1] Ossie Davis said at Maverick's Flat that he had been involved in a similar gathering twenty-five years ago. In the intervening twenty-five years, the image of black people in the various forms of media has changed, but the John Shafts and their women of today are no closer to black reality then the Mantan Morelands and Beulahs of years gone by. I feel that the Black Artists Alliance represents a positive force for change, and I hope that twenty-five years from now another meeting such as the one at Maverick's Flat will not be necessary.

Note: For further information concerning the Black Artists Alliance write P.O. Box No. 7033, Burbank, California 91505.

GOALS

1. We are pledged to the total integration of Blacks into every aspect of media, and are prepared to fight against union iniquities and unequal employment opportunities wherever they may exist in the industry.
2. We are pledged to the in-depth representation of Black life and people in movies, T.V., radio, commercials and stage, etc.
3. We are pledged to professional unity, through the encouragement and respect for one another's talents, through the engendering of personal camaraderie, through the dissemination of knowledge regarding our artistic rights, and through the open exchange of ideas between artists.
4. We are pledged to the development of qualitative creative standards. Our striving is for excellence.
5. We are pledged to the creation of viable alternatives for ourselves as artists and as people.

---

[1] In 1945, according to Peter Noble ("The Negro in Films," London, 1948), "the NAACP set up an organization in Hollywood to advise producers and to analyze screenplays containing Negro characterizations, but, surprisingly, it was fought by Negro artists in Hollywood, who, later on, formed the Institute of Progressive Artists of America." The group's purpose, says Noble, was "to protect and safeguard the interests and employment possibilities of Negro film artists."

Edward Mapp

4   Black Women in Films:
A Mixed Bag of Tricks

[1973]

The sexual dimension of American racism is reflected in the motion picture portrayal of the black woman. Her film image has been defined by others rather than by herself. When she is not a figment of white male fantasy, she is a product of white female thinking. Few black female writers have gained employment in the film industry. The result is a tragic history of stereotyping and a steady procession of mammies, maids, misogynists, matriarchs, madams, and assorted "make-it-for-money" types.

A half-century of screen humiliation for the black woman began with silent films like *The Wooing and Wedding of a Coon* (1905) and *The Masher* (1907). The message conveyed by the latter was that not even a white "skirt chaser" could have romantic inclinations toward a black woman. This theme of contempt for women who possess even a trace of African ancestry endured fifty years later.

In a 1959 version of Fannie Hurst's *Imitation of Life,* the mulatto daughter of a self-sacrificing black maid finds herself a white boy friend. Despite all her efforts at concealing her racial identity including meeting him in town, the boy discovers her dark secret and awards her a brutal thrashing. This was harsher than the penalty meted out to Julie LaVerne, a mulatto character in film versions of *Show Boat*, who was merely forced off the *Cotton Blossom* for passing as white.

The black female as "seductress" is as old as the motion picture

196

medium itself. In 1929 Nina Mae McKinney appeared in *Hallelujah*, an early vintage black musical, in which she seduced a poor black cotton picker and relieved him of his hard earned cash. The seductress usually brought about the complete disruption of the hero's life. He became putty in her hands. Dorothy Dandridge built her career playing the seductress with minor variations in *Porgy and Bess* and *Carmen Jones*. The latter role garnered her an Academy Award nomination as best actress in a leading role in 1954.

Until that time the only black actress to be so honored was Hattie McDaniels, winner of an "Oscar" for best actress in a supporting role as Mammy in the 1939 *Gone With the Wind*. Hollywood, prone to replicate successes and now convinced that audiences would "walk a million miles for one of Mammy's smiles," wrapped a bandanna around the head of each working black actress faster than you can say "Ah's a comin." "Mammy" as portrayed by Hattie McDaniels and Ethel Waters, seemed to dominate her man but always with a touch of comic relief to ease the pain. Although actresses have imbued her with a rebellious spirit, mammy has always been relegated to "her place" in the kitchen or pantry. A mammy should never be confused with a nanny which is a dignified good paying position for whites. A mammy is an undignified low- or non-paying job for blacks. Eldridge Cleaver charges the white man with turning the black woman into a strong self-reliant Amazon and depositing her in his kitchen. As mother surrogate, scapegoat, unpaid servant, the screen mammy is an enigmatic perversion. She developed the curious habit of administering her private brand of welfare to affluent and needy whites alike. In *Imitation of Life* (1934) when she was not giving away a million-dollar pancake recipe to opportunistic whites, she was massaging Claudette Colbert's tired feet. Being mammy to Colbert's daughter left her little time for her own child, who inevitably came to reject her. In the remake of *Imitation of Life* her excuse for working as a maid without salary was, "I like taking care of nice things." A character in that same film summarizes mammy by saying, "I thought she was everybody's Rock of Gibraltar." In *Pinky* (1949), free laundry and professional nursing care were mammy's gifts to an arrogant white woman. The thin line between black mammy and black matriarch may be distinguished largely by whether the old girl is presiding over a white or black household. Certainly, Claudia McNeil's matriarchal exchanges of dialogue with Beneatha in *A Raisin in the Sun* (1961) are not too unlike Mammy's strong words with Scarlet in *Gone With the Wind* (1939).

An inkling of changing times occurred in *Hurry Sundown* (1967) where on her death bed the mammy/matriarch grieves for the sorry thing that has been her life as a white folks' nigger. The suburban maid in *For Love of Ivy* (1968) did not intend to wait until she was too old to pursue a better life. Ivy had no specific goals other than terminating the stagnant and interdependent relationship she shared with her wealthy white employers.

Meanwhile, in films like *Such Good Friends* (1971), whites still tended to be anachronistic in their dealings with mammy. In that modern drama, Dyan Cannon tells her nonconforming black maid, "Sometimes I wonder why we ever ended slavery."

The rebirth of black films in 1971 gave us a new liberated mammy in place of the old. For the first time, mammy is offering aid, advice, and comfort to a black character (Diana Sands) in *Georgia, Georgia* (1972). With authority and determination, she dominates the girl's life even to singing lullabies and brushing her hair. She views the singer's dalliance with a white man as bringing shame upon the black race. The catch here is that mammy's rage, repressed in over fifty years of Hollywood films, is due for deliverance. Her ultimate release is achieved through the impassive strangulation of Georgia, the confused young black heroine.

The ultimate remnant and refinement of the mammy/matriarch may be seen in *Sounder*, an otherwise beautiful film from a performance point of view. Can it be mere coincidence that words such as strength, warmth, and dignity, once used to describe the characterization of "Mammy" in *Gone With the Wind*, are now being applied to the portrayal of Rebecca, the sharecropper's wife in *Sounder*. She wears a bandanna and an oversized faded feedsack dress throughout much of the drama. She toils from dawn to sunset, tilling soil and laundering clothes for white folks. Yet there is no money to buy food for her children. Rather than start her own vegetable garden or put up preserves in her spare moments on Sundays, she joins her family in sports and singing, two pastimes stereotyped for Negroes. Negative attitudes about "happy darkies" are reinforced each time Rebecca meets misfortune with a healthy display of dentures. When her husband is arrested for stealing meat from a smokehouse, she walks miles into town to the jail. Tired and drenched in sweat, she pleads with the sheriff to allow her a visit with her husband. He refuses. Rebecca responds to such stimuli in an almost saintly and superhuman fashion. Neither by rage nor rebellion possessed, she is a good nigger, patient and acquiescent. It is unlikely that white movie audiences, unfamiliar with the code of living forced upon blacks in the South during the 1930s, will recognize the historical context of this story. They are more likely to see Rebecca as a black woman who knows her place. Humility is what numbers of whites seek and do not find in the majority of new black films.

High among the cliches of how the black woman has been presented in films is the "sex object." Sexual titillation and depersonalized sex are not new phenomena in films. Betty Friedan calls attention to the Hollywood version of women as mindless over- or under-dressed sex creatures. Many feminists in the movement that Friedan leads have picketed and demonstrated against motion pictures and advertising they consider sexist. Hitchcock's thriller *Frenzy* was accused of misogyny and sexism but few such charges have been aimed at the recent crop of black films. Perhaps this is because the women's movement is a white family quarrel in which the black woman merely becomes a useful pawn to be discarded when white feminists achieve their goals.

Unlike the seductress who follows a time table for the capitulation of her male prey and who is in command of the situation at all times, the sex object is used and abused without rationale by white and black males in films.

One of the earliest portrayals of the black woman as a suffering sex object occurred in the black film *Scar of Shame* (1928). A black bourgeois groom is ashamed to take his wretched young working class bride home to meet his family. This ostracism leads ultimately to her suicide.

Another black woman whose past doomed her to unhappiness

was *Anna Lucasta* (1959). Anna, an ex-prostitute, struggles to escape the life of sex object despite the negative influence of her father and a former lover, who both find her reformation inconvenient.

Christine, the black female sex object in *Take a Giant Step* (1961), is the mechanism by which a sensitive black boy tests his puberty. Brief references to Christine's past hint at a life infinitely more intriguing than her function in the film of providing an adolescent with an acceptable sexual awakening.

Mabel, a young black whore in *The Pawnbroker* (1965), who disguises her natural hair with a silken wig, is apparently devoid of sexual and ethnic pride. As sex object, she tempts the pawnbroker by unbaring her bosom, hoping to obtain cash for her Puerto Rican lover.

An early Jim Brown cops 'n' robbers movie entitled *The Split* included a brief role for Diahann Carroll as his estranged wife. Although Brown is a crook who has deserted her and messed up her life, she admits to him, "I'm weak with you." Not content with this debasement, the plot calls for her rape/murder at the hands of her white landlord. And on the subject of white landlords, Diana Sands seduces the young blond owner of the tenement in which she dwells in *The Landlord* (1970). Not one to operate in unfamiliar surroundings, she gets him into her own marital bed which is half occupied while her loving black husband is in jail. Not even waiting for her cuckolded spouse to be jailed, Lola Falana, the wife of the black undertaker in *The Liberation of L. B. Jones,* uses her boudoir to fornicate with a redneck sheriff's deputy.

The fantasy image of black women as just so many empty-headed nubile sepia beauties prevails. Precedent for this image emanates from that peculiar institution known as slavery. While strong black males were working in the cotton fields, favored black females were undergoing another type of enslavement by the white masters in the bedrooms of the plantation houses. The pathetic plight of this particular type of sex object is depicted accurately in *The Slaves* (1969), a film in which Dionne Warwick made her screen debut as slave mistress of a white plantation owner. Neither the black movement nor the women's movement seems to have brought about the abolition of female slaves in films. Now she services the robust black slave of the effete white master, a switch that black audiences may see as cinema progress. So we find Brenda Sykes as a pretty black slavemate heaving and howling in the hay with Lou Gossett in *The Skin Game* (1971) and with Fred Williamson in *Nigger Charley* (1972).

In *They Call Me Mr. Tibbs* (1970), a white male character introduces a black prostitute as though she were inanimate, "That is Puff." Puff responds "I love him. He beats me." In another scene, Puff tries to use her body to divert the black detective, Tibbs. These black females, as characterized by film scripts, ask very little in return for their sexual favors.

The talents of two black actresses, Diana Sands and Rosalind Cash, are exploited in *Doctors' Wives* (1971) and *The New Centurions* (1972). Each one appears as a nurse who becomes dedicated mistress to a white man with marital problems, a surgeon and a policeman, respectively. These films carry the insidious message that black women yearn for interracial romantic alliances at any price.

The advent of black films seems in no way to have diminished the incidence of the black woman as sex object. Machismo is alive and well in Hollywood. Women are displayed as nothing more than rings on a merry-go-round of masculine madness. This is not surprising because a popular theme of black films is the male identity crisis. Black females therefore are required to supply temporary relief and distraction for libidinous Shaft, Slaughter, and Super Fly types.

Cotton Comes to Harlem (1970), which launched the black film cycle, gained easy laughs from a situation in which an attractive black woman uses her nude body to escape from the custody of a white police officer.

Viewing some of the rash of black films one might assume the social depth of black feminity to be the whore house. Black whores are displayed blatantly in *The New Centurions, The Hit Man, Across 110th Street,* and *Sweet Sweetback's Baadasssss Song* among others. In the latter film, one whore is actually shown writhing at work in the classic position. She becomes little more than a human being reduced to a sexual robot. When Germaine Greer comments on this sort of self degradation of females in films, her reference is implicit to white women. However, they at least can counteract such stereotypes with a whole gallery of positive screen portraits. No such balance or redress exists for black women. Erotic bath-tub scenes are running a fast second to bedroom scenes when it comes to vacuous brown Barbi dolls in movies such as *Cool Breeze* (1972) and *Super Fly* (1972).

Not sex objects in the traditional sense, most of the black females in *Blacula* (1972) become reluctant blood banks for the evil ambitions of the prince of darkness.

The "docile damsel" has become a staple in black films of the seventies. She is ascribed more sentiment and humanity than the sex object but they both remain sisters in subservience.

In *Buck and the Preacher* (1972), the docile damsel appears as homemaker for the black protagonist. From a plot progression point of view her role is negligible except for one scene in which a white bounty hunter menaces her. The script writer may have considered a black heroine superfluous in a film which already included that rare commodity, a black western hero. Buck, leader of a wagon train moving blacks Northwest after the Civil War, calls her "my woman." Subordinating her own desire to seek refuge in Canada, she risks personal peril in order to stick by Buck.

In a more contemporary setting the docile damsel is seen as the thoroughly dominated girl friend of Mr. T in *Trouble Man* (1972). She cheerfully cancels a scheduled singing engagement in Chicago when Mr. T cannot accompany her. Her career is obviously secondary to being in the apartment and near the telephone when Mr. T visits or rings. She follows his cryptic instructions to the letter without question. If he decides to tell her what he's up to, that's fine. If not, that's all right too.

Doglike loyalty is an unmistakable trait of the docile damsel as in the movie *Melinda* (1972). A steadfast girl is still supportive of her handsome lover after he has thrown her over for a more alluring charmer. In one isolated moment of truth, she warns the fellow, "Just because I love you doesn't mean I'm going to let you shit on me no more." This declaration is an adequate description in reverse of the docile damsel.

The preponderance of "mammies," "sex objects," and "docile damsels" in no way precludes the appearance of positive black female images in films.

Those who heralded the tender and loving relationship between the black husband and wife of *Sounder* as a "film first" have obviously forgotten *Nothing But a Man* (1965), a minor classic among black films. Its black couple, Josie and Duff, are faced with overcoming the obstacles endemic to the black experience in many areas of the country. In helping her husband to overcome, Josie demonstrates a quiet courage which is somewhat alien to Rebecca of *Sounder*. Josie feels there is no need to fear white bigots "if you see them for what they really are."

Obscured by all the acclamation attendant upon Rebecca in *Sounder* is the role of the back country school teacher in the same film. Her character is a statement of personal and ethnic pride. Not only does she care about her young black pupils, she is determined to communicate to them a sense of black history. The boy in *Sounder* comes to her for the education which will somehow free him from a life of poverty and oppression. This sensitive and dedicated professional woman lives in a modest but attractively furnished home. Not all Southern black women were farmers' wives even during the depression.

The black authoress holds the key to the redefinition of the black woman in films.

J. E. Franklin's *Black Girl* (1972) is crammed with full-blown black female characterizations. Mama Rosie is a complex creature who has repressed a lifetime of frustration. Now her hopes are riding on the foster daughter she has reared along with her own girls. We have observed the black woman who cares for other women's children at the expense of her own in *Imitation of Life* and other films but the twist of *Black Girl* is that black children, not whites, are the recipients of Mama Rosie's beneficence. The youngest and most sensitive of her own daughters yearns for a dancing career. Billie Jean is reminiscent of Beneatha, the daughter in *Raisin in the Sun* who is also vocationally ambitious and enmeshed in family problems and pressures. Billy Jean's two elder siblings are bitchy, jealous girls who make Cinderella's step sisters seem like charm-school graduates. *Black Girl* even takes a look at the elderly black woman, the grandmother of the family. She may have passed the climacteric but she is not without a sexual companion. "The Bible is there on the shelf. I'm not yet," she confides.

Maya Angelou's *Georgia Georgia* (1972), gave its title role a range of intricate human emotions. Georgia is a troubled black entertainer "who has just about kicked the habit of being black." Alone and unloved, her defense mechanisms include the sharp answer, the glib retort, and the quick rebuff. She hires a mature black woman to be a combination maid/traveling companion/ mother figure, a woman who can remind her of what she escaped from, presumably the ubiquitous black ghetto. Undergoing a serious "identity crisis," Georgia seeks false security in the arms of a white photographer while resisting any association with her less fortunate black brothers. Self hatred along racial lines is an ugly concept but one which this characterization meets head on.

Some other unpleasant realities are faced by *Lady Sings the Blues* (1972). The bare facts of Billie Holiday's life—girlhood rape, apprenticeship in a brothel, struggle to success, introduction to drugs, and untimely demise—are touched upon briefly in the film. Although the film cannot be taken as serious biography, it does entitle the black female at long last to the full Hollywood treatment with all the glamorous trappings. It is the old rags to riches theme with a lovely black woman presiding over it all for a welcome change. The years have brought us film biographies of Helen Morgan, Ruth Etting, Lillian Roth, Fanny Brice, and countless other white singers but that wondrous quarry of black female performing artists has remained unmined until *Lady Sings the Blues*. This film puts the black actress in the mainstream of motion picture production.

The screen image of the black woman as entertainer is just the first scene in a panorama which must be unfolded. We need films about Angela Davis, Shirley Chisholm, Coretta King, Mary Bethune, Sojourner Truth, Harriet Tubman, Phyllis Wheatley. . . .

The list is endless. Scholarly neglect and racist assumptions have made black women as invisible in motion pictures as they are in society, bringing about what Gerda Lerner calls their double victimization, as blacks and as women.

SECTION V

ESTABLISHING YOUR OWN

James Asendio

1   History of Negro Motion Pictures

[1940]

Twenty years ago [1920], Oscar Micheaux started producing Negro pictures in the east. These pictures have served their purpose, but could hardly be said to have kept pace with the progress of the industry. There have also been several other efforts to produce Negro pictures, but never on the same scale and never with a definite trend toward quality, as is now the case in Hollywood.

In 1915, a Negro youth, just out of school, had his first experience traveling through the Middle West and Mississippi Valley states as a baritone singer in a quartette. This was George Randol's introduction to the stage.

Throughout the intervening twenty-four years, Randol has ever sought to improve the Negro's condition and position in the field of entertainment and the theater. During these twenty-four years, it has been his privilege to know the greater names in the theater and the concert halls. He has watched their owners grow to be stellar attactions and has always had the idea that if pictures were produced that would give Marion Anderson, Roland Hayes, Katrina Yarboro, and other such concert lights, as well as literary geniuses such as Alain Locke of Howard University, Rhodes scholar, and Kelly Miller, dean of Howard University, a vehicle in which to display their wares, there would be attracted to this industry many persons who have much to contribute, regardless of the color of their skins.

After 1,762 consecutive performances with Richard B. Harrison in *The Green Pastures*, where the plan to start an all-Negro motion picture company was evolved during one of the many tours, Randol came West. It was his good fortune to come to Hollywood as an assistant director for Warner Bros. Being inspired by his discussion with Harrison as to the probability of an all-Negro motion picture company, Randol started at once to organize such a company, being greeted, at first, as a person with slightly irresponsible mental faculties.

Persons in Hollywood would look at him with a vacant stare when he talked of all-black motion pictures on a major scale; pat him on the back gently and say, "It was nice to have known you." In other words, the old "brush off."

However, Hal Mohr (member of Local 659, IATSE), winner of the Academy Award for photography in *The Green Pastures*, thought the possibility of making an all-Negro picture would offer new fields of exploration in camera craft. His experience with large groups of colored people in *The Green Pastures* gave him an insight to the very interesting study of screen technique that could be afforded by groups of Negro people with their varied coloring.

Randol was successful in interesting RKO in the production of short subjects starring the Hall Johnson Choir, with the result that in 1937 one of the shorts, *Deep South*, produced under his contract, was runner-up for the Academy Award. By this time, cameramen had come to realize the possibility for rare photographic beauty when groups of Negroes were photographed in typical racial settings. The photography on *Deep South* was really a work of art as handled by Jack McKenzie (member of Local 659, IATSE).

Between pictures at RKO, Randol interested Ralph Cooper and Ben Rinaldo, an agent of Hollywood, and they formed a company to produce the first all-black cast motion picture with modern story, settings, and costumes, released under the title *Dark Manhattan*. This picture became a sensation when shown, even though it was difficult to convince the exhibitors that colored people would pay high prices to see their own race on the screen.

When word reached Hollywood that crowds were standing in unfavorable weather throughout the East to see *Dark Manhattan*, which, by the way was very well photographed by Roland Price, there immediately sprang up a number of companies attempting to make all-Negro pictures.

For a while there was a demand for the product of these new companies, but their lack of experience with the subject matter caused inferior pictures to be made. When people viewed *Dark Manhattan*, they commented favorably upon the photography and compared it with the "B" class pictures then produced by the major studios. When other pictures came along that merely sought to slap together a few images on a film, the public compared the photography of these inferior productions with *Dark Manhattan* and refused to accept them. This lack of photographic perfection was due to the lack of time and cooperation of producers.

During the past three years, important developments have taken place until today colored-cast pictures are now being produced on a major scale. This was brought about four months ago when International Road Shows entered the Hollywood field with an established distribution set-up. They have issued contracts to three producing units for their entire output during the coming year, guaranteeing to the producer an outlet for his products and to the exhibitor a standard grade of pictures, plus a definite delivery schedule, all of which has heretofore been lacking.

Bert Goldberg, vice-president of this company, has surrounded himself with an experienced Hollywood staff, headed by George Randol as chief of production. In this executive position he will be able to give the colored race as well as the race's many white friends the long-awaited opportunity to see the Negro on the screen as he is in life. Using as a foundation *Double Deal*, which critics acclaim as technically perfect and a photographic gem, due to the grand efforts of head-cameraman Mack Stengler (member of Local 659, IATSE), they hope and feel assured that at last colored pictures will take the place they rightfully deserve in the industry.

Editor's Note: According to Wesley Curtwright (Writers' Program, WPA Project, 1940), "the Micheaux Film Corporation was founded in 1918 by Oscar Micheaux and incorporated in Delaware. It was later re-organized as a talking picture company, and incorporated in New York, with capital paid up and no stock for sale. Its officers were: Oscar Micheaux, president; Frank Schiffman, vice-president and secretary; and Leo Brecher, treasurer."

Some of the commercial features made by Micheaux were: *Homesteader* (1919); *Within Our Gates* (1920); *Gonzales Mystery* (1921); *Deceit* (1921); *The Dungeon* (1922); *The Virgin of the Seminole* (1922); *Son of Satan* (1922); *The House Behind the Cedars* (1923); *Jasper Landry's Will* (1923); *Birthright* (1924); *Body and Soul* (1924); *The Devil's Disciple* (1925); *Spider's Web* (1926); *Millionaire* (1927); *When Men Betray* (1928); *Easy Street* (1928); *Wages of Sin* (1929); *Daughter of Congo* (1930); *The Exile* (1931); *Darktown Revue* (1931); *Veiled Aristocrats* (1932); *Black Magic* (1932); *Ten Minutes to Live* (1932); *The Girl from Chicago* (1933); *Ten Minutes to Kill* (1933); *Phantom of Kenwood* (1933); *Harlem after Midnight* (1934); *Lem Hawkins' Confession* (1935); *Temptation* (1936); *Underworld* (1936).

Other black film companies were Reol Motion Pictures Corporation (producer of Lincoln Pictures), directed by Robert Levy, which produced *The Call of His People, The Sport of the Gods, The Jazz Sound, The Burden of Race, Easy Money,* and *The Spitfire.* Charles Allman White produced *Dixie Love, Crimson Fog,* and *Dusky Virgin* between 1931 and 1933. He also produced newsreels featuring Elder Micheaux, the radio evangelist, and William Allen, who found the Lindbergh baby. See also Geraldyn Dismond article, "The Negro Actor and the American Movies" in Section III.

Lindsay Patterson

2   In Movies Whitey Is Still King

[1971]

I've always been willing to admit promptly my mistakes in judgment. Today, unfortunately, too few people are, particularly many of our present politicians who seem bent on plodding a pragmatic and unimaginative course that is surely going to spell doom for everyone everywhere.

In a review of the play *In the Wine Time* somewhat over a year ago, I suggested that maybe someone should give the author (Ed Bullins) ten thousand dollars with the stipulation he leave the country for a year: "Perhaps that way his [useful] anger might not be persuaded to turn into [destructive] hate."

I now humbly apologize to Mr. Bullins. It was rotten advice, but based soundly on precedented history. Writers (and other artists) have always seen the need at some point to escape the social and political chaos of their homelands in order to examine and consider possible solutions objectively, though many, like Eldridge Cleaver, have simply had to flee to save their necks from the guillotine.

However, there was a time when black artists could find a necessary haven free from racism almost anywhere outside the borders of the United States, but that day, like the "good old days" (if there ever was such a thing), is gone.

America has done a magnificent job of exporting, along with her other commodities, the doctrine that to be white is an infinitely more desirable human state than any other. That may be true at

213

present, but as has been repeatedly pointed out, two-thirds of the earth is populated by people with pigmented faces. And since this country has elected to police the world ("making it safe for freedom," our government constantly assures us), then it is obligated to deal with those pigmented faces on equal terms. Although America has never been—by strict definition, at least—a colonial power, it has, more than any other modern nation, divided the world along color lines. And while a good percentage of the responsibility must be laid to our government's political and militaristic policies, the additional percentage belongs at the portals (wherever they are) of American movies.

John Gunther, in the 1941 edition of *Inside Latin America,* wrote:

> In theory, at least Brazil, which has been justly called the greatest melting pot in the world, has no color line. There are no political or legal discriminations against Negroes or mulattoes; even social discrimination is comparatively rare. Anyone who visits the Copacabana beach any day may see white children playing with black and brown, with parents of assorted colors looking on. One President of the country, Nilo Pecanha, was a dark mulatto; there have been a good many fairly eminent Negro or mulatto scientists, politicians, and men of affairs.
>
> On the other hand, Brazil is certainly no paradise for the black man. The Negroes are, by and large, the poorest members of the population; they do the least pleasant kinds of work; they are the exploited class, especially in the north. And people in Rio tell me that a tendency *toward* discrimination has become discernible lately. One thing that caused this was American movies, with their sharp intimation of the color line. Another is Nazi propaganda. Incidentally, Brazilian newspapers never print news of lynchings in the United States, or anything else that might tend to increase race prejudice.

I tried for the fourth time—within as many years—to find a short-term sanctuary from the daily racial enmity in America. Even the most well-intentioned white does not seem to comprehend that living in an area other than a ghetto continues to be a harrowing and frustrating experience. The simple act of walking into a bar and frequently overhearing someone exclaim to a group, "Why doesn't the nigger go where he belongs," or having your change from a purchase thrown and scattered on the counter by a merchant, is more than enough to make you want to run madly down Fifth Avenue at noon brandishing a gun.

My first effort at locating a prejudice-free environment involved an around-the-world trip. In Europe, I discovered that the thirty-year presence and occupation by American armed forces, and the postwar influx of the affluent "silent majority" had racially polluted the minds of many of the Continent's inhabitants. In Paris—the traditional haven for the world's artists—I often barged into discrimination that bore the unmistakable stamp of white America.

Asia was worse. The closer I got to Vietnam, the greater the racial hostility. In Hong Kong particularly (where many armed forces personnel go for rest and recreation), the racial climate seemed as charged as that in most American cities. An American army officer standing in the lobby of my hotel when I arrived shouted to everyone present that he did not like "niggers" and hoped no one else did either. And all the island's residents with whom I came in contact had apparently absorbed the officer's racial attitude.

During a casual conversation with a white American on a Greek island, I remarked that I was black inside, and would always remain so. And for reasons still inexplicable to me, he flew into a violent rage and warned that I would not leave Greece alive.

I made still another attempt at finding what could now be properly termed Utopia. This time I chose to go south of the border, to a small town deep in the interior of Mexico, uncontaminated, I assumed, by white racism. At first glance the town seemed ideal. There were only a handful of American residents, whom one seldom saw, but it soon became apparent that here, too, the long arm of American racism had reached.

The scarcest commodity in town was milk. There was only one dairyman who sold it at an appointed time each day to the public at large, but when I appeared at his hacienda one afternoon he refused—rather waspishly—to sell me any. Outside, a woman explained that the man did not like "Negroes." She was sorry, she said, and added that he was probably the only person in town who felt that way. However, as any minority-group person knows, if there is one bigot around, there are always more.

How did this man who, perhaps, had seen or glimpsed less than a half-dozen American blacks in his life come by his prejudice? The community (like Mexico itself) was a blazing mixture of human colors, with a majority of the residents being as pigmented or darker than I.

Because of the town's remoteness (approximately a hundred miles southwest of Mexico City) and size, there was little to do at night except attend one of the two movie theaters. And to attend regularly, as almost everyone in town does, constitutes a horrifying study in the racial lethalness of American films. Certainly, no people who receive their primary information about "Negroes" from the medium could fail to become terrified of blackness.

I was never aware before that so many Hollywood films had used Africa as a locale. Despite the great political, social, and economic changes occurring there within the last two decades, the films (and all seemed to have been made in the fifties and sixties) persisted in presenting Africa as the lost, dark continent, populated by stupid, bloodthirsty savages.

Beyond Mombasa, perhaps the worst movie ever made, depicted in one scene the most distorted and grotesque caricatures (as anthropologically accurate) of African tribesmen possibly ever drawn. During the scene, as well as others equally bogus, derisive laughter spread throughout the audience, a reaction much like the reaction I repeatedly witnessed (and participated in) among black audiences in the American South during the forties and fifties. Then the gravest insult one could level at a playmate or friend was to accuse him of having African ancestry. ("My folks ain't no damn apes.")

A more recent film, *The Naked Prey*, offered an excellent study of whitey as supreme. How one unarmed white man (Cornel Wilde) could outwit for countless days, on their own terrain, the warriors of an African tribe remains steadfastly beyond my comprehension. But then, none of the films attempted to deal with the African as a complex human with a complex culture.

Highly revealing, too, were such *innocent* products as *To Sir, with Love.* In the United States the film was dismissed by serious critics as corn flakes, but viewing it within the confines of a small, foreign town moves one to a more deadly conclusion. It imposes (in Gunther's words) "a sharp intimation of the color line" by treating blackness as a gimmick (as most of the current "black" Hollywood films do), rather than firm reality.

Needless to say, many of the superbudgeted films like *Star* ignored the existence of the black man altogether. (How can any *musical* film do so?) Others, like the German-made *Uncle Tom's Cabin,* added nothing to the revelation of slavery, but rather perpetrated white history's simplistic version of the institution and the idyllic relationships (the kindly master and Uncle Tom) which probably did not exist. And the list goes on and on with films (most of them third-rate) that either malign the black man or, like *Crack in the World,* set in Africa, contemptuously ignore him altogether.

Just as ominous is Mexico's increasing adoption of the black-white theme in its films and literature. Particularly outrageous is *Memin Pinguin,* a popular weekly black comic-book character who by physical comparison makes the Gold Dust twins look Nordic. Memin (as well as his mother, a black mammy type complete with bandanna) is the prototype of the comic-strip darky who was finally expunged from American films, literature, and art during the early sixties. In a recent issue of the series, mother and son suffer discrimination from a taxi driver ("Why don't the she-bear and her cub get a truck to transport them!"), supposing an act and situation that presently does not exist in Mexico and would not be tolerated, but which certainly does not fail to implant an idea.

And if the few Mexican movies (about 65 percent of the films shown in the town were American made) I saw are indicative of what the film makers in Mexico are into, then there really is great cause for alarm. For the performers are white-faced and the movies as imitative of any out of Hollywood, London, or Rome, virtually ignoring the beauty and splendor of Mexico's vast culture and multiracial population.

Americans—those who care about such things—do not yet seem

fully to realize that the world's people appropriate many of America's ideas and lifestyles. Though Mexicans, like other peoples, profess hatred for the gringo, they are still awed and impressed by his technology, and they tend—especially the rapidly emerging middle classes—to assume and absorb, along with better things, his worst attitudes.

That is the primary reason why black people who, of late, are "making it" to some degree, cannot sit back and graciously denounce racism upon request, or when it personally benefits their careers. Nor can they continue to do their own isolated thing, assuming that the individual image of a successful black will greatly affect the course of all the hopeless and the trapped. They have to come up with some imaginative and collective schemes that will concretely help every black in this country—raise and maintain the esteem of blacks everywhere.

It has always infuriated me that black entertainers, earning tens of thousands of dollars, have not banded together (in recent years, certainly) and formed their own movie company, a large corporation that would employ hundreds of actors, technicians, and writers to produce dozens of films and television series yearly on every aspect of black life. And it can be done! Millions for civil rights activities are raised through benefit performances, and I see no reason why exactly the same method—along with stock participation by the black public—cannot be employed for establishing such a film corporation.

Visually, the central problem for the black man has always been that of one image at a time. Currently, it's the militant image that, by itself, is just as one-dimensional and stereotyped as former ones. No people ever get a sense of their wholeness (and worth) unless they are deluged and inundated by their art to the point where all shades of their personality and character are familiar. And then it becomes unnecessary ever to ask, as *Cotton Comes to Harlem* doggedly does, an artless, dumb, and begging question like, "Is it black enough?"

Blacks in this country have always proclaimed that they know the white man inside out and yet curiously they have failed to use that knowledge for their own economic self-interest, and continue to let whites flagrantly exploit them. Last year (according to *Time* magazine), blacks spent $39 billion on "goods and services," with most of those billions going to further enrich the white community. Clearly, this is an intolerable situation. Blacks must begin to use their economic resources, as imaginatively as they have their creative powers. If they do not, then whites will go on savagely and ruthlessly exploiting them in every way, and who, then, is finally to blame?

Melvin Van Peebles

3   A Black Odyssey:
Sweet Sweetback's Baadasssss Song

[1971]

February 1970 I'm driving north along a highway looking for a
place to turn off into the Mojave. I have this idea about commun-
ing with myself in the bosom of the wilderness, proving once again
that we are part, at least in part, of all that we were programmed
to dance to even way back in good old Sunday school—right—but
anyway, for the last thirty miles or so, ever since I had hit the
"real" desert (or what looked "real" to me, having never been to
the desert before, legit or otherwise, my expertise coming from—
you guessed it) the western wilderness of our pioneer forefathers
et cetera had been fenced off with barbed wire on both sides of
the road with a warning posted at regular intervals saying NO
TRESPASSING AIR FORCE GUNNERY RANGE, or something like that.
From time to time there would be a gate, but I let it slide by; I
could just see myself getting strafed in mid-meditation. Finally
the gunnery range on the left-hand side ended, but I drove on to
give myself kentucky windage against super-piss-poor shots.

AHA!—a road. I turned off the highway. Right away, the road
dwindled into just a trail leading over a little hill. I drive over the
rise and there I am in the real desert, sand-wise and solitude-wise
just like I always imagined it would be. The only thing breaking
the sky-meeting-desert horizon was electricity in the form of an
endless row of huge pylons carrying wires. I gravitated toward the
pylons, being from the city, and parked the car in a little dip. I
got out of the car and squatted down facing the sun. I unbuttoned

my fly, leaned back against the front fender of the car, getting myself comfortable, and pulled out my pecker and began to beat my meat. I was on a mission.

Something was troubling me, some idea was lurking back there in my mind waiting for the coast to clear to be born. That's what I was trying to do with the sun in my face and my prick in my hand, trying to clear my stage, trying to take a shortcut to Purityville so that whatever it was would come out and rap to me. I knew me well enough to realize that I would probably end up going along with the lurking blob back there and I hoped it was at least something I approved of.

I used to not get along with me because the ME I WANTED TO BELIEVE I WAS was always battling with the ME I REALLY WAS. The REALLY WAS always won, naturally, but not before a great deal of time and energy had passed under the old bridge and reams of tension and tape and general bullshit had constipated and polluted me around. Anyway, one day I figured out "Shit," in the name of efficiency, if nothing else, why don't I just do from the start what I am going to end up doing in the end anyway. It sounds simple as can be and maybe for everybody else it is.

When the ME I WANTED TO BELIEVE I WAS was running the show, it vacillated, procrastinated, and the destination was always out of focus, and goals were usually changed in midstream, whereas the ME I REALLY WAS was clear eyed, firm treaded, straight as an arrow and level headed and could always explain concisely and precisely what the ME I WANTED TO BELIEVE was doing wrong. Of course being a guilty bystander of the modern western deification of the "NATURAL," I attributed all my wishy-washy woes and general fuzzy bullshit to the fact that the REAL ME was not at the helm. Anyway, to-make-a-long-story-short, despite Herculean difficulties, I finally managed to install the REAL ME in power. Things improved, but just a little bit, nowheres near the sharp Jack Armstrong-cum-Horatio Alger bulls-eye type progress I had projected. In fact when the REAL ME I just knew was infallible gained control, its clear eyes began to glaze and its firm tread began to wobble and hyperbole continued to be the order of the day. Maybe the

REAL ME had been held in second position so long it had a guilt complex about leading or something.

So I came up with this distilling program. I would decide what I wanted and analyze how to get there with as much dispassion, distance, and intelligence I could muster up. Not only did this help me check out my motives and organize my thoughts, it provided me with a yardstick to judge myself with on the way and it provided me with a beam to stay on course once I had stepped into the forest, leaped into the soup.

I called this my UP-FRONT AIMS PROGRAM; the name wasn't lyricism itself maybe, but the program worked.

Normally when I felt some milestone or other coming on, I would hibernate for a few days or weeks, however long it took, until my spirit was clean enough for my muse's taste. Then my muse would come out and introduce the project or whatever. (Then if the idea passed my inspection, more or less a formality —it always passed, I had the veto power but was afraid to use it— I would give it my up-front aims program processing.)

I was in a time bind, so I was trying this new experimental crash method. I called it semenshock. Maybe I could have brought a girl or a couple of girls with me to ball but that would have meant dividing my attention. That's why I decided on using my good old childhood, Mrs. Thumbs-and-her-four-daughters method. Intellectually, you see, it all made sense but just like years ago, intellectually or not, I was ashamed of getting caught AT IT. I was even ashamed of having the phone ring while I was doing IT. Even if I didn't answer it, I KNEW they would KNOW. Anyway, to make a long story short, that's what and why I was behind a dune, crouched down by the car pounding away at my joint.

Anyway, what am I apologizing for, they have electroshock, so why not semenshock. I even saw this jive-ass movie once where the doctor used racial-shock. This negro soldier had a traumatic war experience and couldn't walk and the doctor couldn't find anything wrong, so in the film's big scene the white doctor calls him a BLACK (a big NO NO at the time) dumb nigger coward and veins stand out on the brother's noble colored features and he struggles to rise! . . . He stands! . . . (Look, he's standing . . . Oh, look he's so angry he doesn't even notice) . . . The brother makes a faltering pace toward the doctor, then another . . . You're walking, the doctor says . . . The brother realizes he is walking and collapses with joy and is caught by the Great White Father once again. (Completely unrealistic because as Uncle Tommy as that nigger had been, he wouldn't have raised his hand to a white man to even save his own Mammy.) Then the doctor apologizes and tells him that he wouldn't really call him nigger except that that was the only way to get him better fast and that there was a war on and that they were short of beds and besides they were all Americans and that the country was beginning to realize what a great contribution its colored folks, etc.

Yum-yum (pound, pound) yum-yum (pound) oh heavenly (pound). Goddamn, just THEN my muse announced it was ready to escort the idea forward.

Here I am, it said, cool it, brother, I said. (It seems my semen scheme was succeeding but I was too heavily occupied to get into it.)

Yum-yum (pound, change hands, pound). Yum—I'll be right with you—yum. Amen-yum. My muse copped an attitude, you suppose to be trying to get in touch with me . . . I'm your reason for being here. Yeah, yum, right (pound, pound) yum-yum, with you.

WHAM, SHAZAM, I leaned forward automatically (with the experience that comes from years of turning my brain matter gray and growing hairs in my palms) to keep from soiling my pants.

My first thought was that the entire thing had been a set-up to rationalize my beating my meat and that I was pretty Goddamn old to be out in the sand and sagebrush masturbating. Then I realized that it had worked after all—that the muse had rolled the stone away from the cave. I peered into me and saw I was tired of the Man (this was new, already?) but there was more. I was going to do my OWN movie.

My ME I WANTED TO BELIEVE I WAS (or maybe it WAS ME) starts right in on its sabotage trying to talk me out of it. Who do you think you are, a big film?

Yes, a big film.

You don't look much like a Director to me, let alone a Producer, standing there with your fly all open. (I zipped up my pants.)

What about the story?

No problem, I got an idea (I lied).

What idea?

A brother . . . A brother getting it all together, you dig . . . and no cop out.

What about bread if it's going to be such a big film? . . . And what do you know about producing, mother fucker?

A Producer produces, mother fucker.

I was walking through the desert. I turned at the top of a mound. The car was tiny in the distance.

I'll get the bread, I'll get it, I told me.

How about the Unions hassling you?

I'll have tight security, what they don't know won't hurt me.

I didn't let myself get intimidated either . . . I'm going to have fifty percent of the folks on the crew too . . . I was really getting into the thing . . . Guerilla Cinema. The idea seemed like it had always existed. I drove back to L.A. It all made sense, in ghetto-wise theory, anyway.

When I did *Watermelon Man,* I had gotten a brother into the producing end. I figured that it would be out of sight if I could pick up the bread from the get-go even before I wrote the script. Usually all the producing cats went around trying to put super-high-priced deals together, "packaging" as they call it:

I'll get such and such a star use L as the Director he'll be hot right after this new one comes out a smash baby my friend knows the prop man and he said the crew stayed in stitches anyway I've got a writer one of the biggest who wants to do the screenplay he'll work on spec he's so excited about the treatment he was playing tennis with Ralphie and he dropped him a hint and he's begging me to let him take it to the front office now . . . (Ad infinitum) . . .

That's packaging, baby.

I went to see the brother and we power-handshaked each other for a half hour and did how-you-doing-my-man and same-old-same-old to each other for another half hour then finally got down to it. I told him about the film and asked him for financing suggestions.

Sure he could help me he knew this actress and she had a friend at the front office of Warner's and with his music connections plus he was going to play tennis with J.D. and he would drop him a hint and he'd be begging to let him take it to the front office . . . etc.

O.K., so you can't win them all; anyway, it was a long shot.

First things first. And the first thing was the script. What did I want to accomplish scriptwise? I wanted to take another step in getting the Man's foot out of my ass.

Actually I knew the answer to that question before I asked it. But I wanted to fulfill fully the questionnaire part of my UP-FRONT AIMS PROGRAM. To get the Man's foot out of my ass means to me logically to get the Man's foot out of all our black asses. This seems to me an apparent truth, but many of the buszwazee brothers don't seem to realize it. They don't seem to understand that they are not free as long as their other brothers are still in slavery. (If they would get out of some of those limousines once in a while and even try and catch a cab or two, the truth would come home to them very rapidly.)

Anyway, next step, how specifically to get the Man's foot out of our ass. The first beachhead, the very first thing that we must do is to reconquer our own minds. The biggest obstacle to the black revolution in America is our conditioned susceptibility to the white man's program. In short, the fact is that the white man has colonized our minds. We've been violated, confused, and drained by this colonization and from this brutal, calculated genocide, the most effective and vicious racism has grown, and it is with this starting point in mind and the intention to reverse the process that I went into cinema in the first fucking place.

"Where is Brer?" I asked me, he was digging TV, movies, and the sounds. But TV was out; television at this stage of the game, as it is practiced in America at least, is not a feasible tool for carrying really relevant ideas to the minds of the disenfranchised. The umbilical cord from the TV program to its sponsor is short and very vital and can be cut abruptly, too abruptly for a program to get away with pushing any extra-uppity ideas. Each thing must be self-contained breadwise. Artistically, we must be guerilla units too. Each project must be a self-contained unit, otherwise it will be subject to the inevitable slings and arrows of outrageous racist economic pressures.

Anyway, storywise, I came up with an idea, why not the direct approach. Since what I want is the Man's foot out of our collective asses, why not make the film about a brother *getting* the Man's foot out of his ass. That was going to be the thing.

Now to avoid putting myself into a corner and writing something that I wouldn't be able to shoot, I made a list of the givens in the situation and tried to take those givens and juggle them into the final scenario.

GIVEN:
1. NO COP OUT.
    A. I wanted a victorious film. A film where niggers could walk out standing tall instead of avoiding each other's eyes, looking once again like they'd had it.

2. MUST LOOK AS GOOD AS ANYTHING CHUCK EVER DID.
    (Very touchy, discouraging, delicate point. One of the problems faced by a black film maker—in fact any American independent film maker who wants to produce his own feature, just more so for a brother—is that Hollywood polishes its product with such a great deal of slickness and expensive perfection that it ups the ante. That is, if I made a film in black and white with poor sound, even if it had all the revolutionary and even story elements that anyone could hope it would have, brother would come out saying, well, shit, niggers can't do anything right. I saw such and such a film in color and 35 mm. and so on and so on, how come we have to make such rinky-dink stuff. Not realizing of

course that the price of freedom is often poverty of means.
Well, I felt that this problem was a little too involved to
attack, so I was determined that the film was going to look
as good as anything one of the major studios could turn
out.)

3. ENTERTAINMENTWISE, A MOTHER FUCKER.
(I had no illusion about the attention level of people brain-
washed to triviality.)
   A. The film simply couldn't be a didactic discourse that
   would end up playing (if I could find a distributor) to an
   empty theater except for ten or twenty aware brothers
   who would pat me on the back and say it tells it like it is.
   B. If Brer is bored, he's bored. One of the problems we
   must face squarely is that to attract the mass we have
   to produce work that not only instructs but entertains.
   C. It must be able to sustain itself as a viable commercial
   product or there is no power base. The Man has an
   Achilles pocket and he might go along with you if at
   least there is some bread in it for him. But he ain't
   about to go carrying no messages for you, especially a
   relevant one, for free.

4. A LIVING WORKSHOP
   A. I wanted 50 percent of my shooting crew to be third-
   world people. (This could conflict with point 2 if a script
   was not developed extremely carefully.) So at best a stag-
   gering amount of my crew would be relatively inexperi-
   enced. Specifically, this meant that any type of film
   requiring an enormous technical sophistication at the
   shooting stage should not be attempted.

5. BREAD
   A. SHORT! SHORT! SHORT!
   B. Normal financing channels probably closed.

6. MONKEY WRENCHING.
   A. I would have to expect a great deal of animosity from the
   film media (white in the first place and right wing in the
   second) at all levels of film making. (I would have to
   double check my flanks at all times and not expose myself
   to the possibility of active racism, in everything from

keeping tight security about the "real" script to choosing
locations to dealing with the labs and perhaps a portion
of the cast and crew too. As costly as it would be, I felt
I would have to leave myself a security margin.)

7. UNKNOWNS AND VARIABLES.
   A. CALIBER OF ACTORS.
   B. CALIBER OF CREW.
   I would have to write a flexible script where emphasis
   could be shifted. In short, stay loose.

I suppose I could have made an infinite list of liabilities and
assets, especially liabilities . . . but anyway.

(ASSET 1.) I kept asking myself what could I do that Hollywood major studios couldn't. The thing that kept occurring to
me was that I could delve into the black community as they would
never be able to do because of their cumbersome technology and
their lack of empathy.

(POSSIBILITY 1.) Something begins to jell. Strange how you
store things. Somewhere I read an interview with this big director
where the interviewer asked how he managed to get away with
such audacious shots. He replied something to the effect that as
long as you kept the story moving, you can put the camera anywhere you want and cut anywhere you desire. WHAMMO. I
decided I would pack the scenario with enough action for three
Goddamn films so I would be able to get away with anything. I
would even use triple or quadruple screen effects like they do to
prop up television detective stories if I had to.

(OPPORTUNITY 1.) Most film makers look at a feature in
terms of image and story, or vice versa. Effects and music (most
directors can't carry a tune in a fucking bucket) are strictly
secondary considerations. Very few look at film with sound considered as a creative third dimension. So I calculate the scenario
in such a way that sound can be used as an integral part of the
film.

I would have to choose a story line strong enough to provide
continuity, but simple enough to give enough room for digression
without losing its directness. I approached the film like you do
the cupboard when you're broke and hungry: throw in every-

thing eatable and hope to come out on top with the seasoning, i.e., by editing.

A couple of the unknowns still bothered me. To keep this strong story line going, I felt I would have to use one actor as the principal vehicle that I could hinge others things onto. Next, I had decided to use cameos, but because of the looseness of their construction, I couldn't foresee the exact running time of the film, so I devised an accordion section for the film that could be lengthened or shortened according to the time consumed by the various other parts of the script.

All this shit swarmed around and around in my head. About this time I had a burden lifted, it dawned on me that I was in charge, and whereas I usually try to impart in my work the idea of getting the Man's foot out of our ass without letting it show to the Man too soon, I did not have to do that this time. So I thought, well, why don't I then, since this could be it, why don't I make a film directly about, accent the positive, what I'm all about, what we are all about. That is, it would be the story itself of a man getting the Man's foot out of his ass that on close examination would fit the necessity of the script for a strong, action-packed story line if it were told in that way. That's where it's at.

(TITLE) The media is a very important part of the message and that's why I called it *SWEET SWEETBACK'S BAADASSSSS SONG*, instead of some phony shit with a subtitle about it being made for brothers and sisters. With that title they would know.

The end is all very well and good and the number-one priority. However, in the meantime, if a way can be devised to make the means productive, you're that much more ahead of the game. I was trying to utilize all the potential of the film and I hoped to get double duty. Not only a film per se, but since I was using a large percentage of disenfranchised people, a self-sustaining workshop situation. When you are funded by a group, when you are not self-sufficient, if you become too relevant for the particular taste of the funding group (at any stage of the game), the Man can pull the economic rug right out from under you. So the film also had this other aspect to it. I looked at it as a workshop situation where people carry the fight onward while at the same time they're gaining the necessary technical knowledge to be even more effective in the struggle for the minds of third-world people and other people of good will.

I got myself a piece of brown wrapping paper and got on the floor where I could work comfortably. I noted all the givens, unknowns, liabilities, assets, and opportunities as best I could. One thing I was sure of, it was going to be done in 35 mm. and in color. Sometimes I get the impression when I'm seeing a movie, that guy set out saying to himself, "Just how much bread can I waste, just how much bread can I utilize on this project?" Sometimes I get the impression that the cost of the film often has more to do with the directors' and producers' egos than with the project itself. Often they want to see how much money they can control, i.e., how much they are loved or how bright they are. Sometimes the other side of the coin is their thing—just how much the cost can be cut down and still have the public sit through ninety minutes of that particular subject. It's sort of a feast-or-famine thing.

I knew we would be very short of bread and so I tried to judge this thing as pessimistically as possible. After devising a low-budget film, I then added touches that would only be found in the most expensive film. In other words, I tried to make a low-budget film without the low budget, but with the advantages of both.

The biggest problem looming in front of me was how I was going to get away with shooting the film with my brand-new reputation as a major film director. I knew I would be watched and the unions could make it extremely difficult for me to make a major film. The answer was so obvious I didn't see it for a few minutes. The unions don't trouble themselves over smut films, that is, pornographic films, which I suppose they consider beneath their dignity, and there is even an entire parallel distribution circuit for these films. So I went to Nutsville to cover my project and told everyone I was making a beaver film. (Beaver is Californese for vagina.)

Voila. There it was on my piece of brown wrapping paper. Then I gave it to my secretary and the final draft was finished on March 6 at 6:20 p.m., 1970. I knew it was March 6 at 6:20 p.m. because

I didn't use the title on the front page, not wanting to freak out the copyright people. I simply put the date. Two weeks and three days had passed since the time when I had leaned my back against the car in the desert and unzipped my fly.

Charles Michener

1   Black Movies

[1972]

MORAL: A BAADASSSSS NIGGER IS COMING BACK TO
COLLECT SOME DUES.
—Postscript to Melvin Van Peebles's film,
Sweet Sweetback's Baadasssss Song

What Van Peebles warned has come to pass. All over the country,
"bad-ass niggers" are collecting dues with a vengeance—and if
you don't believe it, just head downtown for a movie. Outside the
old silver-screen palaces on New York's Times Square, along Chicago's Loop, in downtown Detroit, the crowds are young, mostly
black, and bigger than they've been since Scarlett O'Hara ran
off with Rhett Butler. Inside, the furious action on celluloid is
pointed toward the triumph of black good over white evil; audiences are whooping it up with such glee that projectionists must
jack up the volume during the climaxes, and theater owners are
counting more dollars than they've handled in years. The black
movie explosion is on—and the controversial fallout is just beginning to settle.

Van Peebles set it off—and set the tone—when he vowed more
than two years ago to "get the Man's foot out of all our black
asses" by making a film "about a brother *getting* the Man's foot
out of his ass." The result was the gritty, profane *Sweetback*, a
mythic opus about a black stud's successful revolt against white
society, which grossed $11 million—an amazing success for a movie

235

made and distributed completely outside established industry channels. A couple of months later, Gordon Parks came out with the equally low-budget *Shaft*, about a black private eye, which by year's end had racked up $12 million in North America and single-handedly rescued MGM from near financial ruin.

Never slow to read handwriting that's punctuated with dollar signs, Hollywood quickly took note of two facts: first, whites had begun to flee the inner cities, vacating many big downtown theaters and leaving a vacuum for the burgeoning number of black moviegoers to fill; second, blacks would turn out in far greater numbers for films that featured black heroes and heroines and plenty of sex and violence than they would for white adventure flicks. In short order, the studio bosses began restocking—and re-vamping—their arsenals.

Talented black actors, directors, and writers were suddenly plucked out of studio back rooms, modeling agencies, and ghetto theaters, and turned loose on new black projects. White heroes of scripts that had been lying on the shelf were instantly converted into black heroes and sent scurrying before the cameras. Much of the white trash emerged as black trash and was quickly buried after release. But an astonishing number of black films have been paying off at a rate to put their white counterparts in the shade—and in the process have not only produced the first gold mine in years for a struggling industry, but also have split the United States black community into those who justify or at least discriminate among the films, and those for whom the entire phenomenon is a violent blow to black dignity and social well-being.

Of this year's Westerns [1972], the two biggest nuggets are black —*Buck and the Preacher* ($9 million gross so far), in which Sidney Poitier and Harry Belafonte lead ex-slaves to a new life in the West, and *The Legend of Nigger Charley* ($5 million), in which ex-profootball star Fred Williamson goes from slavery to gunfighting. Tops in the action genre are *Shaft*'s sequel, *Shaft's Big Score* ($10 million), which again features Richard Roundtree as the supercool John Shaft, foiling a gang of white hoods; *Melinda* ($5 million), with Calvin Lockhart as a Los Angeles disk jockey wiping out white gangsters who have murdered his girl friend;

Cool Breeze, a black remake of *The Asphalt Jungle*; *Slaughter*, with Jim Brown also doing in the mob; and the just-released *Hammer*, with Fred Williamson, using his old football nickname, as a boxer who won't go crooked.

A Potential Explosiveness

American International Pictures has a bonanza in the first all-black vampire movie—*Blacula*—which turns America's favorite Transylvanian bloodsucker into an accursed ex-African prince. And *Come Back Charleston Blue*, the sequel to 1970s *Cotton Comes to Harlem*, has already pulled in $7 million with the antics of Godfrey Cambridge and Raymond St. Jacques as Harlem cops who destroy a black dope lord. Finally, there's *Super Fly*, directed by Gordon Parks, Jr., which in a little more than two months is up to $11 million and is currently outgrossing every other movie on the market—black or white—with its offbeat tale of a black cocaine pusher (Ron O'Neal) who not only beats the system—both the mob and the cops—but gets out with a cool half-million.

All this is only the beginning. On their way in the next four months are Van Peebles's film of his Broadway musical play, *Don't Play Us Cheap*, a biography of Billie Holiday, *Lady Sings the Blues*, starring Diana Ross, and a score of entertainments with titles like *Blackenstein*, *Black Gun*, *Black Majesty*, *Blackfather*, *Black Christ*, and *The Werewolf from Watts*, as well as *Hit Man*, *The Book of Numbers*, *Trick Baby*, and *Cleopatra Jones*. In an industry that has recently been producing little more than two hundred films a year, fully one-fourth of those now in the planning stage are black.

A long overdue avenue to success for black talent and a kick for hungry black moviegoers, the phenomenon has nonetheless drawn considerable fire from many black intellectuals, political leaders, and laymen who are mounting protests against the industry and picketing theaters for showing the allegedly pro-drug *Super Fly*. The situation has explosive potential—recently several cars were fire-bombed at the office of American International Pictures in Hollywood, following a meeting with a black group; and there have been reports of an unexploded bomb at Warner Bros. and a burning shed at Fox, which Fox denies.

Many of the talented blacks who are involved in making these movies are torn between conflicting attitudes about their value and significance. Robert Hooks is a leading black actor, a co-founder and director of the outstanding Negro Ensemble Company in New York, who is currently organizing the D.C. Black Repertory Company in predominantly black Washington. Like other serious actors, such as Calvin Lockhart, Rosalind Cash, and William Marshall, Hooks is ambivalent about his participation in the black movie explosion. In the forthcoming *Trouble Man*, he plays T, a ghetto hustler who's hired, like a fast-sword samurai in a Japanese Western, to settle the rivalry between two racket gangs in Los Angeles. "The only interesting subject left for the American stage or screen is the black man," says Hooks. "So these producers have obviously found a good thing to make money on. But for the most part they have been doing these films in bad taste." Still, Hooks hopes that *Trouble Man* (which was directed by black actor Ivan Dixon) will be "a different kind of film."

Charges of Treason

There is no such ambivalence in the attitude of black community leaders such as Junius Griffin, head of the Beverly Hills-Hollywood branch of the NAACP. Says the angry Griffin: "We must insist that our children are not constantly exposed to a steady diet of so-called black movies that glorify black males as pimps, dope pushers, gangsters, and super males with vast physical prowess but no cognitive skills." The danger of this fantasy, adds black critic Clayton Riley, is "to reinforce the ordinary black human being's sense of personal helplessness and inadequacy."

Black Panther chieftain Huey Newton finds the films dangerously counterrevolutionary (though he exempts *Sweetback* and *Buck and the Preacher*): "They leave revolution out or, if it's in, they make it look stupid and naïve. I think it's part of a conspiracy." And Tony Brown, dean of Howard University's school of communications and producer of educational television's "Black

Journal," lays the blame squarely with the blacks themselves. "The blaxploitation films," he says, "are a phenomenon of self-hate. Look at the image of *Super Fly*. Going to see yourself as a drug dealer when you're oppressed is sick. Not only are blacks identifying with him, they're paying for the identification. It's sort of like a Jew paying to get into Auschwitz. Those blacks who contribute to the making of these films," adds Brown, "no matter how they rationalize it, are guilty of nothing less than 'treason.'"

Vigorous Defense

But those involved with the black films countercharge that the critics are obtuse, overwrought, and condescending to their own people. "It's ridiculous," says Gordon Parks, "to imply that blacks don't know the difference between truth and fantasy and therefore will be influenced by these films in an unhealthy way. I knew a black preacher in Chicago and I remember people who wanted to kill their white bosses coming to the prayer meeting and being calmed down by the preacher. These movies are serving the same therapeutic function."

Ron O'Neal, who plays Priest, the victorious pusher in *Super Fly*, argues that the film's critics are simply out of touch. "The plot is so old hat to every kid in Harlem," he says. "Blacks are no longer interested in perpetuating the old myths. The critics of *Super Fly* want to support the myth that crime doesn't pay. But we all happen to know that crime *is* paying off for some people every day." And James Earl Jones, who plays the first black president in *The Man*, says: "If they're going to put the damper on John Shaft let them put it on John Wayne too and they'll find out that there are a lot of people who need those fantasies."

Ex-footballers Jim Brown and Fred Williamson claim that they are doing no more on screen than they did on the gridiron—and for that matter, no more than white screen heroes have been doing all along. "Where were the black critics when Cagney, Bogart, and Raft were doing their thing?" growls Williamson. "When I was a kid, I played Hopalong Cassidy and nobody hit me in the mouth and said, 'Don't be that way.'"

When Williamson was a kid, of course, there were no black Hopalongs to imitate. Black movies had been around since the early talkies (King Vidor's 1929 *Hallelujah* was the first distinguished all-sound film) but until recently, the black image on screen ran through a short spectrum from the shuffling Stepin Fetchit on the one hand, to the noble but amenable Sidney Poitier on the other—both outsiders in an alien society they were bound to accept, both fully acceptable to white sensibilities. Now the tables are turned. In the world of the new black film, the white man is the outsider—and rarely is he acceptable to black sensibilities.

It is a turnabout achieved with little regard for subtlety. When Jim Brown beds down Stella Stevens in *Slaughter*, the camera follows his brawny black hand across her pale white skin with almost palpable relish. The dumb white police sergeant whom Cambridge and St. Jacques dupe in *Charleston Blue* wouldn't survive a day on a real Harlem beat. In the climactic mayhem in *Melinda*, Lockhart not only uses karate and guns to wipe out the white mobsters, but delivers a battery of well-placed kicks to their groins. Some of the turnabout seems merely cosmetic. Who, after all, is Richard Roundtree as John Shaft, with his seedy office, withering wisecracks, and testy police relations, but a darker version of Sam Spade in *The Maltese Falcon?* And aren't Moses Gunn, as the suavely malevolent black syndicate king, and Drew Bundini Brown, as his trigger-happy punk bodyguard, really Sidney Greenstreet and Elisha Cook, Jr. in blackface?

They are and—more importantly—they aren't. For beyond the titillation of sex and violence, beyond the slick reworkings of tried-and-true formulas, what really turns on the black audience was best put by a black girl and boy after they saw *Super Fly* last week in Washington, D.C. "*Super Fly*," said the girl, "is what's happening right here on the street. That's the way it is." "Priest," said the boy, of the film's dope-pushing hero, "is super fine and super bad."

Hot off the Streets

Unlike most white escapist fare with its never-never landscapes of purple sage and alpine luxury, the strongest of the new black films are firmly rooted in the audience's own backyards—*Super Fly, Charleston Blue,* and *Shaft* in the squalid, decayed slums of Harlem, *Melinda* in barren, bleached-out Watts. The spectacular Eldorado Cadillac driven by Priest in *Super Fly* gets quick recognition from some of the Harlem members of the audience, because it actually belongs to K.C., a well-known Harlem pimp who plays himself in the film.

Unlike the James Bond movies' clubby repartee, the last languid gasps of Bulldog Drummond, Jimmy Valentine, and their upper-crust ilk, the sardonic black dialogue is hot off the streets—funky, profane, frankly shocking to many middle-class whites in its sexual references, especially the ubiquitous "mother-f----"—but with a pungent authenticity, especially in the better films such as *Super Fly.* (With an eye toward future TV feasibility, many of the films are shot with alternate scenes and dialogue. Where Roundtree in *Shaft* says "I'm gonna kill that mother-f----," Gordon Parks shot an alternate scene for TV in which Shaft snarls, "I'm gonna kill that granny-dodger.")

It is hard to gauge the true influence of these movies, especially on young blacks. The newest rage among black youths at one Los Angeles high school is to wear their hair straightened and flowing, to sport wide-lapelled midi coats, and to adorn themselves with tiny silver crosses and "coke spoons" around their necks—all à la Priest in *Super Fly.* But more important than clothes or hair is the "super bad" appeal of these movies. "A swift fist and a stiff penis, that's the Shaftian way" is how Clayton Riley sums up their morality. But there is more involved than that. Gordon Stulberg, the much-respected head of Twentieth Century-Fox, believes that "black films give blacks much more opportunity to feel vicariously in control of their environment than whites get from James Bond movies." And indeed, control is first among virtues in these movies: grace under pressure (whether in bed or in the precinct house), mastery of self-defense (by karate or judo), and above all, a hatred for heroin—the main tool of oppression and self-oppression.

At bottom, though, the black films may have more of a political dimension than any of the militant critics suspect. For with the exception of Jim Brown, whose prepotent Slaughter is the only black in an all-white world, the new black heroes are not odd men out, in the white tradition of Cagney, Bogart, and John Garfield, but odd men in—who only venture out of their close-knit black community to become invincible guerrillas in the white community.

Apart from *Super Fly* midi coats, and the like, there is little tangible evidence so far that life on the street has begun to imitate art. But Hollywood's sudden greed for black movies has aroused a sense of power among the new breed of black actors, writers, and directors. Once again, the cue was given by Melvin Van Peebles, who hustled his way past studio brass and the unions to win total and final control over *Sweetback*. Since then, no other black film maker has matched that precedent—though *Super Fly*'s makers successfully imitated Van Peebles's word-of-mouth marketing strategy by previewing the film, not to critics, but to pimps and hairdressers in Harlem.

Even so, black outspokenness about the content of their studio-controlled films is on the increase—and already there have been several notable victories. It was at actor William Marshall's insistence that his role of Blacula was changed from that of a black American paying a social visit to Transylvania to that of an African prince seeking an end to the slave trade—before he falls into the clutches of Dracula. In playing the clap-trappy part, says his costar Vonetta McGee, "Marshall gave so much dignity that you're crying for him in the end."

Fighting for Human Elements

Hired to direct Twentieth's *Trouble Man*, Ivan Dixon discovered that the script had the leading black female character, played by Paula Kelly, jumping in and out of bed like a cat in heat, and called the NAACP in to negotiate a change. And three of the most outspoken black talents around—director Hugh Robertson, writer Lonne Elder III, and actress Rosalind Cash—took one look at MGM's original script for *Melinda* and plunged into a battle that ended with the conversion of hopeless trash into stylish and diverting trash.

"I had to fight and fight for any human elements in the story," recalls Robertson, who previously had edited *Shaft*. "They kept pushing for all sex and violence. I had to insist on the dinner scene between Melinda [Vonetta McGee] and Frankie [Calvin Lockhart] so we could see some kind of relationship between them, not just bring her into the story and suddenly have her dead the next morning. And I had to fight to keep a scene between Frankie and Terry [Rosalind Cash] that shows her as a black woman who's strong and a real person."

Says Cash, a fine stage actress: "I'm proud of what I did with Terry. When I go up to Harlem, the hard-working soul sisters come up to me and say, 'You were for real in that part; I know what that character was all about.' " And Elder, who wrote the prize-winning play *Ceremonies in Dark Old Men*, sums up his Hollywood experience in general by recalling what one big studio executive once said to him: "They want s--- and we're giving them s---."

It's that kind of exploitative—and racist—attitude that has so many veteran black activists up in arms, and to combat it with more than words, they are trying to apply various kinds of pressure to the movie industry. Some of them have rallied to the idea that black films can be used as wedges to make, as one puts it, "the industry pay its dues to the black community"—in money. In Seattle, black owners of a black neighborhood theater have brought suit against a white-owned organization, claiming the right to share in the first-run distribution of *Super Fly*. New York militants have made Harlem virtually out-of-bounds to major film makers with a variety of demands, ranging from an increased proportion of blacks on shooting crews to direct payments to "community organizations."

The Price of Security

And in order to shoot *The Mack* (street slang for glorified pimp) in the Oakland ghetto, white producer Harvey Bernhard had to donate five thousand dollars to the community via the Black Panthers, hired twenty mostly black "security guards" at ten dollars an hour—and still ran into trouble. According to Panther leader Huey Newton, Bernhard's checks bounced and were made good only when Newton threatened to picket. (Bernhard left Oakland prematurely and is now finishing the film in Los Angeles.)

Still other activists are batting around such ideas as a separate rating system for black movies and a black review board to screen scripts before production. Internal bickering has prevented members of the newly formed Coalition Against Blaxploitation in Los Angeles from doing anything with these hot potatoes—out of mindfulness, perhaps, of Jim Brown's fierce admonition: "That's like being under Hitler. I don't want a black or a white Hitler."

Plausible or not, such pressures are having their effect on white movie moguls. MGM's president, James Aubrey, pointedly refused to grant *Newsweek* an interview, leaving the impression that he wanted to lie low until all the controversy had blown over. According to actor Raymond St. Jacques, one group of executives decided to do a black film, then nervously converted all the characters into Puerto Ricans.

As Brown and several other blacks with clout see it, the key to better black films—and bigger payoff to blacks—is to get wealthy blacks involved in the capitalization of new films, just as two black dentists were in the financing of *Super Fly*. "We're allowing white producers to make money off us in our major market like we've done through the years," says Brown. "We've got the capital if blacks would only give it up." Recently, Roy Innes, director of CORE, announced that his organization intended to enter the business, but the wherewithal to do so has not yet appeared. Jesse Jackson of Operation PUSH (People United to Save Humanity) has expressed hopes of organizing black artists, writers, and producers into a cooperative film venture. And Robert Hooks is shaping up Nation Time Productions, to produce worthwhile material in films, TV, theater, and music, using outstanding black talent and money—a project that could amount, he says, "to a black economic revolution in the entertainment industry."

Breaking Out of the Groove

Given the financial track record of so many recent black films—multimillion-dollar earnings on production costs of $750,000 or less—the inducement would seem a natural. But wealthy blacks are notoriously cautious when it comes to entering new fields ("They're the most nouveaux of the nouveaux-riches," complains Elder). For his upcoming *Book of Numbers*, a story about the numbers racket in the 1930s, which he produced, directed, and starred in, Raymond St. Jacques says he went to "every black millionaire in America"—and came up dry. Moreover, what's to guarantee that black-financed films would be any better than the present crop—or, if they were, that blacks would flock to them?

Perhaps the most hopeful portent for better black movies is the almost uniform desire of the new black pantheon of directors, writers, and stars to break out of the sex-and-violence bag. "Unless black films explore other areas of black experience," warns *Melinda*'s superhero Calvin Lockhart, "black films will wind up on the shelf and eventually stop." Sick of films like *Shaft*, Gordon Parks has refused to oversee any more sequels (five more are planned). And rather than doing a sequel to their *Super Fly*, his director son, Gordon, Jr., and screenwriter Philip Fenty are working on a project which, says Fenty, is "totally removed from drugs." Roundtree himself, the ex-model who is perhaps the reigning black superstar, sums up a widespread feeling among his colleagues: "What we want in our movies from now on is to show black people winning because they use their heads, not because they do violence with their hands."

The brilliant young novelist Ishmael Reed, whose novel *Yellow Back Radio Broke-Down* has had two movie options dropped, wants to see movie makers deal with black experience as the young black novelists and playwrights have done. "We can't get that done because they want us to look dumb," he says. "The real problem is with the liberals. Jane Fonda will support the antiwar movement, but Jane Fonda will not ask for reforms in her own profession. Why don't they do more original novels by Afro-Americans instead of putting together hack original screenplays? If we could get the whole range of our experience into movies, I wouldn't mind something like *Super Fly*."

But in the end, it is economics—not good intentions—that will decide the future of black movies. And at the moment, nearly everyone in the business sees the great black hope embodied in a moving little film called *Sounder*. Directed by a white veteran, Martin Ritt, and scripted by Elder, *Sounder* stands apart from the prevailing tide in several important respects: its documentary feel for the historical context of American black experience; its lack of shrillness about white bigotry; its elevation of a black woman as played by Cicely Tyson into a complex, forceful human, not a groovy sex object, and most of all, its quiet, almost mythical tale about a family of Louisiana sharecroppers in the Depression who, in Faulkner's famous words, not only endure but prevail.

But will *Sounder* prevail? Even here blacks are split: some, like actress Tyson and *Newsweek*'s Los Angeles bureau chief, John Dotson, seeing hope in the film's quiet dignity; others smelling ripoff in those very qualities. "*Sounder*," says one black actor, "was made for whites who want to believe that blacks are full of love and trust and patience. It avoids dealing with things like rage and bitterness and the need for some kind of release. That kind of people don't survive here on the streets of New York. I took a girl to see *Sounder* who used to do laundry for white people. She wasn't going to be entertained by a film about black suffering, because she *knows* about black suffering." Replies Miss Tyson: "I think we have come far enough to look back on our lives with pride. It's because of people like those in *Sounder* that we've come as far as we have."

In any case, the black is no longer a bit player on the American movie screen. "Just as we've done with theater and music," Ron O'Neal says, "black people will develop a new art form of movies in this country—given the time and opportunity."

James P. Murray

2 The Subject Is Money

[1972]

I've seen the movie industry in this country as never concerned
with art. Maybe that's a little reactionary, but I just can't see one
example ever of the American movie industry doing anything that
was actually for anything else but money.

—WLIB's David Lampell
Summer, '72

Even as the descendant of a relatively honest tradition in Europe,
the way of pure art in America is a bankrupt way. And this is especially true in film. Just as the commercial publishing houses had
done with literature, and just as the recording industry had done
with music, Hollywood became an industry right after World War
I, joining a list of quotations being traded by major investment
firms on the national stock markets. Many of the moguls who came
to power at the studios were hardly artists, but businessmen with
little or no background in entertainment. And today, some of the
major companies have diversified or merged into huge conglom-
erates: Universal–MCA; United Artists–Transamerica; Paramount
–Gulf & Western; Warner Brothers–Kinney.

In the latest development, several Top-500, multi-oriented corporations have moved investment in feature films to an interesting
end and become involved in motion picture production themselves. The toymakers Mattel joined with producer Robert Radnitz
in bringing the film *Sounder* to the screen. And other corporations

bitten by the movie-making bug include General Electric, Xerox, Bristol Myers, and Boise Cascade as well as *Playboy* and *Reader's Digest* from the literary realm and Wells, Rich, Greene from the advertising world.

So, true to the capitalist system of making a profit, Hollywood has rearranged its priorities and for a while, at least, became successful big business. And during its heyday during the thirties and forties, the high-living moguls virtually ignored black people, both as artists and consumers. And yet, in perhaps one of the greatest ironies of our time, it was black people who brought life back into a dying industry.

Historically, what happened was simple. With the advent of television, movie attendance declined steadily to an ebb of 17.5 million Americans a week in 1971 after a peak of 80 million in 1946. And so did profits. Production and salaries dropped off over the years and unemployment rose.

That high profile, but low energy, youth film era which followed the success of *Easy Rider*, which was supposed to inject new life into the industry, died as rapidly as it had appeared, and by the late sixties, only one in six films was making a profit. Then, some studios faced the additional burden of absorbing costs of a number of completed but unmarketable films—films that were subsequently never released but left to collect dust in their producers' garages.

While all of this happened, more blacks continued to move into the cities of the north and west, and for years, many were not able to afford the luxury of a television. A most popular alternative for a visually oriented people to hours of weekday radio shows, very often in cramped tenements, was a movie downtown on the weekend. And the trend was amplified in the sixties when whites began deserting downtown for the suburbs and apparently different styles of entertainment. Yet, few industry observers were aware of this audience.

It took a "revolutionary" film that, in effect, dared white patrons to walk into the theater, to crystallize the image of a substantial black audience. In 1971, Melvin Van Peebles's *Sweet Sweetback's Baadasssss Song* became the first major black-produced feature film since the 1930 era of men like Oscar Micheaux to draw audiences that were consistently in excess of 80 percent black. And within weeks, a stampede in the ailing industry that had lost hundreds of millions of dollars, was on.

So, producers like John D. F. Black, Roger Corman, Joel Freeman, Sam Goldwyn, Jr., Roger Lewis, Joe Naar, and Sig Shore were among the enterprising whites who became liaison between anxious black artists with ideas or projects and the money-hungry studios and independent distributors. Unfortunately, the role of these men—outsiders to black art—has hardly been questioned enough. The result of their work—by late this fall, close to one-quarter of Hollywood's total planned production was black oriented. In contrast, 1970 saw only 14 of some 400 major features in release as black oriented.

Of course, Hollywood had been importing black actors and actresses, singers and dancers from overflowing New York night-clubs and theaters since the thirties for a different sort of black film. The movie capital had even made a millionaire of Stepin Fetchit and rewarded other blacks with varying degrees of wealth and fame. And the result of the apparent good fortune was a sustained black avalanche of hopeful talent that brought unfamous stage names like Sidney Poitier and Harry Belafonte in the fifties, and Raymond St. Jacques and Ossie Davis in the sixties, to the world of film stardom. And all of this was before the new breed of Richard Roundtrees and Ron O'Neals in the seventies. Over the decades, however, this surge left literally hundreds of others (like their white counterparts) frustrated and quite out of the limelight.

By 1972, the response to those successful black stars had grown until blacks had been computed as representing nearly half the national moviegoing audience, or some $110 million toward the total revenue taken in annually at the nation's box offices.

Every week, *Variety* publishes the cumulative grosses (money taken in at the box offices) for the top fifty domestic money-making films in current run. Some observers have apparently tended to confuse grosses with actual profits. At this writing, *Shaft* appears to have the lead as the most profitable black film, with a gross estimated by director Gordon Parks at between $18 million and

$20 million. His son, Gordon, Jr.'s first effort, *Super Fly* (at over $11 million in some two months) appears well on its way to overtaking that lead, however.

(The problem of more accurately tallying a net gross is muddled by the present system of computing attendance reports from exhibitors across the country.)

From the gross, however, there are a host of postproduction costs, including the theater owner's percentage, promotion and publicity and mailing, and insuring costs for prints of the film. Then, there are production salaries for cast and crew. Members of the technical and support crew are union men and women and they are paid according to a graduated scale. Virtually all the creative talent, including the screenwriter, are represented by skilled agents, who for a 10 percent fee will negotiate each contract. There are also production costs for things like camera rental, film, material to build sets, transportation, and lodging when on location. Finally, there are preproduction costs that must also be budgeted, particularly if rights to a novel, short story or play, from which the screenplay is based, are bought from an independent writer. In 1936, for instance, Margaret Mitchell was paid $50,000 for rights to her novel, *Gone With the Wind.*

So, when the so-called profit has been isolated, it is certainly a comparatively small percentage of the average-grossing film. Still, the question arises: who does get the money when there is a profit?

There are some 13,500 motion picture theaters in the country. Those owned by blacks can be counted on three good hands. (There are none in New York City.) According to one official at Twentieth Century-Fox's New York headquarters, it is theater owners who often manage handsomely when films are successful.

When a given movie is taking care of business, the theater will be automatically reimbursed for the house nut, or the sum of those weekly operational expenses. These standard expenses, which include rent, salaries, insurance, and taxes, range at New York City's first-run theaters from $4,800 (a week) at the tiny Cinema II to $16,500 at the mammoth Rivoli, Loew's State I and II, and the Ziegfeld. Once cleared, the remaining box office intake is split between theater owner and distributor on a percentage basis.

The theaters obviously don't make the house nut during some weeks. Yet whatever the percentages, when a film like *Super Fly* clears that house nut at one theater in one *day* (as it did at the Loew's State II one Sunday last August), it can't be that bad for anyone involved. So, over the past few months, those runaway success black films have been held over with possessive endearment by many pleased, if not impressed, theater owners.

For their role in the overall film-making process, some in the production and distribution segments of the industry feel that theater owners—the only men enjoying direct contact with the consumer and his dollars—are getting over magnificently. And this financial success is felt to be gained sometimes honestly and at other times, not so honestly—as hundreds of lawsuits by distributors charging fast fingers and dishonest accounting clearly prove.

On the other hand, it is claimed that many of the most impressive homes in the Beverly Hills environs belong to agents, production chiefs, and that host of names generally ignored as the screen credits pass at the beginning of each film.

While many own houses or apartments on both coasts and sport better than comfortable living styles, most black artists to the man and woman will deny that they are getting rich from working in movies. They will argue, with justification, that while isolated sums for individual films may appear hefty—in a typical case, a talented artist might work on only six films in twice as many years. Still, it is safe to assume that most of the estimated four hundred black screen artists and technicians in Hollywood who work *regularly* (perhaps forty) will earn between $20,000 and $60,000 a year.

Those estimates preclude the rare black superstar. Sidney Poitier, voted the number-one box office attraction in 1968 by the exhibitors, can still command a salary twice that of any other black actor or actress by virtue of that accolade. Of course, just about the time Poitier became that much of an attraction, the millionaire actor began wisely taking a smaller salary for a percentage of the film's profits. Poitier was paid a reported $750,000 plus 10 percent of the net in the 1969 production, *The Lost Man*. Most recently, his status has changed in that he is currently making (producing, directing as well as starring in) his own films.

Poitier's closest competition comes from Jim Brown, who was paid $37,000 for *Rio Conchos*, while free-lancing as an actor between football seasons in 1963. Brown's going rate for *100 Rifles* in 1969 was $200,000 and 5 percent of the net.

While Diana Sands (for *Georgia Georgia*), Cicely Tyson (for *Sounder*), and Diana Ross (for *Lady Sings the Blues*) are being trumpeted for Oscars, no black actress since Dorothy Dandridge has approached the box office power of Poitier and Brown over a sustained period. Thereby, no actress has come near the salary level of the two superstars.

But superstars notwithstanding, black actors and actresses historically have not had parity with their white counterparts financially. This was due in part to the belief that black films were at best a gamble.

Certainly, many in the industry must have been turned off after Twentieth Century-Fox made a film version of the Broadway hit, *The Great White Hope*, and invested $10 million in the project. For when *Hope* was released in 1970, it was a box office bomb—only managing to generate a gross of $600,000 by the end of the year.

Then, as if to unwittingly substantiate and justify reliance on small budgets, two independent, virtually nonunion films whose total budgets managed to hover beneath the $500,000 mark, turned the industry upside down. *Sweet Sweetback* and *Super Fly* managed to capture the souls of the black audience with their nitty gritty approach to the black image and use of a visual ghetto dialogue. Both films individually grossed over $10 million within three months after they were initially released. And while the industry tended to ignore the creative reasons for those two success stories, they hardly forgot that it all had been done with budgets they used for their better cartoons, trailers, and short subjects. So during last summer, when *Blacula, Melinda,* and *Trouble Man* were in production, rumors of pressure to tighten tight budgets and shorten short production schedules persisted.

Yes, there were definite inconsistencies in the manner in which Hollywood treated the so-called black film boom. While increasing the number of productions, they held off in expending funds they would have undoubtedly used without question in producing comparable Westerns or action features.

If the handful of independent features are thrown in, $700,000 would represent a fair average cost of the black-oriented films produced since 1970. Certainly, the overall Hollywood average must exceed $1 million. The musical *Sweet Charity*, for instance, was made for $8 million.

Money is why the industry has consistently refused to refute or even comment on charges that they are exploiting black audiences, while continuing to make the very same kind of offensive films. (In November, however, Sam Arkoff, president of American International Pictures, did meet with the black press in New York.) The most insidious representation of this defiance, for example, has been that ever-present artistic nemesis, that creative cop-out they call a sequel.

It all started with Sidney Poitier's *In the Heat of the Night*, which was followed by *They Call Me Mister Tibbs* and *The Organization*. *Cotton Comes to Harlem* and *Shaft* were next and now, *Blacula*, *The Legend of Nigger Charley*, *Slaughter*, and *Super Fly* have sequels underway and there is talk of follow-up versions of *Buck and the Preacher*, *Sounder*, and *Across 110th Street*. To their credit, Gordon Parks, Gordon Parks, Jr., and screenwriter Philip Fenty have disassociated themselves from respective future pictures.

And perhaps the most publicized example of this fallacy surrounding black films was the reported $13,500 that *Shaft* star Richard Roundtree received (albeit a newcomer) for his work. Even with the financial success of the second Shaft film, (in which he fought unsuccessfully for a $50,000 salary), Roundtree's scale has hadly matched his box office power.

It should be noted that a film artist's annual income derived solely from film work is dependent on his activity and on the importance of his role in any given project. Still, to those artists harboring idyllic dreams about movie success, there must have been some swooning at the figures press agents casually threw around about certain film stars' salaries (like John Wayne and Elizabeth Taylor), as well as the fantastic sums expended to make those splashy and heralded Hollywood epics. While the era of the epic is a bygone one for all practical purposes, images of those numerals with trails of zeroes certainly still linger in the minds of many.

It is interesting to note that when newcomers to movie making saunter onto the scene, they invariably bring their big budget concepts with them. Motown Records moved to the West Coast, organized a production arm, and simultaneously announced *Lady Sings the Blues* as its first major undertaking. At the time, Motown was undoubtedly the only black corporation in the entertainment world that could make such an investment.

As outlined in the initial releases, a $5 million budget, fully one-third of the production arm's initial outlay, was set aside for the musical biography. But a decision was made to confine filming to California, and the final cost was just over $3 million. Still, *Lady* represents the most expensive black production in the seventies.

With all the activity, the black independent producer has found raising capital outside of Hollywood near impossible. The list of starts and corresponding failures is endless. Among the more recent was the attempt of Ivan Dixon and Sam Greenlee to produce a film version of Greenlee's popular novel, *The Spook Who Sat by the Door*. The production, budgeted just over $800,000 almost died right before filming in Gary, Indiana, was set to begin. (The film was subsequently made on the West Coast.) Then, there is the story of Ossie Davis's Third World Cinema in New York, which, after two years, has failed to get a film project past the preproduction stage even though it has already signed a distribution agreement with Twentieth Century-Fox for its first five films.

Actor Raymond St. Jacques, who was ultimately obliged to sign with Brut Productions, a subsidiary of Fabergé, to finance his *Book of Numbers* (budgeted at $700,000), complained openly of being rebuffed by potential black investors. His anger was symbolic of a growing resentment among black artists. They found the intransigence of those hundreds of wealthy and enterprising blacks who reneged despite the overwhelmiing success record of black films nothing short of ludicrous.

But, perhaps it was the system of realizing that ultimate return that continued to frighten off black film backers.

For as St. Jacques himself indicated last spring, it had taken him some two years after filming *Cotton Comes to Harlem* for his first residual payments to come in. Then, there is the story of the neophyte K-Calb Productions, which struggled to produce the independent *The Bus Is Coming*, despite overwhelming odds. The company watched the trade newspapers as the film inched toward a $4 million gross in its first six months, but president Horace Jackson was forced to threaten legal action to recover his fair share from the distributor.

The industry kept on making their black movies however, and finally last summer there was a backlash against the flood. Besides concerned artists, there were some new voices and the backlash appeared for a few to be symbolic of a lust for power. With the controversy, the so-called black film boom entered yet another stage. It just could not be honestly stated that those negative images were the sole issue to heighten the sense of outrage in some segments of the black community. In all the belated uproar (the black film image had been demeaned for decades), a number of individuals outside the industry itself jockeyed for the position of speaking for the black community and negotiating with the studios.

It was clear in all too many cases that some of the outspoken individuals had noted the potential gain of that symbolic achievement sign of the American dream—money. And that certain group was looking for a piece of the action.

The activity began in New York last May when CORE's Roy Innes called a press conference at his Harlem headquarters and announced the formation of a Harlem Cinema Foundation. The foundation was organized to encourage feature-film makers to work in the black community but in return for seven controversial concessions, which centered around employing more blacks on black-oriented films as well as contributing profits from black films into black banks and a fund to be used for training of apprentices.

The apparent well-intentioned announcement came after Sam Goldwyn, Jr.'s cast and crew of *Come Back Charleston Blue* had been chased out of Harlem following a "misunderstanding" and refused subsequent entry despite a series of negotiating sessions.

At the press conference, several important questions arose. Primary among those was the obvious business gamble in demanding a percentage of a film's profit: suppose the film in question did not make a profit?

Despite pledges of cooperation from several film makers, nothing was heard of the foundation and no black films came to New York for at least six subsequent months, according to Mayor Lindsay's film coordinator.

Still, Innes's newfound interest in the film industry was hardly diminished. By late summer he was being quoted in praise of the depression family tale, *Sounder*. Later, on WNBC-TV's "Today" Show, he debated star Ron O'Neal about the merits of a drug drama called *Super Fly*, a film that had ironically been allowed total freedom while filming in Harlem. He then showed up on another front: Hollywood itself—this during the midst of that vocal backlash—and announced that CORE planned to make a film itself. In still another ironic note, Innis announced plans to seek out funds ($3 million) from Warner Brothers, the same company he had criticized for distributing *Super Fly*.

When attempting to substantiate what has been claimed by the dissidents as a moral base for demanding funds from the industry, problems and confusion arise. What can be easily determined, however, is the fact that large numbers of black people can be found in front of downtown theaters every weekend, usually waiting on long lines, usually paying two to four dollars, usually to see a black film.

What most of the activists claiming retribution from the film industry want is a return from that money spent. Assuming there is a supposed "entertainment" return that should be deducted, how much the activists want (besides the cliché: all we can get) is unclear. It appears that the most popular idea would place funds in a position ultimately to develop a black film industry, primarily through the training of behind-the-camera personnel, a commendable goal once the negotiators have determined the mechanics of such a plan.

The future can be hopeful. With independent producers and production companies taking up the slack, a turnabout in domestic film making has finally arrived. And as reported in *Variety* last

July, the 1972 box office is up in key cities 23 percent or $36 million over 1971.

As of last October, grosses for five key black films were estimated as follows: *Super Fly*—$11 million; *Shaft's Big Score*—$10 million; *Buck and the Preacher*—$9 million; and *The Legend of Nigger Charley* and *Melinda*—$5 million apiece. The total—$40 million. And that total did not consider some twenty-two other first-run black films that had been released by that time. Some of the latter group, like *Blacula, Slaughter, Sounder,* and *Lady Sings the Blues* were drawing crowds enthusiastically. The figures and their impact on the movie industry speak for themselves.

Without resorting to a series of timeworn clichés about the manner in which lust corrupts, some conclusions may be drawn. It was a preoccupation with money—not serious or good films—that made Hollywood the movie capital of the world.

It has been the loss of that money that has challenged Hollywood's status. (Today, India leads the world in film production.) It was the lure of money in part that brought over fifty black actors and actresses, directors and writers from the New York stage to the West Coast film center during the past fifteen years. And most recently the get-rich syndrome has hit a number of suspicious blacks who came to Hollywood blowing clouds of liberation smoke only to wind up imitating the pattern of the white exploiters. Given the nature of the movie industry, this attitude can hardly be characterized as a conspiracy. In Hollywood, every man or woman hustles (if you'll pardon the expression) for himself or herself.

At this crucial point in a tempestuous love affair between black people and the movies, improving images is important. But infinitely more significant is exposing this illicit affection being expressed by some artistically immoral blacks for pieces of green paper.

One cliché needs to be repeated again and again. It is black people who are the victims of this cultural crime. Lest the point be missed, this is not a blanket condemnation of an industry or of a way of making a living for scores of serious artists. Hollywood as an institution—money as an end in itself—cannot be indicted. They are factors, but only people commit crimes. Only people.

Pauline Kael

3   Notes on Black Movies

[1972]

Peggy Pettitt, the young heroine of the new film *Black Girl*, doesn't have a white girl's conformation; she's attractive in a different way. That may not seem so special, but after you've seen a lot of black movies, you know how special it is. The action thrillers feature heroes and heroines who are dark-tanned Anglo-Saxons, so to speak—and not to lure whites (who don't go anyway) but to lure blacks whose ideas of beauty are based on white stereotypes. If there is one area in which the cumulative effect of Hollywood films is obvious, it is in what is now considered "pretty" or "handsome" or "cute" *globally*; the mannequins in shopwindows the world over have pert, piggy little faces.

In the mock documentary *Farewell Uncle Tom*, the Italian movie makers aren't content with simulating the historically re- corded horrors of slavery; they invent *outré* ones, including a slave-breeding farm, so they can mix prurience with their piety about how white Americans are the scum of the universe. On this farm, white Southerners call the black babies "pups," and a slen- der, sensitive young black girl is mated with a huge, shackled Wild Man of Borneo stud while the white owners watch. In order to make us aware of the outrage, the film selects for the terrified girl a black *jeune fille* who resembles Audrey Hepburn. Presumably, if she had larger features we might think the drooling, snarling stud just right for her.

Black Girl is too touching to be considered bad. It is derivative, and its crude techniques seem almost deliberately naïve in the sophisticated medium sound-and-color films, but there is something here struggling to be heard. The film is trying to express a young girl's need to free herself from the patterns of ghetto apathy; it's trying to express black experiences while encased in an inappropriate, TV-shopworn, domestic-drama form (J. E. Franklin's own adaptation of her Off Broadway play). The struggle seems anachronistic. Not just because the cumbrous structure that is falsifying the experiences is the well-made second-rate serious play of thirty years ago, the sort of play that has never got by on the screen (though it still occasionally turns up: *The Subject Was Roses, I Never Sang for My Father*), but because the whole attempt represents the birth pangs of honest and idealistic black movie making—which is like witnessing the birth of something that has already died. *Black Girl* arrives when, after just two years, black movies have reached the same stage of corruption as white punch-'em-and-stick-'em-and-shoot-'em action movies. It isn't in the class of *Sounder*; it's faltering and clumsy, yet the black audience enjoyed it, and in a way, I did, too—I liked watching the people on the screen. They embody different backgrounds and different strategies for survival, and the phenomenal strength of the older actresses in the cast said more than the script itself. However, in casting the older roles and in breaking with the white conventions of beauty by giving Peggy Pettitt the leading role, Ossie Davis, who directed, may not have realized what he was doing to Leslie Uggams, who is also in the picture. Her role requires her to be a model of strength, but Miss Uggams, a TV cutie and a stereotype of the prettiness accepted in the media, seems shriveled and trivialized by that prettiness. A movie that tries to deal with matriarchal black family life, and that features the rich talent of Louise Stubbs as well as that powerhouse Claudia McNeil, can't accommodate media models.

Ossie Davis also directed the first black hit, *Cotton Comes to Harlem*, in 1970—an ingenuous detective comedy that was like a folkloric version of an early-thirties movie. When a sexy black siren outsmarted a white cop by stealing his pants, it was a silly, naïve joke—the tables being turned, and a white man being ridiculed the way black men on screen used to be. The racial humor might have been considered vilely insulting from a white director, but the picture began to suggest the freshness that black performers could bring to movies—just as Ossie Davis himself, when he acted in such movies as *The Hill* and *The Scalphunters*, brought a stronger presence to his roles than white actors did, and a deeper joy. What a face for the camera! He was a natural king, as Louise Stubbs is a natural queen. There seemed to be a good chance that black talent on the screen, on TV, in literature, and in the theater would infuse new life into the whole culture, the way jazz entered American music and changed the beat of American life.

But then the white businessmen saw the buying power of blacks and how easy it would be to do black versions of what was already being done. And they took over, along with the black businessmen-artists, and so we have separate cultures—black-*macho* movies and white-*macho* movies, equally impoverished, equally debased. But movies of this kind are not the only ones that deal with white experience, while for blacks they are virtually all there is. Right now, there are more than fifty in the planning stages or in production, of which about half will probably be completed.

This has happened at the same time that black performers on TV and in movies have got close to us, just as white performers in the past got close to blacks. Despite racial fears, whites obviously accept black performers as part of American life, and respond to them in a new way. (I am told that big-city white families with several kids often have a black child; that is, a kid who wants so badly to be black that he or she talks as if he were, so that if you overhear him you assume he *is* black.)

If the freedom of blacks has always involved a sexual threat to white men—who fear that their wives and daughters would prefer blacks, and imagine that for blacks freedom means primarily sleeping with white women, and turning them into whores—the black-*macho* movies have exploited retaliatory black fantasies. The heroes sleep with gorgeous white girls, treating them with casual contempt. They can have any white women they want, but they have no attachment to them; they have steady, gorgeous, black girls to count on in time of trouble. They act out the white men's worst fears: fully armed and sexually as indomitable as James Bond, they take the white men's women and cast them off.

The black superstud has very different overtones for the black audience from what Bond or Matt Helm had for mixed audiences, because the black movies are implicitly saying to the black audience, "See, we really *are* what the whites are afraid of; they have reason to be afraid of our virility." One would have to be a little foolish to take offense at this when it so obviously serves an ego need, and there's a good deal of humor (and justice) in acting out the white man's fears. (That movie ad showing creamy Raquel Welch's embrace of Jim Brown's beautiful black chest was a great erotic joke.) But there are times when the black hero's condescension to the white women who are eager for his favors becomes mean and confused—when the white women are so downgraded that it seems as if only a stupid, shallow, white tramp could want a black man. Whose fantasy is this? The contempt for white women can be really foul. In *Sweet Sweetback's Baadasssss Song*, the police break into a room where a black man and a white woman are in bed together; the police beat the man while the woman watches and smiles with pleasure. The scene is racist at fairly low levels, since it assumes that the white woman has no feelings (except sadistic ones) about the man she has been making love to—because he's black. But this movie, like the others, posits a black-stud virility, which should insure *some* feeling. Probably the author-director, Melvin Van Peebles, couldn't resist the chance to score an ideological racist point, and what he's saying is that black men shouldn't waste themselves on white women, who are nothing but vicious little beasts, using them.

All weaponry had become phallic in the James Bond pictures, and in the ads for *The Silencers* Dean Martin rode his trusty automatic while girls crowded around him; the black movies feature not only the sexual prowess and the big guns of their black heroes but also an implicit "Anything you can do we can do better." The weapons in the black-*macho* movie ads are a big phallic put-on, but they're also real avengers; they announce to blacks that now we've really got our own. (They're probably also a very effective deterrent to attendance by white males, and the action genre has never attracted many white women. It's not surprising that so few

whites go to black-*macho* movies; they know the show isn't meant
for them, and it's very uncomfortable to be there.) The heroes are
sex-and-power symbols for an audience that has been looking at
white symbols, and so the heroes are revenge figures as well. Sex
means you can get anybody you want, and power is what comes out
of a gun, and money is the key to everything. You can even buy
your way out of your life, change your way of living, if you've got
enough money—as in the fantasy of *Super Fly*. These movies say
that the white man had his turn to play God and now it's ours.
But the movies are controlled by white men, and a big gun is a
macho kid's idea of power.

These films say that the smart black man gets what the white
man has: the luxury goods of a consumer society, including luscious broads. The hero of *Super Fly* says he's got "eight-track stereo
and color TV in every room," and he sneers that it's "the American dream." These films say that there is nothing but consumerism,
so grab what you can; what's good enough for the white man is
good enough for you. The message is the exact opposite of the
Martin Luther King message; he said, in essence, that you must not
let the white man degrade you to his level. King wanted something
better for blacks than the consumer-media society. Since his death,
if black people have been dreaming of something better the media
have blotted it from sight. That dream has been Shafted, Ham-
mered, Slaughtered.

Wartime propaganda films did to the Germans and the Japanese what is done to whites in these films—turned them into every
available stereotype of evil. Whites are made treacherous, cowardly,
hypocritical, and often sexually perverse; the subsidiary black
villains are often sexually kinky, too. And these movies are often
garishly antihomosexual; homosexuality seems to stand for weakness and crookedness—"corruption." They have already developed
some classic clichés: they feature blacks beating up white men with
excessive zeal, and very likely the white villain will rasp "Nigger!"
just before the black hero finishes him off (something many a
black has probably dreamed of doing when he was called "nigger").
Except when we were at war, there has never been such racism in
American films. There have been numberless varieties of conde-

scension and insult, but nothing like this—not since D. W. Griffith made the one terrible mistake of his life in *The Birth of a Nation*, when he showed a black man attempting to rape a young Southern girl, a mistake that shocked the country into awareness of the dangerous power of the emerging art. Only in wartime (and immediately after, in dealing with war themes) have Hollywood movies used this primitive power to encourage hatred of a race or a national group.

The obvious conclusion would seem to be that black people are using the screen to incite race war, but if one examines how the films are made it's apparent that the white companies are making the films for profit, and that the blacks involved are mostly boastful yet defensive about the content. The archetypal black superhero Shaft was, admittedly, lifted out of Dashiell Hammett by Ernest Tidyman, the white writer who got an Academy Award for his screenplay for *The French Connection*; he had tried to latch on to an earlier movement with his book *Flower Power*. These movies use black resentment to turn blacks on to the excitement of getting back at whites; the racism is a slant, a shtick. *Super Fly*, in which the cocaine-hustler hero puts down two weakling black civil-rights representatives who are trying to raise money by telling them that he won't be interested until they buy guns to shoot the whites—a speech calculated to crush the finky, cowardly pair and to get cheers from the audience (and it did when I saw the film)— was produced by a white man (Sig Shore) and is distributed by Warner Brothers, a company headed by a white liberal (Ted Ashley), who probably contributes to civil-rights organizations. With only a few exceptions (*Sweetback* is one), the black films are packaged, financed, and sold by whites, who let the black actors or directors serve as spokesmen for the therapeutic function these films are said to have for the black community—by creating black heroes. Do people actually make movies for therapeutic purposes? Only if wealth can be considered a form of therapy. When their arguments are challenged by CORE and other black groups, the spokesmen generally say that these films are at least providing jobs and training for black actors and technicians, who will then be able to do something better. But when a movie is made that isn't pure exploitation, they can't resist sniping at it and pointing to their own huge grosses as proof that they're giving blacks the right entertainment. This is what big-money success does to people; they want honors, too. The black artists who want to do something worth doing find themselves up against what white artists in films are up against, and with less training and less to bargain with.

If there's anything to learn from the history of movies, it's that corruption leads to further corruption, not to innocence. And that each uncorrupted work must fight against the accumulated effects of the pop appeal of corruption. How is it going to be possible to reach black audiences after they have been so pummelled with cynical consumerism that any other set of values seems hypocritical and phony—a con?

Exploiting black rage is a dangerous game, but the stakes are high for men like Jim Aubrey (president of MGM) and Ted Ashley and their competitors. The movies are made on the cheap, on B-picture budgets, and the profits are enormous. *Shaft*, which cost just over a million dollars, is credited with "saving" MGM, though the slick, black shoot-'em-ups (*Cool Breeze, Melinda*) and the white action films (*Skyjacked*) that Aubrey is producing are far removed from what probably comes to mind when one thinks of the salvation of MGM. (Aubrey's triumph as head of the CBS television network was "The Beverly Hillbillies.") Warner Brothers bought and released *Super Fly*, which cost well under a half-million dollars and has grossed over twelve million, and Warners is now producing its sequel.

Black films are not recapitulating film history; they went immediately from the cradle to this slick exploitation level. For the movie companies, blackness is a funky new twist—an inexpensive way to satisfy the audience that has taken over the big downtown theaters now deserted by the white middle classes. Jokers are now calling Broadway "The Great Black Way."

Among the queasiest racist rationales for a black hero yet is the plot device in *Super Fly* that allows the cocaine hustler (and user, who is also a pimp) to be a black hero: the cocaine he sells goes to whites. This is not only a strange rationale (particularly for a movie produced by a white man and distributed by Warner

Brothers) but a highly specious one. The nonfiction book *Dealer*, Richard Woodley's "portrait of a cocaine merchant," reads almost like the script of *Super Fly*, except that the dealer, who is black, is selling to blacks, because, he explains, a black man dealing downtown would be dangerously conspicuous. In this book, as in the movie, the dealer dreams of getting enough loot to get out of the grind, but in the book it's perfectly clear that he can't—that there's no way. It's easy to see why a fantasy movie made for entertainment and profit should turn him into a winner who fulfills his dreams, and certainly the black audience enjoys his triumph over the white homosexual Mr. Big. And, yes, it's easy to see why the movie made him a man of "principle," who is selling to whites, not blacks, even though it's pretty funny to think that dope hustlers are principled about black people. But the self-righteousness of the men getting rich on this movie is unclean.

The most specific and rabid incitement to race war comes in *Farewell Uncle Tom*, a product of the sordid imaginations of Gualtiero Jacopetti and Franco Prosperi, whose previous films include *Mondo Cane, Women of the World* and *Africa Addio*. Bought for this country by the Cannon Releasing Corporation (*Joe* and soft-core exploitation porn), it had to be toned down, because theater operators were afraid to show a movie featuring a fictional re-creation of slavery, from slave ship to plantation life, and concluding with modern blacks butchering middle-class whites in their homes. The movie, set in the United States but shot mostly in Haiti, was trimmed, and some new scenes were added, so that what was expected to be "the ultimate exploitation vehicle" could be released without violence and damage within the theaters themselves. The limited partnership formed by Cannon's young chairman and president, Dennis Friedland, to acquire the film, includes Evan R. Collins, Jr., Richard Heinlein, Victor Ferencko, Marvin Friedlander, Thomas Israel, Michael Graham, Arthur Lipper, James Rubin, and Steve Wichek; I doubt if any of them are black. There must have been considerable fear of a public outcry about the film, because when they finally opened it they did so with a minimum of publicity.

The film, which purports to be a "documentary" of exactly what

America was like in the days of slavery, includes, in addition to the slave-breeding farm, Southern white women rolling in the hay with their young slaves, a group rape with children watching, and a bizarrely fanciful sequence in which blacks in cages are used for mad scientific experiments, and all this is thrown together with scenes on board a slave ship which can't help affecting you. One's outrage at the voyeuristic hypocrisy of the movie gets all tangled up with one's emotions about the suffering people on the ship. No one has ever before attempted a full-scale treatment of a slave-ship misery; how degrading to us all that by default it has fallen into the hands of perhaps the most devious and irresponsible film makers who have ever lived. They use their porno fantasies as part of the case they make for the slaughter of the whites, who are shown as pasty-face cartoons, then and now. It becomes the blacks' duty to kill whites. "He was a white and so he had to die," Nat Turner says, as he kills a man who has been good to him, and then the film cites Eldridge Cleaver and the Black Panthers and cuts to a modern black on a beach staring at disgusting whites. Unlike the black hits, the film lacks a central figure for the audience to identify with, but the black audience in the theater was highly responsive to Jacopetti's and Prosperi's fraudulent ironies, and in the ads are quotes from black papers saying, "An all time great gut-busting flick," and, "Don't miss *Farewell Uncle Tom*, it is must viewing. Eyeball-to-eyeball confrontation with stark reality and chilling candor." Since the anticipated outcry did not develop, and the film, chopped up and sneaked in as it was, didn't do the expected business, it has been withdrawn, to be brought back in the new year with a new publicity campaign.

The movie hustlers—big studio and little—are about as principled as cocaine hustlers. There is a message implicit in *Super Fly*—everyone is a crook, and we all just want what's best (most profitable) for us—and when the hero pulls off his half-million-dollar haul of cocaine the audience cheers. That's the practicing ethic of the movie business; that's what it lives by, and it gets its cheers from stockholders and the media whenever it pulls off a big box-office haul like *Super Fly*. By now, if a black film isn't racist, the white press joins in the chorus of the exploitation film makers, who claim it's a film not for black people but for white liberals. That's how fast racism can become respectable when it's lucrative.

Are the blacks who participate in these movies naïve enough to believe that they are directing rage only against whites? Since what is being peddled is a consumer value system and a total contempt for ethics or principles, why should the young blacks in the audience make the nice discrimination of the hero of *Super Fly?* Cheat and rob and kill only whites? Surely, when you glorify pragmatic cynicism, blacks in the audience can take the next step; they already know there's less risk in stealing from other blacks and in terrorizing the poor.

When a popular culture is as saturated in violent cyncism as ours, and any values held up to oppressed people are treated with derision as the white man's con, or an Uncle Tom's con, the cynicism can't fail to have its effect on us all. What MGM and Warner Brothers and all the rest are now selling is nothing less than soul murder, and body murder, too.

Selected Filmography

Ace High (Paramount, 1969) with Brock Peters.
Across 110th Street (United Artists, 1972) with Yaphet Kotto, Richard Ward.
Adventures of Huckleberry Finn (MGM, 1939) with Rex Ingram.
Adventures of Huckleberry Finn, The (MGM, 1960) with Archie Moore.
Affectionately Yours (MGM, 1941) with Butterfly McQueen, Hattie McDaniel.
All the Young Men (Columbia, 1960) with Sidney Poitier.
American Aristocracy (Triangle, 1916). Produced by D. W. Griffith, from a story by Anita Loos.
An Affair of the Skin (Independent, 1963) with Diana Sands, Osceolo Archer.
An African in London (Colonial Film Unit, 1943) with Robert Adams.
Angel Levine, The (United Artists, 1970) starring Harry Belafonte.
Angel on My Shoulder (United Artists, 1946). One of the first Hollywood films to show well-dressed blacks in crowd scenes as nonstereotypes.
Anna Lucasta (United Artists, 1958) starring Eartha Kitt, Sammy Davis, Jr., Rex Ingram, Fred O'Neal.
Appaloosa, The (Universal, 1966) with Frank Silvera.
Arrowsmith (Goldwyn, 1932) with Clarence Books.
Autobiography of Miss Jane Pittman (ABC-TV Film, 1974) starring Cicely Tyson.
Bataan (MGM, 1943) with Kenneth Spencer. This World War II action drama received a special award from the NAACP for its nonstereotyped handling of a black soldier.
Battle, The (Biograph, 1911). A D. W. Griffith film which fantasizes events of the Civil War. Predates *Birth of a Nation*.
Battle of Elderbush Gulch, The (Biograph, 1913). Another D. W. Griffith distortion of the Civil War.
Bedford Incident, The (Columbia, 1966) with Sidney Poitier.
Benny Goodman Story, The (Universal, 1957) with Lionel Hampton, Teddy Wilson, Sammy Davis, Jr.

Betrayal, The (Astor, 1948). An Oscar Micheaux film.

Beware (Astor Pictures, 1946) (all black) with Louis Jordan, Frank Wilson, Valerie Black, Ernest Calloway, Milton Woods, Emory Richardson. Produced by Bud Pollard.

Big Fella (Lion-Hammer, 1938) starring Paul Robeson, Elizabeth Welch. An English film.

Biggest Bundle of Them All, The (MGM, 1968) with Godfrey Cambridge.

Birth of a Nation, The (Epoch, 1915) with George Reed. Most of the other actors were whites in blackface. Directed by D. W. Griffith from the novel *The Clansman* by Thomas Dixon.

Birth of the Blues (Paramount, 1941) with Eddie "Rochester" Anderson.

Birthright (Micheaux Film Corporation, 1924) with J. Homer Tutt, Evelyn Preer, Salem Tutt Whitney, Lawrence Chenault, W. B. F. Crowell. Young idealistic Harvard graduate settles in a small southern town where he encounters racial brutality and prejudice.

Blackboard Jungle (MGM, 1950) with Sidney Poitier.

Black Caesar (American International, 1973) with Fred Williamson, Gloria Hendry, Minnie Gentry, D'Urville Martin.

Black Girl (Cinerama, 1972) with Louise Stubbs, Brock Peters, Leslie Uggams. Based on the play by J. E. Franklin. Directed by Ossie Davis.

Black Gunn (Columbia, 1972) with Jim Brown, Brenda Sykes, Vida Blue.

Black Jesus (Plaza, 1971)

Black King, The (Independent, 1932) (all black) with Vivian Baber, Mary Jane Watkins, Harry Gray, Knolly Mitchel. Directed by Bud Pollard.

Black Magic (Micheaux Film Corporation, 1932)

Black Rodeo (Cinerama, 1972)

Black Waters (World Wide, 1920) with Noble Johnson. English and Dominions film.

Blacula (American International, 1972) starring William Marshall.

Blonde Venus (Herald Pictures, 1940) (all black) starring Lena Horne, Ralph Cooper.

Body Disappears, The (Warner Brothers, 1942) with Willie Best.

Body and Soul (Micheaux Film Corporation, 1925) starring Paul Robeson, Julia Theresa Russell, Mercedes Gilbert. About an evil minister.

Boogie Woogie Dream (Negro Marches On, 1944) (all black) with Lena Horne, Albert Ammons, Pete Johnson, Teddy Wilson. Produced by Jack and Dave Goldberg.

Booker T. Washington (Encyclopedia Britannica, 1966). Narrated by John Hope Franklin.

Borderline (Pool, 1930) starring Paul Robeson, Eslanda Goode Robeson. English film.

Bowery to Broadway (Universal, 1945) with Ben Carter, Mantan Moreland.

Brewster's Millions (Edward Small, 1946) with Eddie "Rochester" Anderson.

Bright Road (MGM, 1953) starring Dorothy Dandridge, Harry Belafonte, Philip Hepburn.

Broken Strings (International Roadhouse) (all black) starring Clarence Muse. Produced and directed by Bernard B. Ray.

Brother John (Columbia, 1971)

Brute, The (Micheaux Film Corporation, 1925) starring Evelyn Preer, Lawrence Chenault.

Buck and the Preacher (Columbia, 1972) starring Harry Belafonte, Sidney Poitier, Ruby Dee.

Burn! (United Artists, 1970)

Bus is Coming, The (Marvin, 1971)

Cabin in the Cotton, The (Warner Brothers, 1933) with Clarence Muse, Snowflake.

Cabin in the Sky (MGM, 1943) (all black) with Lena Horne, Ethel Waters, Eddie "Rochester" Anderson, Rex Ingram, Kenneth Spencer, Ernest Whitman, Mantan Moreland, Oscar Polk, Louis Armstrong, Buck and Bubbles, Willie Best, Duke Ellington, John Sublett.

Cairo (MGM, 1942) with Ethel Waters, Reginald Owen, Dooley Wilson.

Captain Blood (Warner Brothers, 1936) with Rex Ingram.

Carmen Jones (Twentieth Century Fox, 1954) with Harry Belafonte, Dorothy Dandridge, Pearl Bailey, Diahann Carroll, Olga James.

Carnival in Rhythm (Warner Brothers, 1944) (all black) starring Katherine Dunham and her troupe.

Casablanca (Warner Brothers, 1943) with Dooley Wilson.

Castle Keep (Columbia, 1969) with Al Freeman, Jr.

Cat Ballou (Columbia, 1965) with Nat "King" Cole.

Change of Mind (Cinerama, 1969) with Raymond St. Jacques.

Charley-One-Eye (Paramount, 1973) with Richard Roundtree.

Chasing Trouble (Monogram, 1940) with Mantan Moreland, Frankie Darro.

Cincinnati Kid, The (MGM, 1966) with Cab Calloway.

Cleopatra Jones (Warner Brothers, 1973) with Tamara Dobson, Benie Casey, Brenda Sykes. Screenplay by Max Julien and Sheldon Keller.

Coffy (American International, 1973) with Pam Grier, Booker Bradshaw.

Come Back Charleston Blue (Warner Brothers, 1972) starring Raymond St. Jacques, Godfrey Cambridge.

Comedians, The (MGM, 1969) with Cicely Tyson, James Earl Jones, Raymond St. Jacques, Roscoe Lee Browne.

Connection, The (Films Around the World, 1962). From the play by Jack Gelber.

Cool Breeze (MGM, 1972)

Cool World, The (Independent, 1963). About young adults in Harlem.

Coon Town Suffragettes (Independent, 1914) (all black). Produced by Sigmund Lubin.

Cotton Comes to Harlem (United Artists, 1970) starring Raymond St. Jacques, Godfrey Cambridge, Redd Foxx.

Coward, The (Triangle, 1915). One of the few silent films in which a black was portrayed sympathetically. In this case, a minister.

Crowning Experience, The (Moral Rearmament, 1960) (all black). The life of Mary McLeod Bethune.

Dark of the Sun (MGM, 1968) with Jim Brown.

Dark Romance of a Tobacco Can (Essanay, 1911)

Dark Town Jubilee (Independent, 1914) (all black) starring Bert Williams.

Darktown Revue (Micheaux Film Corporation, 1931)

Daughter of Congo (Micheaux Film Corporation, 1930) with Kathleen Noisette, Loretta Tucker, Clarence Reed, Willor Lee Guilford.

Death of a Gunfighter (Universal, 1969) starring Lena Horne.

Deceit (Micheaux Film Corporation, 1923) with Evelyn Preer, William E. Fontaine, George Lucas, Norman Johnston, Cleo Desmond.

Defiant Ones, The (United Artists, 1957) starring Sidney Poitier.

Detroit 9000 (General Film, 1973) with Hari Rhodes, Vonetta McGee.

Devil's Disciple, The (Micheaux Film Corporation, 1926) with Evelyn Preer, Lawrence Chenault.

Dirty Dozen, The (MGM, 1967) with Jim Brown.

Dixie Jamboree (PRC, 1945) with Louise Beavers, Ben Carter.

Dr. George Washington Carver (MGM, 1945) with Clinton Rosemond. Documentary.

Double Deal (Negro Marches On, 1938) (all black) with Florence O'Brien, Shelton Brooks, Edward Thompson, Maceo Sheffield, F. E. Miller, Edgar Washington, Freddie Jackson, Jeni Le Gon, Monte Hawley, Charles Hawkins. Produced by Jack Goldberg, directed by William Wellman, from a screenplay by Arthur Hoerl.

Dungeon, The (Micheaux Film Corporation, 1922) with William E. Fountaine, Shingzie Howard, J. Kenneth Goodman, W. B. F. Crowell, Earle Browne Cook, Blanche Thompson. About a man who has murdered eight of his previous wives and is about to murder the ninth.

Dutchman (Independent, 1967) with Al Freeman, Jr. From the play by LeRoi Jones.

East of Borneo (Universal, 1932) with Noble Johnson.

Easy Street (Micheaux Film Corporation, 1930) with Richard B. Harrison.

Edge of the City (United Artists, 1957) with Sidney Poitier.

Emperor Jones, The (Krimsky-Cochran, 1933) with Paul Robeson, Frank Wilson, Fredi Washington, Rex Ingram. From the Eugene O'Neill play.

End of the Road (Allied Artists, 1970) with James Earl Jones.

Enter the Dragon (Warner Brothers, 1973) with Jim Kelly.

Farewell Uncle Tom (Cannon, 1972)

Final Comedown, The (New World, 1972)

Finian's Rainbow (American International, 1968) with Frederick O'Neal.

Five on the Black Hand Side (United Artists, 1973) with Clarice Taylor, Leonard Jackson, Virginia Capers, Glynn Turman, D'Urville Martin, Richard Martin, Sonny Jim. Screenplay by Charlie L. Russell, based on his play. Produced by Brock Peters and Michael Tolan.

Flame in the Streets (Atlantic, 1962) with Earl Cameron, John Willis.

Float like a Butterfly, Sting like a Bee (Grove Films, 1969). About Muhammad Ali nee Cassius Clay.

Florian Slappey Series, The (Independent, 1925–26) (all black). Produced and conceived by Octavius Roy Cohen.

Flying Down to Rio (RKO Radio, 1933) with Etta Moten, Clarence Muse.

Follow the Boys (Universal, 1944) with Louis Jordan, Louise Beavers, Nicodemus Stewart (played an officer of a black battalion).

For Love of Ivy (Cinerama, 1968) with Sidney Poitier, Abby Lincoln, Leon Bibb.

For Massa's Sake (Pathe, 1911)

Fox Movietone Follies of 1929 (Twentieth Century Fox, 1929) with Stepin Fetchit. His film debut.

Free, White and Twenty-One (American International, 1964) with Frederick O'Neal.

Gangsters on the Loose (Herald Pictures, 1948) with Ralph Cooper, Teresa Thompson.

Ganja and Hess (Kelly-Jordan, 1973) with Duane Jones, Marlene Clark, Bill Gunn, Sam Waymon, Leonard Jackson. Written and directed by Bill Gunn. Cameraman, James E. Hinton.

Georgia, Georgia (Cinerama, 1972) starring Diana Sands.

Ghost Breakers (Paramount, 1940) with Willie Best, Noble Johnson.

Girl from Chicago (Micheaux Film Corporation, 1933)

Go Man, Go (United Artists, 1954) with Sidney Poitier. About Harlem Globetrotters.

Golden Boy (Columbia, 1940) with Clinton Rosemond.

Gone Are the Days (Hammer Brothers, 1963) with Ossie Davis, Ruby Dee, Godfrey Cambridge. Directed by Nicholas Webster. Based upon the play *Purlie Victorious* by Ossie Davis.

Gone With the Wind (MGM, 1939) with Hattie McDaniel (won Oscar as best supporting actress), Oscar Polk, Ben Carter, Eddie "Rochester" Anderson, Butterfly McQueen (film debut).

Goodbye, My Lady (Warner Brothers, 1956) with Sidney Poitier.

Gonzales Mystery (Micheaux Film Corporation, 1921)

Gordon's War (Twentieth Century Fox, 1973) with Paul Winfield, Gilbert Lewis, Nathan C. Heard. Directed by Ossie Davis.

Greatest Thing in Life, The (Independent, 1918). Some claim that D. W. Griffith made this film to make amends for *Birth of a Nation*. It includes a scene in which a white soldier holds and kisses his black comrade as he dies.

Great Life, The (Warner Brothers, 1941) with Hattie McDaniel.

Great White Hope, The (Twentieth Century Fox, 1970) starring James Earl Jones.

Green Pastures, The (Warner Brothers, 1937) (all black) with Rex Ingram, Eddie Anderson, Clinton Rosemond, Frank Wilson, George Reed, Edna Mae Harris.

Guess Who's Coming to Dinner? (Columbia, 1968) with Sidney Poitier, Beah Richards.

Halls of Anger (United Artists, 1970) with Calvin Lockhart.

Hammer (United Artists, 1972) with Fred Williamson.

Harder They Come, The (New World, 1973) starring Jimmy Cliff.

Harlem After Midnight (Micheaux Film Corporation, 1931)

Harlem Globe Trotters, The (Columbia, 1951) with Dorothy Dandridge, Harlem Globetrotters team.

Harlem on the Prairie (Buell, 1939). Lays claim as the first black western.

Heart Is a Lonely Hunter, The (Warner Brothers–Seven Arts, 1968) with Cicely Tyson.

Hearts in Dixie (Twentieth Century-Fox, 1929) (all black) with Clarence Muse, Stepin Fetchit, Mildred Washington.

Helldorado (Twentieth Century-Fox, 1935) with Stepin Fetchit.

Hello, Dolly (Twentieth Century-Fox, 1969) with Louis Armstrong.

Henry Brown Farmer (U.S. Dept. of Agriculture, 1942). Narration by Canada Lee.

Hickey and Boggs (United Artists, 1972) starring Bill Cosby.

Hit (Paramount, 1973) starring Billy Dee Williams.

Hit Man (MGM, 1972) with Bernie Casey, Pamela Grier, Lisa Moore, Sam Laws.

Home of the Brave (United Artists, 1949) with James Edwards.

Homesteader (Micheaux Film Corporation, 1922) with Evelyn Preer.

Honkey (Mahler, 1971)

Honour of His Family (Biograph, 1910). Directed by D. W. Griffith.

House Behind the Cedars, The (Micheaux Film Corporation, 1927) with Andrew S. Bishop, Shingzie Howard, William Crowell, Lawrence Chenault, Douglas Griffin. Script by Charles Chesnut.

House with Closed Shutters (Biograph, 1910). Directed by D. W. Griffith.

Huckleberry Finn (Paramount, 1932) with Clarence Muse.

I Escaped from Devil's Island (United Artists, 1973) starring Jim Brown.

I Was a Fugitive from the Chain Gang (Warner Brothers, 1933) with Everett Brown.

Ice Station Zebra (MGM, 1968) with Jim Brown.

If He Hollers Let Him Go! (Cinerama Releasing, 1968) starring Raymond St. Jacques, Barbara McNair.

Imitation of Life (Universal, 1934) with Louise Beavers, Fredi Washington, Hazel Washington.

Imitation of Life (Universal, 1959) with Juanita Moore.

In Slavery Days (Rex, 1913) starring Margarita Fischer, a white actress who was known for her blackface comedienne roles. She also played roles in the film versions of *Uncle Tom's Cabin*.

In the Heat of the Night (Mirisch Corporation, 1967) with Sidney Poitier, Beah Richards. Title song by Ray Charles, musical score by Quincy Jones.

In This Our Life (Warner Brothers, 1942) with Hattie McDaniel, Ernest Anderson. Film placed on the Honor Roll of Race Relations for 1942 for its sympathetic treatment of young ambitious black man falsely accused of manslaughter.

Intruder in the Dust (MGM, 1949) with Juano Hernandez, Elzie Emmanuel.

Island in the Sun (Twentieth Century-Fox, 1957) with Harry Belafonte, Dorothy Dandridge.

It Happened One Sunday (Associated British, 1945) with Robert Adams.

Jericho (Dark Sands) (Buckingham, 1937) with Paul Robeson, Orlando Martins, Eslanda Goode Robeson, Princess Kouka.

Jesus Christ Superstar (Universal, 1973) with Carl Anderson as Judas Iscariot.

Jezebel (Warner Brothers, 1938) with Eddie "Rochester" Anderson, Theresa Harris.

Jimi Hendrix (Warner Brothers, 1973). Live performances of Jimi Hendrix from 1966–70, including appearances at Monterey, Isle of Wight, and Woodstock festivals.

Jimi Plays Berkeley (New Line, 1973). Musical documentary about Jimi Hendrix.

Joanna (Twentieth Century-Fox, 1969) with Calvin Lockhart.

Joe Louis Story (United Artists, 1953) with Coley Wallace, Hilda Simms.

Judge Priest (Twentieth Century-Fox, 1935) with Hattie McDaniel, Stepin Fetchit.

Judge's Story, The (Thanhauser, 1911). A southern judge shows sympathy for an accused black.

Keep Punching (Independent, 1941) (all black) with Henry Armstrong.

Kentucky Minstrels (Universal, 1935) (blackface) English.

King of the Zombies (Monogram, 1941) with Leigh Whipper, Mantan Moreland.

King Solomon's Mines (Gaumont, 1937) with Paul Robeson, Robert Adams. English film.

Lady Sings the Blues (Paramount, 1972) with Diana Ross, Billy Dee Williams, Richard Pryor. Miss Ross was nominated for Academy Award.

Landlord, The (United Artists, 1970) with Pearl Bailey, Diana Sands, Lou Gossett. Based on the novel by Kristine Hunter.

Last of the Mobile Hot-Shots (Warner Brothers, 1970) with Robert Hooks.

Learning Tree, The (Warner Brothers–Seven Arts, 1969) with Kyle Johnson, Estelle Evans, Alex Clarke. Directed by Gordon Parks from his novel.

Legend of Nigger Charley, The (Paramount, 1972) with Fred Williamson.

Lem Hawkins' Confession (Micheaux Film Corporation, 1935)

Let No Man Write My Epitaph (Columbia, 1960) with Bernie Hamilton, Ella Fitzgerald. From Willard Motley's novel of the same name.

Let the Good Times Roll (Columbia, 1973). Documentary of the rock 'n roll era in the 1950s. Featuring Chuck Berry, Little Richard, Chubby Checker, Bo Diddley, the Shirelles, the Coasters.

Liberation of L. B. Jones (Columbia, 1970) with Roscoe Lee Browne.

Lifeboat (Twentieth Century Fox, 1944) with Canada Lee.

Lilies of the Field (United Artists, 1962) with Sidney Poitier. Poitier won Oscar as Best Actor.

Limit, The (Cannon, 1972)

Littlest Rebel, The (Twentieth Century-Fox, 1936) with Bill Robinson, Willie Best. A Shirley Temple epic.

Live and Let Die (United Artists, 1973) with Yaphet Kotto, Geoffrey Holder, Brock Peters, Gloria Hendry.

Long Ships, The (Columbia, 1964) with Sidney Poitier.

Lost Boundaries (Film Classics, 1949) with Canada Lee.

Lost Lady, The (First National, 1932) with Clarence Muse, Nina Mae McKinney, Noble Johnson.

Lost Man, The (Universal, 1969) with Sidney Poitier, Al Freeman, Jr., Leon Bibb.

Lydia Bailey (Twentieth Century Fox, 1951) with Juanita Moore, William Marshall.

McMasters, The (Chevron, 1971)

Major Dundee (Columbia, 1965) with Brock Peters.

Malcolm X (Warner Brothers, 1972). Documentary about the great man.

Man, The (Paramount, 1972) starring James Earl Jones.

Man and Boy (Levitt Pickman, 1972)

Mark of the Hawk, The (Universal–International, 1958) with Sidney Poitier, Eartha Kitt.

Maryland (MGM, 1940) with Hattie McDaniel, Ben Carter, Clarence Muse, George Reed, Ernest Whitman, Clinton Rosemond.

Meet Me in Las Vegas (MGM, 1957) with Lena Horne.

Melancholy Dame (Cohen, 1929) (all black) with Evelyn Preer, Spencer Williams. Directed and written by Octavius Roy Cohen. First black talking film.

Melinda (MGM, 1972) with Calvin Lockhart, Vonetta McGee, Roslind Cash. Screenplay by Lonnie Elder III, directed by Hugh Robertson.

Member of the Wedding (Columbia, 1953) with Ethel Waters.

Memory for Two (Columbia, 1946) with Eddie "Rochester" Anderson, Louise Franklin.

Men of Two Worlds (Two Cities, 1946) with Robert Adams, Orlando Martins, Eseaz, Tunji Williams. English film.

Midshipman Easy (British Lion, 1935) with Robert Adams.

Mildred Pierce (Warner Brothers, 1946) with Butterfly McQueen.

Millionaire, The (Micheaux Film Corporation, 1927) with Grace Smith, J. Lawrence Crimer, Cleo Desmond, Lionel Monagas, William Edmonson, Vera Brocker, S. T. Jacks, E. G. Tatum. About a man who makes his fortune in South America, returns to Harlem where a girl connected with gangsters tries to trap him into marriage.

Mingus (Filmmakers, 1968). About Charlie Mingus.

Mr. Creeps (Toddy Pictures, 1938) (all black) with Mantan Moreland, F. E. Miller.

Murder on Lenox Avenue (Negro Marches On, 1941) (all black) with Mamie Smith, Alex Lovejoy, Alberta Perkins, George Williams, Dene Larry, Norman Astwood, Gus Smith, Edna Mae Harris. Story by Frank Wilson, lyrics and music by Donald Heywood, directed by Arthur Dreifuss.

Mystery in Swing (Negro Marches On, 1938) (all black) with Marguerite Whitten, Sybil Lewis, Josephine Edwards, Monte Hawley, Bob Webb, F. E. Miller, Halley Harding, Jess Lee Brooks. Produced and directed by Arthur Dreifuss.

Native Son (Independent, 1951) with Richard Wright, Willa Pearl Curtiss. Based on the novel by Richard Wright.

New Orleans (Majestic–United Artists, 1947) with Billie Holiday, Louis Armstrong.

Night and Day (Warner Brothers, 1946) with Hazel Scott, Clarence Muse.

Night of the Quarter Moon (MGM, 1959) with Nat "King" Cole, James Edwards, Billy Daniels, Marguerite Belafonte.

Nigger, The (Twentieth Century-Fox, 1915)

No Way Out (Twentieth Century-Fox, 1950) with Sidney Poitier, Frederick O'Neal, Ruby Dee, Ossie Davis.

Nothing But a Man (Independent, 1965) with Gloria Foster, Ivan Dixon, Abby Lincoln.
Nothing Sacred (Selznick, 1938) with Hattie McDaniel.
Octoroon, The (Kalem, 1913)
Odds Against Tomorrow (United Artists, 1959) with Harry Belafonte, Carmen De Lavallade. Screenplay by John O. Killens.
Of Mice and Men (Hal Roach, 1940) with Leigh Whipper.
Off to Bloomingdale Asylum (Independent, 1902). According to some film historians, the first film in which a black character appeared. A French film.
On Velvet (Columbia, 1938) with Nina Mae McKinney.
On with the Show (Warner Brothers, 19—) with Ethel Waters (film debut).
100 Rifles (Twentieth Century-Fox, 1969) with Jim Brown.
One Mile from Heaven (Twentieth Century-Fox, 1938) with Fredi Washington, Bill Robinson, Eddie "Rochester" Anderson.
One Potato, Two Potato (Independent, 1964) with Bernie Hamilton.
One Tenth of Our Nation (American Film Centre, 1940). Documentary about black education in the South.
Organization, The (United Artists, 1971) with Sidney Poitier.
Ouanga (Paramount, 1935) with Fredi Washington.
Our Gang (Hal Roach Comedies, 1930) with Farina, Stymie Mathew Beard.
Ox-Bow Incident, The (Twentieth Century-Fox, 1943) with Leigh Whipper.
Panama Hattie (MGM, 1943) with Lena Horne.
Paradise in Harlem (Negro Marches On, 1939) (all black) with Mamie Smith, Frank Wilson, Edna Mae Harris, Sidney Easton, Alex Lovejoy, George Williams, Merritt Smith, Norman Astwood. Screenplay by Frank Wilson, produced by Jack Goldberg, directed by Joseph Seiden.
Paris Blues (United Artists, 1961) with Sidney Poitier, Diahann Carroll.
Patch of Blue (MGM, 1966) with Sidney Poitier, Ivan Dixon.
Pawnbroker, The (Landau, 1965) with Thelma Oliver, Roscoe Lee Browne, Brock Peters, Juano Hernandez. Musical score by Quincy Jones.
Pennies from Heaven (Columbia, 1937) with Louis Armstrong, Charles Wilson.
Penrod and Sam (Warner Brothers, 1937) with Philip Hurlic.
Petrified Forest, The (Warner Brothers, 1936) with Slim Johnson, John Alexander.
Phantom of Kenwood (Micheaux Film Corporation, 1933)
Pinky (Twentieth Century-Fox, 1949) with Ethel Waters, Frederick O'Neal, Nina Mae McKinney.
Pittsburgh Kid, The (Republic, 1942) with Ernest Whitman, Henry Armstrong, Etta McDaniel. Directed by Octavius Roy Cohen.
Place Called Today, A (Avco Embassy, 1972)
Place to Live, A (Philadelphia Housing Association, 1941). Documentary on housing.
Porgy and Bess (Columbia, 1959) with Sidney Poitier, Dorothy Dandridge, Sammy Davis, Jr., Pearl Bailey.
President's Analyst, The (Paramount, 1967) with Godfrey Cambridge.
Pressure Point (United Artists, 1962) with Sidney Poitier.

Prestige (RKO-Radio, 1932) with Clarence Muse.
Prisoner of Shark Island, The (Twentieth Century-Fox, 1936) with Hattie McDaniel, Ernest Whitman.
Proud Valley, The (Ealing, 1940) starring Paul Robeson. An English film.
Putney Swope (Cinema V, 1969)
Quiet One, The (Film Documents, 1949) with Estelle Evans, Donald Thompson.
Raisin in the Sun, A (Columbia, 1961) starring Sidney Poitier, Claudia McNeil, Diana Sands, Ruby Dee. Based upon the Lorraine Hansberry play.
Rastus Series (Independent, around 1910) (all black) Includes such titles as Rastus in Zululand.
Red Ball Express (Universal, 1952) with Sidney Poitier.
Reivers, The (Cinema Center, 1969) with Rupert Crosse.
Right On (Concept East Ltd., 1971)
Rio Conchos (Twentieth Century-Fox, 1966) with Jim Brown.
Riot, The (Paramount, 1969) with Jim Brown.
Road to Mandalay, The (MGM, 1926) with Clarence Muse.
Robinson Crusoe (1922) with Noble Johnson as Friday.
Safari (Paramount, 1940) with Clinton Rosemond, Ben Carter.
Sahara (Columbia, 1944) with Rex Ingram. For his role as a Sudanese soldier, Ingram received a special award from the Motion Picture Committee for Unity, as the "most outstanding" black actor of the year.
Sailor Takes a Wife, The (MGM, 1946) with Eddie "Rochester" Anderson. Film was censored by Memphis Board because star Robert Walker tipped his hat to a black.
St. Louis Blues (Paramount, 1939) with Maxine Sullivan.
St. Louis Blues (Paramount, 1958) with Nat "King" Cole, Eartha Kitt, Pearl Bailey, Cab Calloway, Ella Fitzgerald.
Salt and Pepper (United Artists, 1968) with Sammy Davis, Jr.
Sambo Series (Independent, 1909–11) (all black) Produced by Sigmund Lubin.
Sanders of the River (Independent, 1935) starring Paul Robeson, Nina McKinney. An English film.
Sapphire (J. Arthur Rank, 1959) with Gordon Heath.
Save the Children (Paramount, 1973). Musical documentary of Black Expo '72 in Chicago. Featuring Marvin Gaye, the Staple Singers, the Temptations, the O'Jays, Rev. James Cleveland, Curtis Mayfield, Roberta Flack, Gladys Knight and the Pips, the Jackson Five, and Rev. Jesse Jackson, organizer of the Exposition.
Scalphunters, The (United Artists, 1968) with Ossie Davis.
Scream Blacula Scream (American International, 1973) with William Marshall, Don Mitchel, Pam Grier.
Sepia Cinderella (Herald Pictures, 1957) (all black) with Billy Daniels, Sheila Guyse, Ruble Blakey, Water Fuller, John Kirby, Fred Gordon. Directed by Arthur Leonard from a screenplay by Vincent Valentini, produced by Jack Goldberg.
Shaft (MGM, 1971) starring Richard Roundtree, Moses Gunn.
Shaft's Big Score (MGM, 1972) starring Richard Roundtree.
Shaft in Africa (MGM, 1973) starring Richard Roundtree, Vonetta McGee.

Show Boat (Universal, 1936) with Paul Robeson, Hattie McDaniel, Clarence Muse.

Show Boat (MGM, 1951) with William Warfield.

Singing Kid, The (Warner Brothers, 1936) with Cab Calloway.

Siren of the Tropics (Negro Marches On, 1937) with Josephine Baker.

Skin Game (Warner Brothers, 1971) with Lou Gossett.

Slaughter (American International, 1972) starring Jim Brown.

Slaughter's Big Rip-Off (American International, 1973) with Jim Brown, Brock Peters, Gloria Hendry.

Slave, The (Biograph, 1909) (blackface). A D. W. Griffith film.

Slaves (Walter Reade, 1969) with Ossie Davis, Dionne Warwicke.

Slender Thread, The (Paramount, 1966) with Sidney Poitier.

So Red the Rose (Paramount, 1936) with Daniel Haynes, Clarence Muse, George Reed.

Something to Shout About (Columbia, 1943) with Hazel Scott (film debut).

Son of Satan, A (Micheaux Film Corporation, 1924) with Andrew S. Bishop, Ida Anderson. About the experience of a man spending a night in a haunted house.

Song of Freedom (Lion–Hammer, 1937) with Paul Robeson, Robert Adams, Orlando Martins, Elizabeth Welch. An English film.

Song of the South (RKO–Disney, 1947) with Hattie McDaniel, James Baskett.

Soul of Nigger Charlie, The (Paramount, 1973) with Fred Williamson, D'Urville Martin, Denise Nicholas.

Soul Soldier (Fanfare, 1972)

Soul to Soul (Cinerama, 1971) with Ike and Tina Turner.

Sound and the Fury, The (MGM, 1959) with Ethel Waters as Dilsey.

Sounder (Twentieth Century-Fox, 1972) with Cicely Tyson, Paul Winfield, Kevin Hooks. Tyson and Winfield were nominated for Academy Awards, as was Lonnie Elder III, who wrote the screenplay.

Spider's Web (Micheaux Film Corporation, 1927) with Lorenzo McLane, Evelyn Preer, Edward Thompson, Grace Smythe, Marshall Rogers, Henrietta Loveless, Billy Gullport. About a lecherous white man who tries to force his attention on a black girl in a small Mississippi town, and her aunt who is accused of murder in Harlem.

Spirit of Youth (Independent, 1937) (all black) with Joe Louis, Clarence Muse.

Spook Who Sat By the Door, The (United Artists, 1973) with Lawrence Cook, Paula Kelly, Janet League. Screenplay by Sam Greenlee from his novel, produced by Greenlee and Ivan Dixon, directed by Dixon.

Spy 13 (MGM, 1934) with the Mills Brothers.

Stand Up and Fight (MGM, 1939) with Clinton Rosemond.

Stigma (Cinerama, 1972)

Stormy Weather (Twentieth Century-Fox, 1943) (all black) with Lena Horne, Bill Robinson, Cab Calloway, Katherine Dunham, Harold Nicholas, Fayard Nicholas, Ada Brown, Dooley Wilson, Babe Wallace, Ernest Whitman, Zuttie Singleton, F. E. Miller, Nicodemus. Directed by Andrew Stone from a story by Jerry Horwin and Seymour Robinson.

Story of Temple Drake (Paramount, 1933) with Hattie McDaniel (film debut).

Story of a Three Day Pass, The (Sigma III, 1968). Written and directed by Melvin Van Peebles.

Sunday Sinners (Negro Marches On, 1941) (all black) with Mamie Smith, Alex Lovejoy, Earl Sydnor, Sidney Easton, Edna Mae Harris, Cristola Williams, Norman Astwood, Gus Smith, Alberta Perkins. From a story by Frank Wilson. Directed by Arthur Dreifuss with music and lyrics by Donald Heywood.

Super Fly (Warner Brothers, 1972) with Ron O'Neal, Curtis Mayfield.

Super Fly T.N.T. (Paramount, 1973) with Ron O'Neal, Roscoe Lee Browne, Sheila Frazier, Robert Guillaume.

Sweet Jesus, Preacher Man (MGM, 1973) with Roger E. Mosley, Sam Laws.

Sweet Sweetback's Baadasssss Song (Cinemation, 1971). Written, directed, produced, and starred in by Melvin Van Peebles.

Symbol of the Unconquered (Micheaux Film Corporation, 1925) with Lawrence Chenault, Walker Thompson, Iris Hall, E. G. Tatum, Jim Burris, Mattie Wilkes, Lee Whipper. Beautiful girl goes west to claim her dead grandfather's mine and meets trouble.

Synanon (Columbia, 1965) with Eartha Kitt, Bernie Hamilton.

Take a Giant Step (United Artists, 1960) with Ruby Dee, Johnny Nash, Fred O'Neal, Beah Richards.

Tales of Manhattan (Twentieth Century-Fox, 1943) with Paul Robeson, Ethel Waters, Eddie "Rochester" Anderson, Clarence Muse, George Reed, the Hall Johnson Choir.

Talk of the Town, The (Columbia, 1942) with Rex Ingram.

Tamango (Hal Roach, 1959) with Dorothy Dandridge, Alex Cressan.

Tarzan's Perils (1951) with Dorothy Dandridge.

Tell No Tales (MGM, 1939) with Theresa Harris, Clinton Rosemond.

Temptation (Micheaux Film Corporation, 1936)

Ten Minutes to Kill (Micheaux Film Corporation, 1933)

Ten Minutes to Live (Micheaux Film Corporation, 1932)

Ten Nights in a Barroom (Coloured Players, 1920) with Charles Gilpin.

They Call Me Mister Tibbs (Columbia, 1971) with Sidney Poitier, Barbara McNair.

They Died with Their Boots On (Warner Brothers, 1942) with Hattie McDaniel.

They Won't Forget (Warner Brothers, 1937) with Clinton Rosemond.

Thief of Bagdad, The (Independent, 1941) with Rex Ingram, Adelaide Hall. An English film.

Thousands Cheer (MGM, 1943) with Lena Horne, Hazel Scott.

Tick Tick Tick (MGM, 1970) with Jim Brown.

Tiger Bay (British Lion–Wyndham, 1933) with Orlando Martins.

To Sir, with Love (Columbia, 1967) with Sidney Poitier.

Top of the Heap (Fanfare, 1972)

Travels with My Aunt (MGM, 1972) with Lou Gossett.

Trick Baby (Universal, 1973) with Mel Stewart.

Trouble Man (Twentieth Century-Fox, 1972) with Robert Hooks. Directed by Ivan Dixon.
Uncle Jasper's Will (Micheaux Film Corporation) with William E. Fountaine, Shingzie Howard.
Uncle Tom's Cabana (MGM, 1947). Film short.
Uncle Tom's Cabin (Thomas Edison, 1903) (blackface)
Uncle Tom's Cabin (Thanhauser, 1909) (blackface)
Uncle Tom's Cabin (World, 1914) with Sam Lucas as Uncle Tom.
Uncle Tom's Cabin (Paramount, 1918)
Uncle Tom's Cabin (Universal, 1927) with James B. Lowe as Uncle Tom.
Underworld (Micheaux Film Corporation, 1936)
Uptight (Paramount, 1968) with Raymond St. Jacques, Julian Mayfield, Frank Silvera, Ruby Lee, Juanita Moore, Max Julien, Roscoe Lee Browne. Script by Ruby Dee, Julian Mayfield, and director Jules Dassin, from the novel *The Informer*.
Vanishing Virginian, The (MGM, 1943) with Leigh Whipper, Louise Beavers.
Veiled Aristocrats (Micheaux Film Corporation, 1932)
Virgin of the Seminole, The (Micheaux Film Corporation, 1922) with William E. Fountaine, Shingze Howard.
Volcano (Paramount, 1926) with Clarence Muse.
Wages of Sin (Micheaux Film Corporation, 1929)
Warm December, A (National General, 1973) with Sidney Poitier, Esther Anderson.
Watermelon Man (Columbia, 1970) with Godfrey Cambridge, Mantan Moreland. Directed by Melvin Van Peebles.
Wattstax (Columbia, 1973). Record of an all-black music festival held in the Los Angeles Coliseum on August 20, 1972. Featuring Issac Hayes, the Staple Singers, Jimmy Jones, Little Milton, Richard Pryor, the Emotions, Albert King, Luther Ingram, Johnnie Taylor, Rufus Thomas, Carla Thomas.
Way Down South (Sol Lesser, 1939) with Clarence Muse, Lilian Yarbo, Stymie Beard, Marguerite Whitten, Hall Johnson Choir, Ralph Morgan, Allan Mowbray, Steffi Duna, Sally Blane, Jack Carr. Screenplay by Langston Hughes, based on a story by Clarence Muse, directed by Bernard Vorhaus.
We've Come a Long Way (Negro Marches On, 1945). Documentary on black progress. Narration by Elder Micheaux, produced and directed by Jack Goldberg.
When Men Betray (Micheaux Film Corporation, 1928)
White Bondage (Warner Brothers, 1937) with Eddie "Rochester" Anderson.
White Hunter (Twentieth Century-Fox, 1937) with Ernest Whitman, Ralph Cooper.
Within Our Gates (Micheaux Film Corporation, 1920)
You Can't Take It with You (Columbia, 1939) with Lilian Yarbo, Eddie "Rochester" Anderson.

Bibliography

Adler, Renata. "The Negro That Movies Overlook." *The New York Times,* March 3, 1968.

Asendio, James. "History of Negro Motion Pictures." *International Photographer,* no. 12, January 1940.

Baldwin, James. "Carmen Jones: The Dark Is Light Enough." *Notes of a Native Son.* Boston: Beacon, 1965.

————. "Sidney Poitier." *Look,* July 23, 1968.

Bart, Peter. "The Still Invisible Man." *The New York Times,* July 17, 1966.

Blakeston, Oswell. "Black Fanfare." *Close Up* (London), August 1929.

Brown, Sterling. "The Negro in the Movies." *Negro Poetry and Drama.* Washington, D.C.: Associates in Negro Folk Education, 1937.

Browne, Nick. "Would You Believe Belafonte as a Jewish Angel?" *The New York Times,* April 27, 1969.

Canby, Vincent. "The Movies That Still Haunt Hollywood." *The New York Times,* January 26, 1969.

Carter, Elmer Anderson. "Of Negro Motion Pictures." *Close Up* (London), August 1929.

Cripps, Thomas R. "Death of Rastus: Negro in American Films Since 1945." *Phylon,* fall 1967.

Crowther, Bosley. "The Birth of a Nation." *The New York Times* magazine, February 7, 1965.

Curtwright, Wesley. "Motion Pictures of Negroes." Microfilm. Carnegie Study. Schoemburg Collection. New York, 1940.

———. "Brief Outline of Negro Actors in America." Microfilm. Carnegie Study. Schoemburg Collection. New York, 1940.

Dismond, Geraldyn. "The Negro Actor and the American Movies." *Close Up* (London), August 1929.

Draper, Arthur. "Uncle Tom Will You Never Die?" *New Theatre,* January 1936.

Fisher, Ethel. "Behind the Camera with Men of Two Worlds." *Film Quarterly* (London), autumn 1946.

Flatley, Guy. "Sidney Poitier as Black-Militant." *The New York Times,* November 10, 1968.

Golden, Herb. "The Negro and Yiddish Film Boom." *Variety*, January 3, 1940.

Green, Paul. "A Letter from Paul Green." *Close Up* (London), August 1929.

Harrison, William. "The Negro and the Cinema." *Sight and Sound* (London), spring 1939.

Harwick, Leon. "The Negro Looks at Hollywood." *Hollywood Quarterly,* spring 1946.

Hirsch, Foster. "Uncle Tom's Becoming a Superhero." *Readers & Writers,* November–January, 1968.

Holly, Ellen. "How Black Do You Have to Be." *The New York Times,* September 15, 1968.

Horne, Lena and Schickel, Richard. *Lena.* New York: Doubleday, 1965.

Jacobs, Lewis. *The Rise of the American Film.* New York: Harcourt, Brace, 1939.

Johnson, Albert. "The Negro in American Films: Some Recent Works." *Film Quarterly,* summer 1965.

———. "Beige, Brown or Black." *Film Quarterly,* fall 1959.

Kael, Pauline. *Kiss Kiss Bang Bang.* New York: Little Brown, 1968.

————. "Notes on Black Movies." *New Yorker* magazine, December 2, 1972.

Klemesrud, Judy. "Calvin: Champagne Yes, Coca-Cola No." *The New York Times,* April 19, 1970.

————. "Cicely, the Looker from Sounder." *The New York Times,* October 1, 1972.

————. "Fred—'Don't Compare Me with Sidney.'" *The New York Times,* March 18, 1973.

Mason, Clifford. "Why Does White America Love Sidney Poitier So?" *The New York Times,* September 10, 1967.

Mattox, Michael. "The Day Black Movie Stars Got Militant." *Black Creation,* winter 1973.

Murray, James P. "The Subject Was Money." *Black Creation,* winter 1973.

Neal, Larry. "Beware of Tar Baby." *The New York Times,* August 3, 1969.

Nelsen, Anne K. and Hart, M. "The Prejudicial Film: Progress and Stalemate, 1915–1967." *Phylon,* summer 1970.

Noble, Peter. *The Negro in Films.* London: Skelton Robinson, 1948.

Patterson, Lindsay, ed. *Anthology of the American Negro in the Theatre.* Washington: Publishers, 1967.

Peterson, Maurice. "Book of Numbers." *Essence Magazine,* January 1973.

Pool, Rosey E. "The Negro Actor in Europe." *Phylon,* fall 1953.

Potamkin, Harry Alan. "The Aframerican Cinema." *Close Up* (London), August 1929.

Reddick, Lawrence D. "Educational Programme for the Improvement of Race Relations in Films. . . ." *Journal of Negro Education,* summer 1944.

Riley, Clayton. "What Makes Sweetback Run?" *The New York Times,* May 9, 1971.

Sanders, Charles L. "Sidney Poitier: Man Behind the Superman." *Ebony,* April 1968.

Stebbins, Robert. "Hollywood's Imitation of Life." *New Theatre,* July 1935.

Stern, Seymour. "The Birth of a Nation." Monograph. Museum of Modern Art and British Film Institute, London and New York, 1946.

Stone, Judy. "Jim Brown, Fighting Southern Sheriff." *The New York Times,* July 26, 1969.

Weales, Gerald. "Pro-Negro Films in Atlanta." *Films in Review,* November 1952.

Wesley, Richard. "Which Way the Black Film." *Encore Magazine,* January 1973.

White, Walter. "A Letter from Walter White." *Close Up* (London), August 1929.

Index